Remaking
Home Economics

Remaking Home Economics

Resourcefulness and Innovation in Changing Times

Edited by **Sharon Y. Nickols** *and* **Gwen Kay**

The University of Georgia Press
Athens and London
Published in cooperation with the
College of Family and Consumer Sciences,
University of Georgia

Most University of Georgia Press titles are
available from popular e-book vendors.

Printed in the United States of America
19 18 17 16 15 P 5 4 3 2

Library of Congress Cataloging-in-Publication Data

Remaking home economics : resourcefulness and innovation in changing times /
edited by Sharon Y. Nickols and Gwen Kay.
pages cm
Includes bibliographical references and index.
ISBN 978-0-8203-4806-3 (hardcover : alk. paper) —
ISBN 978-0-8203-4807-0 (pbk. : alk. paper) —
ISBN 978-0-8203-4808-7 (ebook)
1. Home economics. I. Nickols, Sharon Y. II. Kay, Gwen.
TX295.R37 2015
640—dc23

2014045431

British Library Cataloging-in-Publication Data available

Contents

Acknowledgments

Many chapters in this volume were originally delivered as papers at the multidisciplinary conference "Home Economics: Classroom, Corporate, and Cultural Interpretations Revisited" held February 27–28, 2012, at the University of Georgia, Athens.

Substantial support for the conference was provided by a state-of-the-art conference grant from the Office of the Provost, University of Georgia, with additional financial and logistics assistance from the College of Family and Consumer Sciences, the Janette M. Barber Distinguished Professorship Endowment, the Institute for Women's Studies, and the Honors Program.

Additional chapters were added in order to broaden the original historical emphasis of the conference. Lisa Bayer, the director of the University of Georgia Press, and members of the staff provided invaluable encouragement throughout the development of this volume. Additional support from the College of Family and Consumer Sciences at the University of Georgia is greatly appreciated.

The editors express appreciation to the authors and their support staffs, and to the anonymous reviewers of the prospectus and the full manuscript. Many other colleagues shared ideas and cheered this effort. Special thanks are extended to Samuel Nickols and Jef Sneider, our husbands, for their encouragement throughout the development of this book.

Sharon Y. Nickols and Gwen Kay

Remaking
Home Economics

Introduction

SHARON Y. NICKOLS *and* GWEN KAY

A 1986 questionnaire to majors in the College of Home Economics at the University of Georgia asked students how they felt about the name "home economics," and whether a new name might be desirable. The students overwhelmingly advocated a different name. Many echoed the sentiment of one anonymous respondent, who posited that with a new name, "people wouldn't think we just cook and sew—my courses are a lot harder than that. I'd like respect for my hard work" (College of Home Economics Archives n.d.). Over and over, on campuses throughout the country (and for many years), students, faculty, and administrators have repeated this sentiment almost verbatim: home economics is more than cooking and sewing.

Indeed, home economics is, and always was, much more than cooking and sewing, but the field seems caught in a triple bind. First, the subjects in its academic programs and its professional practice focus on matters of daily living—how, where, and when people meet their basic human needs. Despite the reality that being well nourished, clothed, sheltered, and nurtured are extremely complex goals to achieve on a personal level, not to mention the large economic, social, and institutional structures interacting with these life processes, such concerns have been largely taken for granted (until a crisis occurs). The dismissal of the entire field of home economics is based on the presumption that cooking and sewing are easy and are readily acquired skill sets requiring no education, training, or preparation. This ignores the chemistry, biology, nutrition, and budgetary elements of food preparation, as well as the community issues of food security and public health; and it ignores the chemistry, the ecological and social aspects of textile processing, and the construction and marketing of clothing, as well as the global issues of environmental sustainability and the working conditions of those who make apparel.

Second, home economics has been populated largely by women, and work done by women has been devalued throughout history. In addition to food and apparel (aka cooking and sewing), home economics was, and still is, concerned with child development, family relationships, and aging; with housing and interior spaces conducive to efficient and healthy living; and with the management of household assets. In the distant past, these activities were primarily domestic in scope, presumably required no formal education, and were consequently undervalued. During the past century these components of daily life became increasingly intertwined with formal structures outside the home, thus offering home economics graduates the opportunity to provide education, products, and services for individuals and families. Fulfilling these employment opportunities contributed to the social and economic development of families and communities, and to the success of the employing businesses and institutions. Nevertheless home economics employees were seldom fully recognized or equitably paid for their expertise. Today, more men are earning college degrees in specialized areas of home economics and assuming leadership roles than ever before, yet the field continues to be perceived as the domain of women.

Third, as the college programs and employment opportunities of home economics grew, specialized knowledge relating to subjects within its scope rapidly expanded. As a multidisciplinary field, home economics addressed issues related to daily living by applying concepts from the physical and social sciences, the arts and humanities, and its own specialized areas of study. Research, teaching, and the professional practices of these specializations led to new nomenclature and identities. Although still historically affiliated with home economics, departments in colleges, the colleges themselves, and occupations that developed from the specialized areas adopted names deemed more suitable to contemporary circumstances. As a consequence, a vague understanding of home economics persists in the United States, while its contemporary manifestations continue to evolve, frequently without explicit connections to their foundation in home economics. In various chapters of this book, names that replaced "home economics" are used, as are the titles of specialized areas within the field. For consistency, "home economics" is used generically in most of the book to refer to the field of study and the practice of the profession, but other contemporary names (human sciences, family and consumer sciences, human ecology) fit better in some chapters.

The knowledge and skills of home economics are embedded in a host of daily living situations (e.g., credit counseling, childcare centers, nutrition guidelines, time management seminars, universal design, ready-to-wear garment finishes, food labels), yet the field is neither well understood nor widely recognized by the public. Public uncertainty about the nature of the field co-exists with a lack of understanding that home economics knowledge and experience could contribute to preventing or solving many current problems.

Adding to these conundrums, the inseparable nature of the field of home economics and those who develop and deliver its programs is often confusing. Is this book about the field of home economics or about its practitioners (those whose occupations are grounded in the subject matter)? The answer is both. As seen in many other studies of women's historical roles (e.g., Bernhard et al. 1994; Frankel and Dye 1991; Osterud 2012; Walker and Sharpless 2006), the activities and the actors are so interwoven that the story unravels if these two elements are separated.

Understanding the past as prologue to the future is a tenet of historical scholarship. This book is intended to foster dialogue across disciplines in higher education and to facilitate discussions with a broader audience about the role of home economics (in its past, current, and future manifestations) in addressing perennial problems of daily life and about the changes that have remade and are remaking home economics.

The perception that home economics has vital information is reflected in news media as "bring back home ec" and in the exclamation point that ends many conversations about how to solve the lack of knowledge and skills to meet the challenges of contemporary living (Graham 2013; Grossman 2003; Lichtenstein and Ludwig 2010; Traister 2014; Veit 2011). The idea that home economics could solve, or even prevent, an obesity epidemic, vast household debt, elder neglect, a housing crisis, waste and the pollution of natural resources, and a variety of other social ills is not unlike the passion that birthed the field of study. Despite being misunderstood, trivialized, and underresourced, home economics has been addressing the persistent problems of daily life for more than a century. What is it about home economics that makes this subject and the field itself so enduring?

As Elias (2008) observed, many of the issues raised by the pioneers of home economics remain contested in the twenty-first century. They are at the core of daily life, and thus they are relevant across a wide spectrum, from students contemplating fields of study and careers, to practicing professionals, to policy makers, to members of households themselves. In their twenty-first-century form they include questions about the extent to which the aspirations for home economics have been achieved, altered, or subverted. The chapters in this book deepen the analysis and dialogue by looking at probing questions: What did home economics contribute to solving issues of daily life? What does the field have to contribute now? What were the career experiences of home economists? How have home economists provided leadership in shaping or reshaping cultural values, educational institutions, and agencies? The nexus of these historical and contemporary issues in the profession are addressed in

Remaking Home Economics: Resourcefulness and Innovation in Changing Times.
This book builds on the collective efforts of researchers from history, home
economics, women's studies, and women in science who collaborated two decades ago on *Rethinking Home Economics: Women and the History of a Profession* (Stage and Vincenti 1997). Both books provide a platform for researchers
to further explore historical and contemporary aspects of the profession, while
this volume provides a foundation to understand the past and to probe the
challenges and rewards of careers related to meeting the needs of individuals,
families, and communities in a fast-changing global environment.

Why is *Remaking Home Economics: Resourcefulness and Innovation in Changing Times* timely and important? One reason is that we need to further explore
the complexities of home economics so as to arrive at a more comprehensive
understanding of the field and its challenges and contributions. "Home economics has not fared well at the hand of historians," proclaimed Sarah Stage
(1997, 1). The scathing dismissal of home economics by feminist activists and
others from the 1960s through the 1980s contributed to a gulf between home
economists and scholars in other disciplines. Although Susan Strasser carefully described the philosophical discussions at the Lake Placid Conferences
and the commitment of early home economists to improving conditions of
daily life in *Never Done: A History of American Housework* (1982), most of that
book is an account of how new products and the imposition of industrial production concepts on the household by "management experts," some of whom,
such as Christine Frederick, were mistakenly identified with home economics,
increased the workload of women during the early to mid-twentieth century.
In *Perfection Salad: Women and Cooking at the Turn of the Century* (1986), Laura
Shapiro criticized home economists for their role in product development and
food marketing, but she gave no attention to the role of corporations in product promotion, home economists' contributions to the study of nutrition and
dietetics, nor the limited employment opportunities for those educated professional women. Ruth Schwartz Cowan in *More Work for Mother* (1983) and
Glenna Matthews in *"Just a Housewife"* (1987) reported how the introduction of
household appliances and management advice tested and promoted by home
economists increased the work of "housewives," the wives and mothers who
were indeed "married" to the house and the culturally idealized family of the
early to mid-twentieth-century United States. Cowan's study ends with the
1950s while Matthews's book is primarily a criticism (sometimes justified) of
the opinions and advice of the early twentieth-century home economists.

For the most part, any exploration of home economics occurred, if at all,
in the silos of academia. In the 1990s historians and women's studies scholars
were drawn to home economics and the women who populated the field as
a topic of study because it offered experiences "rich with insights into gendered domains in the professions, business, and academia" (Stage 1997, 5).

The publication of *Rethinking Home Economics: Women and the History of a Profession* (Stage and Vincenti 1997) marked a synthesis of new perspectives and the collaboration of practitioners and historians. Subsequently, historians Megan Elias (*Stir It Up: Home Economics in American Culture*, 2008) and Carolyn Goldstein (*Creating Consumers: Home Economists in Twentieth-Century America*, 2012) provided twentieth-century contextual information about culture, thus leading to a better understanding of the historical roles of home economists.

Feminist scholar Josephine Donovan's work (2004) also has provided context for the study of a profession largely occupied by women. She delineated "cultural feminism," in which there are three basic elements: women have been assigned to the domestic sphere and to caring labor, women have been concerned with production for use (versus production for exchange), and women have not had substantial political power in society, which has led to an ethic that is life affirming and focused on the concrete details of life. This is an apt description of home economics for much of its history. Today's human sciences professionals, both women and men, put the human experience at the center of their scholarship and practice while working within an ecological framework.

In the field of home economics Kappa Omicron Nu, an honor society for the profession, has recorded the contributions to family and consumer sciences by leaders and other practitioners. Four issues of the *Kappa Omicron Nu Forum* were devoted to biographies and autobiographies on the theme "Legacies for the Future" (9[2], 10[1], 11[2], and 17[1], available at www.kon.org/archives/forum/forum_archives.html#f9a). The purpose of these special issues was to provide a record of the contributions of leaders who helped shape the field of home economics, in the belief that their experiences and insights could inspire others and help inform the future (Nickols 1996). Also sponsored by Kappa Omicron Nu, *African American Women: Contributions to the Human Sciences* (Miller, Mitstifer, and Vaughn 2009) is a collection of forty-four essays documenting the struggles and accomplishments of Black women in home economics, notably at historically Black colleges and universities, and the familial and cultural contexts that shaped their intellectual contributions, personal mentoring relationships, and careers in home economics.

Several historical milestones also have drawn new attention to the place of home economics in the United States. The centennial of the American Association of Family and Consumer Sciences (AAFCS) in 2009 prompted a focus on history from within the profession. The 150th anniversary in 2012 of the Morrill Act that created the land-grant colleges and the 100th anniversary in 2014 of the Smith-Lever Act that codified the Cooperative Extension Service also have created interest. Upon their creation, most land-grant colleges immediately admitted women and soon offered domestic science courses. Cooperative Extension offered a prime career opportunity for women graduating with home economics degrees in the early 1900s. Betty Friedan's *The Feminine Mystique* (1963), a book that shook the foundations of assumptions about women's personal fulfillment and well-being, and called into question their entrapment in domestic responsibilities, had its 50th anniversary in 2013.

Issues addressed by home economists persist in contemporary society and are often matters of public concern. Just as domestic manuals written by both men and women proliferated in the 1800s (e.g., Beecher 1841; Beecher and Stowe 1869; Fowler and DePuy 1880; Parloa 1898), today the ubiquitous presence of television programs, magazines, websites, and "apps" on cooking, home décor and repair, personal finances, and human relationships attests to an abiding interest in personal and family well-being (for further discussion, see Leavitt 2002). Few media programs are hosted by someone with formal education in home economics, but the popularity of these programs reflect the public's desire to be informed (or perhaps entertained) about all things domestic.

As the twenty-first century has unfolded, a growing interest in learning and practicing the household skills lost in a pervasive consumer culture has become apparent. Books such as Jane Zimmerman's *Made from Scratch: Reclaiming the Pleasures of the American Hearth* (2003), Shannon Hayes's *Radical Homemakers: Reclaiming Domesticity from a Consumer Culture* (2010), and *Making It: Radical Home Ec for a Post-Consumer World* (2010) by Kelly Coyne and Erik Knutzen gained popularity. While these authors were not particularly informed about or supportive of home economics, the emphasis on personal action and gaining skills to achieve individual and family well-being is consistent with the calls to bring back home economics. A large proportion of this current attention is on food. For example, the Institute of Domestic Technology (IDT), established in 2011, focuses exclusively on food, and most of its faculty are restaurateurs and cookbook authors (www.instituteofdomestictechnology.com). While not grounded in the multidisciplinary field of home economics, IDT members support the make-it-from-scratch, understand-your-food ethos. In this cultural milieu, the contributors to *Remaking Home Economics: Resourcefulness and Innovation in Changing Times* recognize the opportunity to further explore, not just the past, but also recent trends and future directions related to the "ever timely and forever complex" field of home economics (Gentzler 2012). Multidisciplinary perspectives inform the entire volume.

This book is organized around four themes in past and current home economics: home economics philosophy, social responsibility, and outreach to the public; food and clothing; gender and race in career experiences and preparation; and responses to challenges of identity and continuity of the field. Some chapters deal with a specific, limited time period, while others cover more than a century. Topics are often interwoven, just as the profession and its practitioners are inextricably linked. This book is not a compendium of all the areas covered by human ecology. Food and clothing have a prominent role because they are the subjects the public most often identifies with home economics. Other fields are briefly referenced, yet they deserve in-depth discussion in the future.

As an area of study and professional practice that is complex and multifaceted, home economics calls for joint endeavors among scholars from a variety of perspectives. Hopefully, this volume will provoke new understandings and new questions that will continue the custom and necessity of innovating and remaking home economics.

REFERENCES

Beecher, Catharine E. 1841. *A Treatise on Domestic Economy*. New York: Harper and Brothers.

Beecher, Catharine E., and Harriet Beecher Stowe. 1869. *The American Woman's Home*. New York: J. B. Ford.

Bernhard, Virginia, Betty Brandon, Elizabeth Fox-Genovese, Theda Perdue, and Elizabeth H. Turner, eds. 1994. *Hidden Histories of Women in the New South*. Columbia: University of Missouri Press.

College of Home Economics [Family and Consumer Sciences] Archives. N.d. Hargrett Rare Book and Manuscript Library. University of Georgia, Athens.

Cowan, Ruth Schwartz. 1983. *More Work for Mother: The Ironies of Household Technology from the Open Hearth to the Microwave*. New York: Basic.

Coyne, Kelly, and Erik Knutzen. 2010. *Making It: Radical Home Ec for a Post-Consumer World*. New York: Rodale.

Donovan, Josephine. 2004. *Feminist Theory: The Intellectual Traditions*, 3rd ed. New York: Continuum.

Elias, Megan J. 2008. *Stir It Up: Home Economics in American Culture*. Philadelphia: University of Pennsylvania Press.

Fowler, C. H., and W. H. DePuy. 1880. *Home and Hearth and Home Economics*. New York: Phillips and Hunt.

Frankel, Noralee, and Nancy S. Dye , eds. 1991. *Gender, Class, Race and Reform in the Progressive Era*. Lexington: University of Kentucky Press.

Friedan, Betty. 1963. *The Feminine Mystique*. New York: Norton.

Gentzler, Yvonne S. 2012. "Home Economics: Ever Timely and Forever Complex." *Phi Kappa Phi Forum* 92(2): 4–7.

Goldstein, Carolyn M. 2012. *Creating Consumers: Home Economists in Twentieth-Century America*. Chapel Hill: University of North Carolina Press.

Graham, Ruth. 2013. "Bring Back Home Ec! The Case for a Revival of the Most Retro Class in School." *Boston Globe*, October 12, http://www.bostonglobe.com/ideas/2013/10/12/bring-back-home/EJJi9yzjgJfNmgxWUIEDgO/story.html (accessed October 15, 2013).

Grossman, Jennifer. 2003. "Food for Thought (and for Credit)." *New York Times,* September 2, A23.

Hayes, Shannon. 2010. *Radical Homemakers: Reclaiming Domesticity from a Consumer Culture.* Richmondville, N.Y.: Left to Write Press.

Leavitt, Sarah. 2002. *From Catharine Beecher to Martha Stewart: A Cultural History of Domestic Advice.* Chapel Hill: University of North Carolina Press.

Lichtenstein, Alice H., and David Ludwig. 2010. "Bring Back Home Economics Education." *Journal of the American Medical Association* 303(18): 1857–1858.

Matthews, Glenna. 1987. *"Just a Housewife": The Rise of Domesticity in America.* New York: Oxford University Press.

Miller, Julia R., Dorothy I. Mitstifer, and Gladys Gary Vaughn, eds. 2009. *African American Women: Contributions to the Human Sciences.* East Lansing, Mich.: Kappa Omicron Nu.

Nickols, Sharon Y. 1996. "Guest Editor's Message." *Kappa Omicron Nu Forum* 9(2): 3–6.

Osterud, Grey. 2012. *Putting the Barn Before the House: Women and Family Farming in Early Twentieth-Century New York.* Ithaca, N.Y.: Cornell University Press.

Parloa, Maria. 1898. *Home Economics: A Guide to Household Management Including the Proper Treatment of the Materials Entering into the Construction and the Furnishings of the House.* New York: Century.

Shapiro, Laura. 1986. *Perfection Salad: Women and Cooking at the Turn of the Century.* New York: Farrar, Straus and Giroux.

Stage, Sarah. 1997. "Home Economics: What's in a Name?" In *Rethinking Home Economics: Women and the History of a Profession,* edited by Sarah Stage and Virginia B. Vincenti, 1–13. Ithaca, N.Y.: Cornell University Press.

Stage, Sarah, and Virginia B. Vincenti, eds. 1997. *Rethinking Home Economics: Women and the History of a Profession.* Ithaca, N.Y.: Cornell University Press.

Strasser, Susan. 1982. *Never Done: A History of American Housework.* New York: Pantheon.

Traister, Rebecca. 2014. "Feminists Killed Home Ec. Now They Should Bring It Back—for Boys and Girls." *New Republic,* May 28, www.newrepublic.com/article/117876/feminists-should-embrace-home-economics (accessed May 30, 2014).

Veit, Helen Zoe. 2011. "Time to Revive Home Ec." *New York Times,* September 5, http://www.nytimes.com/2011/09/06/opinion/revive-home-economics-classes-to-fight-obesity.html (accessed February 2, 2012).

Walker, Melissa, and Rebecca Sharpless, eds. 2006. *Work, Family, and Faith: Rural Southern Women in the Twentieth Century.* Columbia: University of Missouri Press.

Zimmerman, Jean. 2003. *Made from Scratch: Reclaiming the Pleasures of the American Hearth.* New York: Free Press.

I. Home Economics Philosophy, Social Responsibility, and Outreach

Home economics, from its earliest manifestation as a movement for education and the improvement of living conditions to its current multifaceted components, is a complex profession and field of study. Understanding the origins of the field is critical to an appreciation of its current form and to a belief in its future relevance. Throughout its history, home economics has been a synthesis of the theoretical and the practical, engaged in heuristic, exploratory study from the classroom and laboratory to people in their daily lives. General and specialized academic programs for students, educational program delivery to the public, structured careers and entrepreneurial endeavors, research, and public policy advocacy are all components of home economics. The chapters in this part provide an overview of the development of the focus of home economics and of one comprehensive system for the delivery of home economics–based knowledge.

Chapter 1, "Knowledge, Mission, Practice: The Enduring Legacy of Home Economics" by Sharon Y. Nickols and Billie J. Collier, is an omnibus presentation of the origins of home economics, including the derivation of its original name, the philosophical perspectives expressed by its founders, the current approach to core concepts in the field, and the overarching characteristics of home economics over time. The professional practice of the field has been built on a variety of research methods, the results of which have contributed to services and products for the public, educational programs, and public policy. Over the twentieth century the need for specific expertise to address the spectrum of topics under the home economics rubric led to specialization in academic programs and in the profession itself. This chapter sets the stage for the discussion of resourcefulness and innovation as home economics has responded to specific aspects of serving the public during changing times.

Chapter 2, "Extending Knowledge, Changing Lives: Cooperative Extension Family and Consumer Sciences" by Jorge H. Atiles, Caroline E. Crocoll, and Jane Schuchardt, provides an example of the inseparable relationship between research, educational programming, and public service that characterizes home economics. The authors discuss the early synergy between home economics and Cooperative Extension, adaptations in information delivery over the century of the field's existence, and prospects for the future. Cooperative Extension represents the democratization of education through informal learning and an emphasis on personal and community efficacy. Stakeholders at the local, state, and federal levels combine resources to address ongoing and timely issues.

Science and social responsibility have been intertwined, persistent themes in home economics over the decades. Home economics is grounded in science and steeped in Progressive Era ideals. The harmony between science and social responsibility is illustrated by two towering figures in early home economics: Caroline Hunt, profiled in chapter 3, and Ellen H. Swallow Richards, profiled in chapter 11. In chapter 3, "Home Economics in the Twentieth Century: A Case of Lost Identity?," Rima D. Apple argues that the gendered nature of home economics and its alliance with women of the Progressive Era were its strengths as the profession embraced improving the human condition as its mission. However, school curricula shifted during the century to a focus on the knowledge and skills needed by individuals in a consumer-oriented society, creating challenges to the identity and focus of the field that are still faced by home economics today.

1. Knowledge, Mission, Practice

The Enduring Legacy of Home Economics

SHARON Y. NICKOLS *and* BILLIE J. COLLIER

A preschool teacher engaging young children in learning activities appropriate for their stage of development. A dietitian providing nutrition education and counseling to clients in the Women, Infants and Children supplemental nutrition program. An apparel designer developing comfortable and attractive clothing for elderly consumers. An interior designer planning functional and pleasant spaces with renewable and recycled materials. A financial counselor helping people manage their credit and reduce debt. A textile scientist developing biodegradable fibers for use in wound dressings. A team of housing, exercise science, adolescent development, and financial literacy personnel from community agencies planning a residential facility for youth aging out of foster care. What do all these individuals have in common? They are the modern face of professionals in home economics. While these present-day roles may seem distinct and specialized, the conceptual foundation and preparation for them came out of the home economics tradition as it developed over the past century.

Formalized as a field of study in the early twentieth century, home economics has gone through transitions in its knowledge base, name, and practice. Throughout these changes three elements have been constant: an interdisciplinary knowledge base; a mission intended to elucidate, enlighten, and empower; and the multidisciplinary practices of the profession, including teaching, research, and service to others. Much like engineering, home economics is a mission-oriented field of study and professional practice. The ultimate goals are to address human needs by interventions that prevent or solve problems that affect the way people live their lives. The majority of the public may see only the activities of the women and men who work in the various careers associated with the field; however, home economics has a rich history of philosophical reflection and self-assessment of its intellectual foundation and purpose.

The goal of this chapter is to explain the foundation of home economics deriving from its philosophy and mission, and to describe its contemporary practice. In order to fully appreciate the field as it is today, it is important to have an understanding of the historical context and intellectual history upon which it was built.

Origins of Home Economics

The precursors of the field of home economics can be traced to the mid-1800s, including projects of innovative thinkers such as Sir Benjamin Thompson (Count Rumford) and Catharine Beecher (1846). An American-born British loyalist, inventor, and advisor to Bavaria, Count Rumford "organized industrial schools for soldiers' children, built workhouses for the poor, . . . and concocted the inexpensive but nutritious Rumford's soup of barley, peas, potatoes, and beer for the indigent and incarcerated," as well as inventing improved household heating systems (Gentzler 2012, 5; Hunt 1942).

Catharine Beecher, along with other prolific writers in her family, made a significant impact on the domestic and social values of mid-1800s New England and beyond (Leavitt 2002). She established in 1823 the Hartford (Connecticut) Female Seminary, where "domestic education" had a prominent role in the curriculum. Through her books and other writings Beecher sought to uplift women's roles as manager of the household and as moral guide for family members. Beecher's *A Treatise on Domestic Economy*, first published in 1841, went through fifteen editions and was considered the mid-nineteenth century's "standard domestic textbook" (Tonkovich 2002). Beecher, with her sister Harriet Beecher Stowe, revised and updated the book, which was then published as *The American Woman's Home; or, Principles of Domestic Science* (Beecher and Stowe 1869), an encyclopedia of advice based on their interpretation of principles of science, common sense, and religion, and their advocacy for women's education. These works were immensely impactful because they acknowledged and embraced the tremendous influence that the labor of women had on the overall welfare of the family unit, and they began to publicize best practices for household management. The seeds of modern principles of efficiency and sustainability are present in these works.

Land-grant colleges established by the Morrill Act of 1862 provided access to advanced education focusing on applied science and practical knowledge. The fledgling land-grant institutions of Kansas, Iowa, and Illinois pioneered in domestic science courses in the 1870s (Bevier and Usher 1906; Craig 1945; Gunn 1992; Miller 2004). Instructional sessions were offered for rural women at the farmers institutes of southern and midwestern colleges, and Martha Van Rensselaer developed a reading course for farmers' wives through Cornell's rural outreach program (Holt 1995; Scholl 2008, 2011, 2013). Research supported by the U.S. Department of Agriculture addressed issues of human nutrition and other aspects of household well-being, thus establishing a research foundation for home economics (Goldstein 2012; Rossiter 1982).

Training programs intended to address the poor economic conditions of African Americans were established by missionaries following the Civil War through the 1880s, some of which developed into collegiate home economics programs. Hampton Institute in Virginia and Spelman College in Georgia are examples. The original programs for both men and women at Hampton Institute emphasized labor as a force for self-sufficiency and moral development; and in keeping with nineteenth-century gender roles, household work was the focus for women students (Miller 2004). Eventually, the coursework for women adopted the emphasis on science and other characteristics of the Progressive Era. The new field of domestic science provided women students at Hampton Institute with the knowledge and degrees and thus the authority "to claim specialized expertise in fields such as teaching, social service, and science" (ibid., 61). Spelman Seminary was created in 1883 in Atlanta to educate African American women (Guy-Sheftall and Steward 1981). An industrial department focused on teaching skills in dressmaking, millinery, needlework, and cooking was established to educate students for "self reliance and self-support" (Standards Committee 1933). A curriculum leading to a bachelor of science degree was developed in 1924 to prepare teachers of home economics; the two-year household arts diploma was discontinued. The emergence of a strong African American middle class in Atlanta contributed to vocational education being supplanted by an emphasis on the liberal arts at Spelman College.

The second Morrill Act (1890) authorized federal funding for land-grant institutions in the southern states with the charge to provide education for African Americans in agriculture, the mechanical arts, and domestic science. Twelve of the sixteen schools had been founded prior to 1890, either by freed African Americans themselves or by state legislatures (Whitaker et al. 2009). Land-grant status and later federal appropriations eventually enabled the 1890 institutions to strengthen their academic offerings and establish research programs (Fahm 1990; Williams and Williamson 1985). Carrie Lyford, reporting on the development of home economics in 1923, made special mention of the extension work of the 1890 colleges: "The extension demonstrations by the Negro agents are unquestionably among the most important lessons in homemaking carried on in the South today" (qtd. in Miller, Mitstifer, and Vaughn 2009, 29; also see Harris 1997).

Cooking schools, training programs, and services targeting low-income women of the crowded cities of New England were based on the Progressive Era philosophy of human betterment and the desire to reduce the drudgery of women's lives (Bevier and Usher 1906; Craig 1945; Hunt 1942; Leavitt 2002; Schneider and Schneider 1993). Emily Huntington, the matron of the Wilson Industrial School for Girls in New York City's crowded East Side tenement district, launched the Kitchen Garden movement in 1875 to teach academic concepts and domestic skills to children (James, James, and Boyer 1971; Miller 2004). Progressive Era philanthropist Grace Hoadley Dodge provided organizational and financial backing for many of the city's improvement programs, including the Kitchen Garden Association. In 1887, Dodge financed a teacher-training program, which later became Teachers College, to prepare teachers for the children of the poor (Katz 1980). Teachers College became a leading force in the academic development of domestic science and household arts, which were eventually combined as home economics (Miller 2004). Many of the early educators in home economics earned degrees from Teachers College or were faculty members there.

The systematization of the academic discipline of home economics coalesced during the series of conferences held in Lake Placid, New York, between 1899 and 1908. The proceedings of the Lake Placid Conferences on Home Economics, compiled in eight volumes, provide a detailed record of the thoughts, experiences, and recommendations of the individuals and committees that undertook the task of framing the academic field and its professional practice. (The Lake Placid Conference proceedings are available at http://hearth.library. cornell.edu.) A constitution for the American Home Economics Association (AHEA) was approved at a dinner on New Year's Eve 1908, or perhaps shortly after midnight in 1909 (Baldwin 1949).

By the late nineteenth century, a variety of names had been in use at the various programs across the country, including domestic science, household arts, home science, and household economics. One of the urgent business items at the first Lake Placid Conference was to reach agreement on a name for the emerging field. Consensus was reached on the name "home economics" for the general subject, "so that it should find a logical place in the college and university course" (Lake Placid Conference 1901, 4–5; Baldwin 1949; Weigley 1974). Although home economics was chosen as the general term, alternative names were suggested as appropriate for courses designed for younger pupils and yet different nomenclature was suggested for high school students (Lake Placid Conference 1901). This emphasis on home economics in higher education at the turn of the twentieth century should not be overlooked. It underscores the field's thorough grounding in the basic physical and social science disciplines and the applied nature of studies gaining acceptance during this period.

The word "economy" is derived from the Greek words *oikos* (house) and *nemein* (to manage). Although the contemporary understanding of "economy" pertains to the structure of economic life in a country or period of time, and "economics" is defined as the "description and analysis of the production, distribution, and consumption of goods and services" (Merriam-Webster n.d.), the most basic meaning of "economics" is the management of the household. The words "home economics" actually are redundant when *oikonomia* is literally translated. Based on extensive philosophical discussion, the Lake Placid Conference participants settled on "home economics" for the field of study they were developing.

As home economics evolved during the twentieth century, alternative nomenclature also evolved. "Human ecology" echoed earlier concepts as eco-systems thinking grew more prevalent. "Family" became a more descriptive term for the profession than "home," and "family and consumer sciences" was adopted. "Human sciences" captured the expansion in subject areas and collaborations in institutions of higher education. Each contemporary name reflects a perspective that focuses on some aspect of the relevant philosophy and practice. When wrestling with the problems presented by a sometimes negative, and no longer apt, image of home economics, leaders have returned to some of the thoughts of Ellen Richards and her colleagues at Lake Placid.

Philosophy and Knowledge

Ever the philosopher as well as a pragmatic researcher, Ellen Swallow Richards introduced her conceptualization of "oekology," eventually spelled ecology, as an environmental science that included humans, and not just land and plants as determined by the (male) scientists of the 1890s (Clarke 1973). She advocated for "oekology," emphasizing the environment-human relationship, as she initiated reform movements to address water and air quality, the circumstances of poor immigrants, and shoddy goods and adulterated food in the marketplace (Clarke 1973; Kwallek 2012; Miles 2009; Stage 1997; also see Meszaros, this volume). Richards's visionary understanding of the relationship between humans and their environment continues to be highly relevant today.

In *Sanitation in Daily Life*, Richards (1907, v) declared, "*Human ecology* is the study of the surroundings of human beings in the effect they produce on the lives of men. The features of the environment are natural as climate, and artificial, produced by human activity, as noise, . . . dirty water, and unclean food." Furthermore, the study of the environment has two aspects: "municipal housekeeping—the cooperation of citizens" in securing a clean and safe environment, and "family housekeeping" to create a healthful home. Richards was the first to use the term "human ecology." In her view, an understanding of human ecology led directly to two missions: educating about science for better living, and living in harmony with the environment.

At the fourth Lake Placid Conference, a committee on courses of study in colleges and universities, composed of Marion Talbot and Alice Peloubet Norton, University of Chicago; Isabel Bevier, University of Illinois; and Mary Roberts Smith, Stanford University, presented a definition of home economics: "Home economics in its most comprehensive sense is the study of the laws, conditions, principles and ideals which are concerned on the one hand with man's immediate physical environment and on the other hand with his nature as a social being, and is the study specially of the relations between those two factors" (Lake Placid Conference 1902, 70–71). Two points of clarification were made: home economics is a philosophical subject because of its emphasis on relationships; and the subjects upon which it builds are empirical (i.e., economics, sociology, chemistry) and are concerned with events and phenomena (ibid., 71). (For profiles of other leaders at the Lake Placid Conferences on Home Economics, see Meszaros and Braun 1983.)

This definition and the points of clarification are enduring core concepts of the field. While not explicitly stated in the 1902 definition, it was understood that the focus was on the family household and the interaction of individuals and families with the natural, material, and social environments.

The development of home economics was greatly influenced and facilitated by the reform movements of the Progressive Era (see Apple, this volume). This period from the late 1800s to the 1920s was one of broad cultural change in which the philosophy of pragmatism with an emphasis on action and experimentation was adopted (Roark et al. 2009). Basic beliefs were that human intelligence could shape, change, and improve society, and thus expertise and scientific management were emphasized. During this period, President Theodore Roosevelt advocated conservation of natural resources, and progressive educators adopted John Dewey's theory that students learn by doing. Growing interest in adult self-improvement and lagging development in rural areas led to passage of the Smith-Lever Act in 1914, which was aimed at improving agricultural productivity and the conditions of rural living through demonstrations and club activities (Scholl 2013; also see Atiles, Crocoll, and Schuchardt, this volume).

The "girl question" in vocational education prompted lively debate in congressional hearings early in the twentieth century as legislators considered how to apportion resources and what kinds of programs to support (Powers 1992). The complex attitudes held by both men and women about women's roles within and outside the home, which were largely framed by social class and experience, influenced the discussions of whether home economics was "general" or "vocational" education. Eventually the Smith-Hughes Act of

1917 provided federal funding to expand home economics offerings in public schools throughout the country and financial aid for faculty at the college level to educate and supervise these home economics teachers (Apple 1997; Powers 1992).

Paralleling the professionalization of other fields, the American Dietetic Association began a series of moves in the 1920s aimed at the special credentialing of practitioners, thus validating the rigor of academic preparation for nutrition-related careers (ACEND 2013). With their emphasis on food and nutrition, home economics colleges played a major role in the development of dietetics.

As the public turned to science to solve problems, home economics expanded its scope and influence (Elias 2008; Schneider and Schneider 1993; Stage and Vincenti 1997). For example, rayon and acetate, the first man-made fibers—touted as "artificial silk"—found a ready market in the early decades of the twentieth century, but also were often of inferior quality (Collier, Bide, and Tortora 2009). The textile industry and government agencies turned to home economists with specialized knowledge and training in fibers, fabrics, and clothing to develop standards and help consumers in their purchasing decisions. The Office of Home Economics in the U.S. Department of Agriculture, elevated to the Bureau of Home Economics in 1923, served as a generator of standardized consumer information based on research. The American Standards Association, the leading voluntary standards organization in the United States, often turned to the bureau, as well as to the American Home Economics Association, for technical expertise on food, clothing, and household appliances (Goldstein 2012; see Pundt 1980 for other AHEA activities related to standards). Research discoveries by faculty in the emerging departments of home economics at colleges and universities also were translated into practical applications. For example, a multistate regional project, the Southern Rural Housing Project, sought to establish standards for kitchens (e.g., arrangement of work areas, height and depth of cabinets for efficient use of human energy, adequate storage) in order to reduce women's workload in the home (Gassett 1957).

Research contributed to the professionalization and specialization of home economics during the first half of the twentieth century (Goldstein 2012; Stage and Vincenti 1997). The first director of the Bureau of Home Economics, Louise Stanley, was committed to strengthening "home economics as a research field for women" (Goldstein 2012, 63), and she built a platform and staff around this goal. Because the research and information dissemination positions in government agencies were considered to be jobs appropriate for women, home economics graduates with the right degrees and training were assured of being hired. Even as these positions provided an opening wedge for the employment of home economics graduates, the concentration of women in these positions had the consequence of gender segregation in the workforce and the continuation of home economics as a field dominated by women. Women were a primary constituency of the bureau (see Moran, this volume).

Stanley organized divisions in the bureau, emphasizing the generation of new knowledge as a guiding principle. This inevitably led to hiring scientists who were asked to concentrate their studies on one of the areas of focus in home economics. With her background in biochemistry, Stanley initially led the Division of Food and Nutrition, which studied the nutritional value of foods as well as preparation and preservation techniques. Under the leadership of Ruth O'Brien, the Division of Textiles and Clothing tested the properties and performance of textiles and apparel products, and prepared bulletins for use by consumers. Hildegarde Kneeland headed the Division of Economics, whose staff used social science methods to study consumer behavior in the context of the family, the marketplace, and broader social and economic conditions.

The physical sciences dominated home economics during its early years, but as psychology and the behavioral sciences advanced, child development gained prominence in the field (Grant 1997). Courses in the care of children were added to the home economics curriculum, and textbooks were published on the care of children (Goodspeed and Johnson 1929) and family relationships (Groves, Skinner, and Swenson 1932). Child development laboratories were established in home economics colleges, and mothers' study clubs were offered through home economics outreach agencies. The Children's Bureau in the U.S. Department of Labor launched a program for "better babies" to promote the health and growth of children, even encouraging contests and awarding certificates at county and state fairs from 1915 through the early 1920s (Holt 1995). Cooperative Extension home economics personnel often collaborated in these efforts.

Economic productivity increased immensely in the 1950s and a host of new items became available, including family housing in the suburbs, automobiles, and air conditioning (Roark et al. 2009). Many household tasks became mechanized (e.g., laundry, dishwashing); television provided entertainment at home; and economist John Kenneth Galbraith (1958) described the United States as "the affluent society." An idealized "American family" was popularized through the new medium of television. "In place of the traditional emphasis on work and savings, the consumer culture encouraged satisfaction and happiness through the purchase and use of new products" (Roark et al. 2009, 1003).

Throughout the 1950s and 1960s home economics was still one of the few collegiate paths for women; and home economics graduates found professional employment as opportunities expanded from teaching and research to jobs in business, industry, and communications (Goldstein 2012; Leavitt 2002). As jobs increased in number and diversity, home economics programs responded by offering more specialized majors with courses that corresponded to the positions graduates would seek. One area of rapid growth in higher education enrollment was fashion merchandising. The proliferation of retail stores offered opportunities for young (predominantly) women who had knowledge of apparel and accessory products and who could manage the procurement, distribution, and selling of these products. Careers in journalism attracted home economics graduates, especially as writers for women's magazines and as editors for the family living and food pages of newspapers (Elias 2008). Advice about the design of houses and home décor grew increasingly technical and specialized as another area of home economics, interior design, became professionalized (Leavitt 2002). The Foundation for Interior Design Education Research (FIDER) was established in 1971, and as enrollments in home economics interior design programs grew, educators incorporated courses into the curriculum to meet FIDER credentialing and state licensing standards (Garber-Dyar, Golwitzer, and Memken 1994).

Concurrently, other changes were brewing as men developed interest in certain specializations in home economics, notably human development, family studies, and nutrition. Between 1955 and 1963 the number of men earning doctorates in home economics increased markedly, with about 17 percent of all doctoral degrees, and 49 percent of those in child development and family relations, being awarded to men (Rossiter 1995). While men joined the faculty ranks of colleges of home economics, their presence did not attract an increase in male students at that time.

Throughout the field's history, home economics leaders reexamined the philosophy and mission of home economics. At mid-century, in the midst of the aforementioned changes, the philosophy and basic tenets of the founders were reaffirmed: "Home economics synthesizes knowledge drawn from its own research, from the physical, biological, and social sciences and the arts and applies this knowledge to improving the lives of families and individuals" (*Home Economics: New Directions* 1959, 4). The document *New Directions* also described the many settings in which individuals with degrees in the field were engaged, reflecting the continuing trend of specialized knowledge, organized by subject area, to address the problems of daily life.

The image of a stable and comfortable life in the United States dramatically changed in the 1960s and 1970s. Pivotal books brought to public attention specific social and environmental issues. Betty Friedan addressed perplexing issues in women's lives in *The Feminine Mystique* (1963); Michael Harrington revealed the extent of poverty in the nation in *The Other America* (1962); and Rachel Carson described the dangers of abusing the natural environment in *Silent Spring* (1962). The civil rights movement forced U.S. society to confront racial injustice. When the Civil Rights Act of 1964 was written, it was amended to include gender. Women's roles in society continued to change over the next decades as increasing numbers of women, especially married women and mothers, entered the paid labor force. This transition was unremarkable as a gradual shift, yet it was so momentous in its cumulative effect that labor economists characterized it as a "subtle revolution" (Smith 1979). In a little more than a generation (approximately 1945–1975), the size of the U.S. employed female labor force more than doubled.

In 1975, another AHEA committee, New Directions II, affirmed the founders' definition of the field and asserted that the focus of home economics is the family in its various forms. They defined a "family" as "a unit of intimate transacting and interdependent persons who share some values and goals, responsibility for decisions and resources and have commitment to one another over time" (Bivens et al. 1975, 26). This definition emphasized interaction and interdependence, rather than structure or legalities. It was a definition ahead of its time, and has been increasingly appropriate as family configurations became more and more diverse during the following decades. Well into the twenty-first century, the definition of a family remains one of the most pressing societal and political issues. Restating the founders' ecological philosophy, New Directions II (Bivens et al. 1975, 27) declared, "The core of home economics is the family ecosystem: the study of the reciprocal relations of [a] family to its natural and man-made environments, the effect of these singly or in unison as they shape the internal functioning of families, and the interplays between the family and other social institutions and the physical environment."

Concurrent with the seventy-fifth anniversary of the AHEA in 1987, the association published a compilation of essays on the areas of study and practice in home economics (child development, clothing, textiles, food, nutrition, family economics, housing, home management) (East and Thomson 1987). The authors described the growth of knowledge in the various subject areas, while affirming the interrelationships among them.

During this period, Marjorie Brown (1985, 1993) and Brown and Beatrice Paolucci (1979) critiqued home economics philosophy and practice. They advocated critical science (an adaptation of critical theory) as a tool for home economics professionals to examine the profession itself as well as the culture in which it functioned. Vincenti and Smith (2004) and McGregor (2012) have condensed and interpreted Brown's philosophy and language for contemporary scholars and practitioners. Rather than assume that the problems families face are just about daily tasks, Brown's terminology "practical perennial problems" encourages home economics practitioners and students to consider what should be done to meet human needs, taking into account the conditions in society and the recurring concerns faced by each generation over long periods of time and across cultures. These challenges require deliberative thought and reasoned action that can be both intellectually and morally defended. Brown's approach was widely championed by home economics teacher educators, and it provided the impetus for revisions in home economics school curricula (Johnson and Fedje 1999).

The issue of nomenclature for the field of home economics has been discussed throughout its history. At a conference in Scottsdale, Arizona, in 1993 "family and consumer sciences" was chosen (see Kay, this volume; Elias 2008). Subsequently, AHEA formally changed its name to the American Association of Family and Consumer Sciences (AAFCS). Affiliated organizations for teachers, Cooperative Extension personnel, and one college administrators association also adopted "family and consumer sciences." The title Board on Human Sciences was selected by administrators representing home economics units institutionally affiliated with the national land-grant and state universities association. The youth organization linked to school home economics programs replaced Future Homemakers of America with Family, Career, and Community Leaders of America in 1999 (Vincenti and Browne 2009).

As the twenty-first century approached, family and consumer sciences professionals were acutely aware of the trends that were reshaping U.S. society. Among them were technology, especially the development of digital communications systems; globalization; change from a production to a service economy; increased ethnic diversity and aging of the population; concern about environmental sustainability; changes in patterns of work; and, especially relevant to the profession, dramatic alterations in family composition and roles (Baugher et al. 2000). A think tank was convened in 2000 to establish a forward-looking framework to encompass the body of knowledge for family and consumer sciences.

Based on these deliberations, a Body of Knowledge Task Force further refined the concepts developed by the group. The model was introduced at the 2001 AAFCS Commemorative Lecture (Anderson and Nickols 2001) and was further elaborated in the association's research journal (Nickols et al. 2009). It builds on the integrative focus that has been a characteristic of home economics throughout its history. This body of knowledge model was adopted as the intellectual frame of reference for accreditation by the AAFCS's Council for Accreditation (2010) and is used as a basis for curricula, specific courses in academic units, outreach, and service programs.

The Venn diagram in figure 1.1 depicts the integrative nature of the field of family and consumer sciences. The central concept is basic human needs

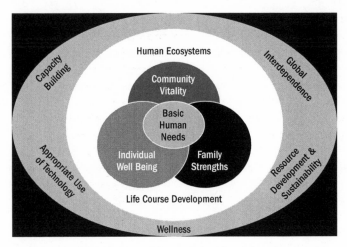

FIGURE 1.1. Family and Consumer Sciences Body of Knowledge

with individual well-being, family strengths, and community vitality seen as interdependent and essential features of a satisfying quality of life. Two core concepts—human ecosystems and life course development—are integrative elements (i.e., necessary for understanding the interdependent systems of human and natural environments and the transitions and trajectories that individuals and families experience through their lifetimes). The outer sphere of the diagram is composed of crosscutting themes, reflecting issues in the social, economic, political, technological, and natural environments. The current crosscutting themes are the appropriate use of technology, wellness, resource development and sustainability, global interdependence, and capacity building. While the core concepts are enduring within the profession, the practice of the profession occurs in an ever-changing environment, and thus the crosscutting themes will likely change over time (Anderson and Nickols 2001). With this orientation, the field is well positioned to address emerging trends and to collaborate with allied professions.

The body of knowledge conceptual framework lends itself to "transdisciplinary" applied research because it "incorporates the pragmatic and humanistic philosophical traditions of human ecology" and encourages diverse research approaches (Faust et al. 2014). The integrative framework allows for studying the individual in the context of the family or studying the family in the context of the community.

Empirical research continues as a mainstay in family and consumer sciences research methods. Many of the questions addressed require experimental study conducted in a laboratory. Other experimental designs involve human subjects with specific characteristics, while survey research is based on sampling from the population. Qualitative research approaches involve the researcher(s) interacting directly with the individual or family. Often this is a follow-up to a survey that identified salient issues for a target population, such as the elderly, at-risk families, or low-income consumers. For example, family scientists have been at the forefront of work with military families who are experiencing the loss of a loved one, separation during deployment, or reintegrating after active duty (Nelson Goff, Crow, and Reisbig 2009; Wick and Nelson Goff 2014; Wilson et al. 2011). The holistic approach of developing interventions that involve not only the military member, but also his or her family and environment, is a model that can be applied to other human sciences issues in keeping with the enduring mission of home economics.

The body of knowledge framework encourages researchers and practitioners alike to reach across domains of methodology or subject matter to address the crosscutting themes of wellness or sustainability. Examples abound of human scientists teaming with engineers, chemists, economists, or political scientists to work on renewable products or public policy to promote sustainability. The national and international emphasis on wellness has brought together health professionals from diverse fields to explore both behavioral and physical aspects of wellness. In this effort, human scientists are often leaders in the prevention and intervention realm (see Lewis, Laing, and Foss, this volume). Common interests have paired dietitians and nutritionists with exercise scientists as they study the synergistic and beneficial effects of diet and exercise on health. Indeed this latter collaboration has led to bringing the nutrition and exercise science fields together, sometimes in the same academic unit (Haymes and Dorsey 1998). The integrative and interdisciplinary approach of human ecology to the promotion of healthy lifestyles and the prevention of disease means that the field is well positioned to play a critical role in any national, comprehensive health care reform initiative.

An Enduring Mission

Documents spanning more than a century of home economics affirm the intent of the field to be empowerment and intervention. Words such as "promote," "improve," "strengthen," "empower," and other proactive terminology are used to describe the mission of home economics. A mission is an entity's reason for existing and a guide for its actions, and it is a feature of a profession along with its particular knowledge and skills. The mission of home economics is fulfilled through a variety of practices and applications.

The various units of today's home economics (e.g., colleges, departments, agencies, professional associations) have mission statements that reflect the educational and proactive intentions appropriate to their function. For many the mission statement is a version of "improving the quality of life for individuals and families." One outcome of the Scottsdale conference was the motto "Empowering Individuals, Strengthening Families, Enabling Communities" ("Conceptual Framework" 1994). More recently, an alliance of family and consumer sciences organizations adopted the guiding principle: "Creating Healthy and Sustainable Families" (AAFCS n.d.).

Several distinguishing traits originating from the philosophy and mission of home economics characterize practitioners of the profession and the field itself. The practice of the profession is not just transmitting knowledge; it also involves the attitudes and values of those in the field. Participants at the Lake Placid Conferences explored these concepts. Benjamin Andrews, a professor of household economics at Teachers College in New York City, attended the Lake Placid Conference in 1907 and observed: "So far home science has concerned itself chiefly with material factors. The home and the family are not fundamentally a material thing, they are a personal or spiritual life participated in by individuals" (Lake Placid Conference 1907, 152). Marion Talbot, Alice Chowan (from Canada), and Isabel Bevier also promulgated concepts that promoted the home as a nurturing environment and home economics as a field of study that included moral and intellectual freedom (Lake Placid Conference 1908; also see Brown 1984).

This strong sense of identity with the mission has been coined the "soul" of the profession (Anderson and Nickols 2001; Baugher 2001). Many professionals in home economics explain that they are "called" to their field of study and their careers. Their practice of the profession is inextricably bound to an identity that expresses their core values and is supported by ethical, responsible, and altruistic concerns for the well-being of the public (East 1980; Nickols 2001). Don Bower (2001, 21) asserted that the nature of home economics "begins with our commitment to using the physical and social sciences to nurture families and communities. Beyond that, however, our soul has to be linked to the fact that women predominate in our disciplines" and many have "felt the sting of oppression, whether based on gender, ethnicity, or even the discipline itself" (also see Nerad 1999; Ralston, this volume). The strength-based approach of empowerment through knowledge with the ultimate goal of well-being for individuals, families, and communities (often expressed as a calling to make a positive difference) continues to sustain the practitioners of family and consumer sciences despite the fluctuations in public understanding and support of the profession.

Modern Faces of Home Economics

Today's family and consumer scientists, grounded in the integrative knowledge base of the field, continue to carry out the mission of improving the quality of life. Apple and Coleman (2003, 122) observed that as the field has become more specialized "graduates of postsecondary programs rarely consider themselves home economists or even family and consumer professionals. Rather they identify with a more narrow profession such as nutrition, or child development, or personal finance." They suggested that this narrowing "often ignores the ideals of social responsibility that the early leaders promoted." Contrary to this conclusion, many graduates select careers traditionally associated with home economics that respond to specific human needs, while others create careers as social entrepreneurs—individuals who pursue innovative solutions to social issues that will create and sustain social values (Social Entrepreneur n.d.). Furthermore, current students are engaged in service-learning programs, practicum experiences, and family policy courses that foster a human ecological understanding. When describing what they hope to accomplish through their careers, strong overtones of the home economics reformist tradition and mission are evident.

The values of the past and a sense of mission are still present in the work of contemporary professionals. We have selected five profiles to provide a sampling of the modern face of home economics. The first is about HOPE, which shows how today's family and consumer professionals are addressing problems such as homelessness, which requires an understanding of human development, personal values, housing, and consumer economics.

HOPE Community

Homelessness is a problem plaguing many communities today. Families are increasingly a large part of that population. As social and volunteer services struggle to assist, keeping families intact and helping them maintain resilience is challenging. Enter Dr. Lenore McWey and her students in the College of Human Sciences at Florida State University. They are taking this challenge locally by providing parenting education to families in the HOPE (Housing Opportunities and Personal Empowerment) Community, a transitional housing program in Tallahassee and part of the Big Bend Homeless Coalition. McWey uses an evidence-based parenting education program called the "Incredible Years," developed by Dr. Carolyn Webster-Stratton. This interactive parenting education prepares parents and children with better communication and coping skills as they make transitions. In recognition of the value of this service, the Department of Family and Child Sciences received President Barack Obama's Volunteer Service Award in 2011. The HOPE Community program illustrates not only the efficacy of interventions in the context of the family, but also the moral "rightness" of the home economics mission of creating healthy and sustainable families. McWey (pers. comm.) expresses the "personal calling" tradition in home economics: "It has been a great privilege to work with HOPE community families. When I see the parents laughing and playing with their children, I am reminded of how much more I have received from

this project than I have given." McWey earned a PhD in marriage and family therapy at
Florida State University and previously taught at Virginia Tech.

Professionals in child development advocate for the well-being of children
by providing for quality childcare and early childhood education. The ability
to reach vast audiences to teach about personal well-being and social responsibility benefits from the entrepreneurial expertise of home economists like
Janice Hamilton, who have remade their careers.

Janice Hamilton: From Corporate America to Entrepreneur

"To do good while doing well"—that's the mission of Janice Hamilton's company,
CarrotNewYork. She and her team stimulate action for positive personal change and
social responsibility in health and wellness, environmental sustainability, peer relationships, financial literacy, and nutrition. They reach their audience—children
and youth—through videos, interactive games, posters, comic books, websites, and
"anything digital." CarrotNewYork's clients include government agencies (USDA, FDA,
FEMA), corporations (Visa, Colgate-Palmolive), and associations (Ad Council, Autism
Speaks). CarrotNewYork's programs have been trans-created for eighty countries in
over thirty languages. Hamilton began her career in traditional home economics areas (bachelor's degree in home economics education from Marymount College, master's degree in clothing and textiles from Kansas State University). She joined McCall
Pattern Company and then Butterick Fashion Marketing Company, and later was the
director of consumer marketing for Singer. Hamilton (pers. comm.) says, "In 1980, my
entrepreneurial spirit led to the launch of JMH Education Marketing. I am committed
to stimulating positive social change and social responsibility through education, so
I rebranded the company to CarrotNewYork and launched into new delivery methods."
Carrot's programs have garnered numerous awards, including an Emmy. In keeping
with Hamilton's social good philosophy, CarrotNewYork's policies enable its employees to achieve a healthy work-life balance.

Dietitians and nutritionists are leading the fight against obesity through
their work in schools, hospitals, and clinics, educating the public about the
many factors that influence healthy eating behavior. Food scientists like Dr.
Yun-Hwa Hsieh are at the forefront of efforts to maintain a healthful and safe
food supply both in the United States and abroad, while respecting consumers' cultural contexts.

Yun-Hwa Hsieh's Global Contributions to the Quality of Life

Dr. Yun-Hwa "Peggy" Hsieh, the Betty M. Watts Professor of nutrition, food, and exercise sciences in the College of Human Sciences at Florida State University, is an innovative teacher and researcher. She has developed antibodies for detecting trace amounts

PHOTO 1.1. Yun-Hwa Hsieh, Betty M. Watts Professor of nutrition, food, and exercise sciences, researches food composition. Photograph courtesy College of Human Sciences, Florida State University.

of contaminants, working to minimize the hidden risks of allergens and other prohibited ingredients in food. She holds many patents, and her antibodies are incorporated in commercial, easy-to-use assay kits available to food processors, restaurants, government regulators, and schools. Hsieh's work has garnered international attention for detection of the protein elements that cause the spread of mad cow disease and for pork- and blood-derived materials that are strictly forbidden for many around the world. Countries with large Muslim populations are interested in Hsieh's methods. She has been hosted by the Sultanate of Brunei and appointed to the advisory committee of its Halal Industry Innovation Centre. Her expertise is helping the organization to develop test methods to ensure that citizens have access to the halal foods that meet their dietary restrictions. As she works with populations around the globe, Hsieh is motivated by a sensitivity to different cultures and a desire to help people everywhere enhance their quality of life. Like many of the first home economists, she strives to improve food safety and inform the public. Hsieh earned a PhD in human sciences at Florida State University; she previously taught at Auburn University.

In the 1970s and 1980s, home economists advocated for women's financial rights (e.g., credit in women's own names, pay equity), and they continue to advocate for family-oriented policies in the workplace. Today, the integrative nature of the profession also is evident in the holistic approach of family financial advisors, like Bluestem Financial Advisors.

Holistic Financial Planning

"I aim to make the financial planning process an educational one, giving my clients the tools to reach their financial goals, and providing audiences [with] information to help them make smart decisions in each stage of life," says Dr. Karen Folk (pers. comm.). Her co-owner and partner in Bluestem Financial Advisors, Jacob Kuebler, declares, "Young professionals are often overlooked, but as these clients' work and family life becomes more complex, I help them develop a clear track to meet their goals; I am passionate about that" (Kuebler, pers. comm.). Folk and Kuebler are both certified financial planners. Understanding how things fit together—the interaction of people, environments, events, and resources—is characteristic of professionals in family and consumer sciences. Using this holistic perspective, personal financial planners serve as effective guides for financial decision making and as trusted managers of assets. Two historical pillars of home economics, home management and consumer economics, are the foundation for personal financial planning. Folk earned a PhD in family and consumption economics at the University of Illinois, Urbana-Champaign (UIUC) and a master's degree in consumer economics at Oklahoma State University. Kuebler holds a bachelor's degree from UIUC in agricultural and consumer economics and a master's degree in personal financial planning from the College of Human Ecology, Kansas State University. Both Folk and Kuebler are active in consumer-oriented organizations of financial planners with high professional standards and a strong sense of social responsibility.

PHOTO 1.2. Karen Folk and Jacob Kuebler of Bluestem Financial Advisors review financial plans with clients. Photograph courtesy Bluestem Financial Advisors, LLC.

Apparel development and marketing professionals and interior designers with degrees in human ecology demonstrate their commitment to sustainability by increasingly adopting socially responsible production policies and green practices in selecting materials. Family and consumer sciences educators and volunteers facilitate community development and guide communities seeking to understand and influence public policy (Anderson 2004). Family policy analysis conducted by human ecology professionals broadens political discourse by bringing a holistic, multidimensional, lifespan framework to the development of laws and regulations that otherwise have been viewed from individualistic or single-solution perspectives (Anderson 2004; Bogenschneider and Corbett 2010). Family and consumer sciences graduates build on subject matter knowledge and international experiences as they join think tanks and global action agencies.

Khadija Hill and Resources for the Future

The launching pad for Khadija Hill's desired career in policy analysis and environmental sustainability was, she says, "the value placed on family and education in rural Georgia where I grew up" (Hill, pers. comm.). Engagement in a service-learning project that took an interdisciplinary team of women students and faculty to a remote area of Tanzania provided Hill with insight about the cohesiveness among her multiple interests in the environment, women's roles, consumer decision making, and social policy. After graduating in 2009 with a bachelor of science degree in family and consumer sciences from the University of Georgia, her goal was to create a career of service in promoting healthy, prosperous, thriving families and communities, and to gain an understanding of the day-to-day workings of the social, political, and economic structure. "I understood I must be in the best environment to accomplish that, so

PHOTO 1.3. Khadija Hill applies her consumer sciences degree and her passion for international environmental sustainability and the well-being of families at Resources for the Future in Washington, D.C. Photograph by Ellen A. Walter, courtesy Resources for the Future.

I relocated to the center of American policy and governance, Washington, D.C., and looked for a job," she recalls. She found Resources for the Future (RFF), and RFF recognized Hill's credentials and passion. RFF is a think tank, conducting nonpartisan research, developing policy briefs, and facilitating dialogue on environmental and economic issues affecting communities locally and globally. Hill began her work at RFF as a research staff assistant and was then promoted to development officer for individual giving. Hill affirms: "Family and consumer sciences prepared me so well for this work—it's my passion!"

Home economics has remade itself throughout its history. The field is broad and complex, increasingly requiring more specialized knowledge, yet continuing to address issues that are interrelated in complicated ways in daily life. The contemporary manifestations of home economics are found in diverse settings. Attempts to shed the connotations and clichés of the past by selecting different names for the field that are believed to be more suitable and accurate have not necessarily enlightened the public. Yet students, both women and men, continue to find their calling in family and consumer sciences. Strong programs of research and public service at institutions of higher education extend the reach of the profession. In the practice of modern professionals the knowledge and mission of the field continue. They are an enduring legacy.

ACKNOWLEDGMENTS

This chapter benefited from the insights of John Buckwalter, the dean of the College of Human Ecology at Kansas State University, and Gladys Shelton, the interim state program leader for 4-H and Family at North Carolina A&T State University's Cooperative Extension. We express our appreciation to them and to the individuals featured in the vignettes.

REFERENCES

AAFCS (American Association of Family and Consumer Sciences). N.d. "Creating Healthy and Sustainable Families," www.AAFCS.org/aboutus/FCSbrand.asp (accessed April 17, 2014).

ACEND (Accreditation Council for Education in Nutrition and Dietetics). 2013. *Policy and Procedures Manual.* Chicago: Academy of Nutrition and Dietetics.

Anderson, Carol L., ed. 2004. *Family and Community Policy: Strategies for Civic Engagement.* Alexandria, Va.: American Association of Family and Consumer Sciences.

Anderson, Carol L., and Sharon Y. Nickols. 2001. "The Essence of Our Being: A Synopsis of the 2001 Commemorative Lecture." *Journal of Family and Consumer Sciences* 93(5): 15–18.

Apple, Rima D. 1997. "Liberal Arts or Vocational Training? Home Economics Education for Girls." In *Rethinking Home Economics: Women and the History of a Profession*, edited by Sarah Stage and Virginia B. Vincenti, 79–95. Ithaca, N.Y.: Cornell University Press.

Apple, Rima D., and Joyce Coleman. 2003. "'As Members of the Social Whole': A History of Social Reform as a Focus of Home Economics, 1895–1940." *Family and Consumer Sciences Research Journal* 32(2): 104–126.

Baldwin, Keturah E. 1949. *The AHEA Saga.* Washington, D.C.: American Home Economics Association.

Baugher, Shirley L., ed. 2001. "The Soul of the Profession." *Journal of Family and Consumer Sciences* 93(3): 17.

Baugher, Shirley L., Carol L. Anderson, Kinsey B. Green, Sharon Y. Nickols, Jan Shane, Laura Jolly, and Joyce Miles. 2000. "Body of Knowledge of Family and Consumer Sciences." *Journal of Family and Consumer Sciences* 92(3): 29–32.

Beecher, Catharine E. 1846. *A Treatise on Domestic Economy, for the Use of Young Ladies at Home and at School*, rev. ed. New York: Harper and Brothers.

Beecher, Catharine E., and Harriet Beecher Stowe. 1869. *The American Woman's Home.* New York: J. B. Ford.

Bevier, Isabel, and Susannah Usher. 1906. *The Home Economics Movement.* Boston: M. Barrows.

Bivens, Gordon, Margaret Fitch, Gwendolyn Newkirk, Beatrice Paolucci, Em Riggs, Satenig St. Marie, and Gladys Vaughn. 1975. "Home Economics—New Directions II." *Journal of Home Economics* 67(3): 26–27.

Bogenschneider, Karen, and Thomas J. Corbett. 2010. "Family Policy: Becoming a Field of Inquiry and Subfield of Social Policy." *Journal of Marriage and Family* 72(3): 783–803.

Bower, Don. 2001. "Soul Shaping Borne of Personal Experience." *Journal of Family and Consumer Sciences* 93(3): 21.

Brown, Marjorie M. 1984. "Home Economics: Proud Past—Promising Future." *Journal of Home Economics* 76(4): 48–54, 27.

———. 1985. *Philosophical Studies of Home Economics in the United States: Our Practical-Intellectual Heritage.* Vols. 1 and 2. East Lansing: Michigan State University.

———. 1993. *Philosophical Studies of Home Economics in the United States: Basic Ideas by Which Home Economists Understand Themselves.* East Lansing: Michigan State University.

Brown, Marjorie, and Beatrice Paolucci. 1979. *Home Economics: A Definition.* Alexandria, Va.: American Home Economics Association.

Carson, Rachel. 1962. *Silent Spring.* Boston: Houghton Mifflin.

Clarke, Robert. 1973. *Ellen Swallow: The Woman Who Founded Ecology.* Chicago: Follett.

Collier, Billie J., Martin Bide, and Phillip G. Tortora. 2009. *Understanding Textiles.* Upper Saddle River, N.J.: Pearson/Prentice Hall.

"The Conceptual Framework for the 21st Century." 1994. *Journal of Family and Consumer Sciences* 86(4): 38.

Council for Accreditation, American Association of Family and Consumer Sciences. 2010. *Accreditation Documents for Undergraduate Programs in Family and Consumer Sciences*, http://www.AAFCS.org/education/accreditation.html (accessed March 30, 2014).

Craig, Hazel T. 1945. *The History of Home Economics*. New York: Practical Home Economics.

East, Marjorie. 1980. *Home Economics: Past, Present, and Future*. Boston: Allyn and Bacon.

East, Marjorie, and Joan Thomson, eds. 1987. *Definitive Themes in Home Economics and Their Impact on Families, 1909–1984*. Washington, D.C.: American Home Economics Association.

Elias, Megan J. 2008. *Stir It Up: Home Economics in American Culture*. Philadelphia: University of Pennsylvania Press.

Fahm, Esther Glover. 1990. "Home Economics—Our Roots, Our Present, Our Future." In *Historically Black Land-Grant Institutions and the Development of Agriculture and Home Economics, 1890–1990*, edited by Leedell W. Neyland, 190–252. Tallahassee: Florida A&M University Foundation.

Faust, Victoria, Cynthia R. Jasper, Ariel Kaufman, and Margaret J. Nellis. 2014. "Cooperative Inquiry in Human Ecology: Historical Roots and Future Applications." *Family and Consumer Sciences Research Journal* 42(2): 267–277.

Friedan, Betty. 1963. *The Feminine Mystique*. New York. Norton.

Galbraith, John Kenneth. 1958. *The Affluent Society*. New York: Houghton Mifflin.

Garber-Dyar, Connie, Nancy G. Golwitzer, and Jean Memken. 1994. "Codes and Standards in Interior Design Curricula of College and University Home Economics Programs." *Journal of Family and Consumer Sciences* 86(3): 37–44.

Gassett, Lorna J. 1957. *Space Allowances for Meal Preparation and Service in the Southern Rural Home*. Bulletin 274. Knoxville: University of Tennessee Agricultural Experiment Station. http://trace.tennessee.edu/utk_agbulletin/189 (accessed May 5, 2014).

Gentzler, Yvonne S. 2012. "Home Economics: Ever Timely and Forever Complex." *Phi Kappa Phi Forum* 92(2): 4–7.

Goldstein, Carolyn M. 2012. *Creating Consumers: Home Economists in Twentieth-Century America*. Chapel Hill: University of North Carolina Press.

Goodspeed, Helen G., and Emma Johnson. 1929. *Care and Training of Children*. Philadelphia: Lippincott.

Grant, Julia. 1997. "Modernizing Mothers: Home Economics and the Parent Education Movement, 1920–1945." In *Rethinking Home Economics: Women and the History of a Profession*, edited by Sarah Stage and Virginia B. Vincenti, 55–78. Ithaca, N.Y.: Cornell University Press.

Groves, Ernest R., Edna L. Skinner, and Sadie J. Swenson. 1932. *The Family and Its Relationships*. Philadelphia: Lippincott.

Gunn, Virginia Railsback. 1992. "Educating Strong Womanly Women: Kansas Shapes the Western Home Economics Movement, 1860–1914." PhD diss., University of Akron.

Guy-Sheftall, Beverly, and Jo Moore Steward. 1981. *Spelman: A Centennial Celebration, 1881–1981*. Charlotte, N.C.: Delmar.

Harrington, Michael. 1962. *The Other America: Poverty in the United States*. New York: Simon and Schuster.

Harris, Carmen. 1997. "Grace Under Pressure: The Black Home Extension Service in South Carolina, 1919–1966." In *Rethinking Home Economics: Women and the History of a Profession*, edited by Sarah Stage and Virginia B. Vincenti, 203–228. Ithaca, N.Y.: Cornell University Press.

Haymes, Emily M., and Jodee L. Dorsey. 1998. "The Florida State University Program." *Quest* 50: 116–120.

Holt, Marilyn Irvin. 1995. *Linoleum, Better Babies, and the Modern Farm Woman, 1890–1930*. Albuquerque: University of New Mexico Press.

Home Economics: New Directions: A Statement of Philosophy and Objectives. 1959. American Home Economics Association. AAFCS Archives, Rare and Manuscript Collections, Carl A. Kroch Library, Cornell University, Ithaca, N.Y.

Hunt, Caroline L. 1942. *The Life of Ellen H. Richards, 1842–1911*. Washington, D.C.: American Home Economics Association.

James, Edward T., Janet Vilson James, and Paul S. Boyer. 1971. *Notable American Women 1607–1950: A Bibliographical Dictionary*. Vol. 2. Cambridge, Mass.: Belknap.

Johnson, Julie, and Cheryl G. Fedje, eds. 1999. *Family and Consumer Sciences Curriculum: Toward a Critical Science Approach*. Peoria, Ill.: McGraw-Hill.

Katz, Esther. 1980. "Grace Hoadley Dodge: Women and the Emerging Metropolis, 1856–1914." PhD diss., New York University.

Kwallek, Nancy. 2012. "Ellen Swallow Richards: Visionary on Home and Sustainability." *Phi Kappa Phi Forum* 92(2): 8–11.

Lake Placid Conference on Home Economics. 1901. *Proceedings of the First, Second, and Third Conferences*. Lake Placid, N.Y.: n.p.

———. 1902. *Proceedings of the Fourth Conference*. Lake Placid, N.Y.: n.p.

———. 1907. *Proceedings of the Ninth Conference*. Lake Placid, N.Y.: n.p.

———. 1908. *Proceedings of the Tenth Conference*. Lake Placid, N.Y.: n.p.

Leavitt, Sarah A. 2002. *From Catharine Beecher to Martha Stewart: A Cultural History of Domestic Advice*. Chapel Hill: University of North Carolina Press.

Lyford, Carrie Alberta. 1923. "Home Economics in Negro Schools." *Journal of Home Economics* 15(11): 634–637.

McGregor, Sue L. T. 2012. "Marjorie Brown's Philosophical Legacy: Contemporary Relevance." *Kappa Omicron Nu Forum* 19(1). http://www.kon.org/archives/forum/19-1/mcgregor3.html (accessed April 5, 2014).

Merriam-Webster. N.d. "Economics." www.merriam-webster.com/dictionary/economics (accessed April 10, 2014).

Meszaros, Peggy S., and Bonnie Braun. 1983. "Early Pioneers." *Journal of Home Economics* 75(3): 4–8.

Miles, Joyce B. 2009. *The Life and Legacy of Ellen Swallow Richards*. DVD available from American Association of Family and Consumer Sciences, Alexandria, Va.

Miller, Elisa. 2004. "In the Name of the Home: Women, Domestic Science, and American Higher Education, 1865–1930." PhD diss. University of Illinois.

Miller, Julia R., Dorothy I. Mitstifer, and Gladys Gary Vaughn, eds. 2009. *African*

American Women: Contributions to the Human Sciences. East Lansing, Mich.: Kappa
Omicron Nu.

Nelson Goff, Briana S., J. R. Crow, and A. M. J. Reisbig. 2009. "Primary Trauma of
Female Partners in a Military Sample: Individual Symptoms and Relationship
Satisfaction." *American Journal of Family Therapy* 37: 336–346.

Nerad, Maresi. 1999. *The Academic Kitchen: A Social History of Gender Stratification at
the University of California, Berkeley.* Albany: State University of New York Press.

Nickols, Sharon Y. 2001. "Keeping the Betty Lamp Burning." *Journal of Family and
Consumer Sciences* 93(3): 35–44.

Nickols, Sharon Y., Penny A. Ralston, Carol Anderson, Lorna Browne, Genevieve
Schroeder, Sabrina Thomas, and Peggy Wild. 2009. "The Family and Consumer
Sciences Body of Knowledge and the Cultural Kaleidoscope: Research
Opportunities and Challenges." *Family and Consumer Sciences Research Journal*
37(3): 266–283.

Powers, Jane Bernard. 1992. *The "Girl Question" in Education: Vocational Education for
Young Women in the Progressive Era.* Washington, D.C.: Falmer.

Pundt, Helen. 1980. *AHEA: A History of Excellence.* Washington, D.C.: American Home
Economics Association.

Richards, Ellen. 1907. *Sanitation in Daily Life.* Boston: Thomas Todd.

Roark, James L., Michael P. Johnson, Patricia Cline Cohen, Sarah Stage, Alan Lawson,
and Susan M. Hartmann. 2009. *The American Promise: A History of the United
States,* 4th ed. Boston: Bedford/St. Martin's.

Rossiter, Margaret. 1982. *Women Scientists in America: Struggles to 1940.* Baltimore,
Md.: Johns Hopkins University Press.

———. 1995. *Women Scientists in America: Before Affirmative Action, 1940–1972.*
Baltimore, Md.: Johns Hopkins University Press.

Schneider, Dorothy, and Carl J. Schneider. 1993. *American Women in the Progressive
Era, 1900–1920.* New York: Facts on File.

Scholl, Jan. 2008. "Early FCS Extension Specialist: Martha Van Rensselaer." *Family and
Consumer Sciences Research Journal* 37(2): 149–156.

———. 2011. "Martha Van Rensselaer: Family and Consumer Sciences Champion."
Journal of Family and Consumer Sciences 103(3): 11–18.

———. 2013. "Extension Family and Consumer Sciences: Why It Was Included in the
Smith-Lever Act of 1914." *Journal of Family and Consumer Sciences* 105(4): 8–16.

Smith, Ralph E., ed. 1979. *The Subtle Revolution: Women at Work.* Washington, D.C.:
Urban Institute.

Social Entrepreneur. N.d. www.ashoka.org/social_entrepreneur (accessed May 5,
2014).

Stage, Sarah. 1997. "Ellen Richards and the Social Significance of the Home Economics
Movement." In *Rethinking Home Economics: Women and the History of a Profession,*
edited by Sarah Stage and Virginia B. Vincenti, 17–33. Ithaca, N.Y.: Cornell
University Press.

Stage, Sarah, and Virginia B. Vincenti, eds. 1997. *Rethinking Home Economics: Women
and the History of a Profession.* Ithaca, N.Y.: Cornell University Press.

Standards Committee. 1933. *History: Home Economics in Georgia*. Georgia Home Economics Association. AAFCS Archives, Rare and Manuscript Collections, Carl A. Kroch Library, Cornell University, Ithaca, N.Y.

Tonkovich, Nicole, ed. 2002. *The American Woman's Home*. New Brunswick, N.J.: Rutgers University Press.

Vincenti, Virginia, and Lorna Browne. 2009. *The Heritage of Home Economics*, pt. 3: *1980s–2000s*. Audiovisual program available from Kappa Omicron Nu, East Lansing, Mich.

Vincenti, Virginia, and Frances Smith. 2004. "Critical Science: What It Could Offer All Family and Consumer Sciences Professionals." *Journal of Family and Consumer Sciences* 96(1): 63–70.

Weigley, Emma Seifrit. 1974. "It Might Have Been Euthenics: The Lake Placid Conferences and the Home Economics Movement." *American Quarterly* 26(1): 79–96.

Whitaker, William H., Jr., M. Virlyn Williams, M. Evelyn Fields, Dannie L. Keepler, Bonita Y. Manson, and Sheila M. Littlejohn. 2009. "Historically Black Colleges and Universities: The Development of Family and Consumer Sciences in HBCUs." In *African American Women: Contributions to the Human Sciences*, edited by Julia R. Miller, Dorothy I. Mitstifer, and Gladys Gary Vaughn, 3–21. East Lansing, Mich.: Kappa Omicron Nu.

Wick, S., and Briana S. Nelson Goff. 2014. "A Qualitative Analysis of Military Couples with High and Low Trauma Symptoms and Relationship Distress Levels." *Journal of Couple and Relationship Therapy* 13: 63–88.

Williams, Thomas T., and Handy Williamson Jr. 1985. "Teaching, Research, and Extension Programs at Predominantly Black Land-Grant Institutions." *Southern Journal of Agricultural Economics* 17(1): 31–41.

Wilson, S. R., K. Wilkum, S. M. Chernichky, S. M. MacDermid Wadsworth, and K. M. Broiarczyk. 2011. "Passport Toward Success: Description and Evaluation of a Program Designed to Help Children and Families Reconnect after a Military Deployment." *Journal of Applied Communication Research* 39: 626–655.

2. Extending Knowledge, Changing Lives

Cooperative Extension Family and Consumer Sciences

JORGE H. ATILES, CAROLINE E. CROCOLL, *and* JANE SCHUCHARDT

Four federal legislative acts between 1886 and 1914 created a unique educational system for the general public in the United States. The culmination of this legislation was the Cooperative Extension Service, a partnership among federal, state, and local governments to deliver knowledge from institutions of higher education to the people for individual and community action. The concept and the institutional structure have endured for over a hundred years. This chapter chronicles the history, current form and function, and future prospects of Cooperative Extension's family and consumer sciences.

Legislative History of Land-Grant Colleges and Cooperative Extension

On May 15, 1862, President Abraham Lincoln established the Department of Agriculture and called it "the people's department." That same year, Lincoln signed the first Morrill Act into law, which created institutions in each state that would educate people in agriculture and other practical professions. Introduced by Vermont congressman Justin Smith Morrill, the land-grant act was intended to make education available to people of all social classes. The law granted each state thirty thousand acres of public land per senator and representative. Proceeds from the sale of the land were to be put in endowment funds to provide support for each state's land-grant college (Bliss 1960; Cochrane 1993).

In 1887, Congress passed the Hatch Act, named for Congressman William Hatch of Missouri, to provide funding for agricultural experiment stations affiliated with the land-grant colleges. The emphasis of the experiment stations was to study and promote the efficient production and use of agricultural products. However, experiment station personnel soon realized that research insights alone were not sufficient to convince farmers to adopt new scientific technologies. Furthermore, many of the farmers in the most critical need of new farming knowledge were unable to read or write (Danbom 2006; Eppright and Ferguson 1971).

The second Morrill Act, passed in 1890, provided funding to the former Confederate states to support their land-grant colleges. It prohibited racial discrimination by any college receiving these funds, requiring that they be distributed "equitably." The states circumvented the anti-discrimination provision by designating separate institutions for persons of color. These colleges, established for African Americans throughout the South, are now known as the 1890 land-grant institutions (Hurt 2002; Rasmussen 1989).

On May 8, 1914, the Smith-Lever Act formalized the Cooperative Extension Service (hereafter, Cooperative Extension), providing for state matching of federal funds to establish a network of county educators connected to the land-grant colleges. The purpose of the legislation, sponsored by Senator Hoke Smith of Georgia and Representative A. F. Lever of South Carolina, was to give "instruction and practical demonstrations in agriculture and home economics to persons not attending . . . college" (Rasmussen 1989, 49). An agreement with the states, drafted shortly after passage of the act, stipulated that not only Smith-Lever-related extension work, but all extension-related work associated with the U.S. Department of Agriculture (USDA) in a state would be carried out through the state college of agriculture. Smith-Lever initially provided $10,000 annually to the agricultural colleges exclusively for Cooperative Extension with the added provision that funding could increase according to growing demand so long as states agreed to match these funds (Hurt 2002; Rasmussen 1989). The inclusion of home economics in Smith-Lever legislation may have been due, in part, to the results of a nationwide USDA survey reporting the hardships of rural women, to which one respondent in her plea for health information for farm homes declared, "Surely, citizens are entitled to as much protection as cattle" (USDA Report 105, 1915, qtd. in Babbitt 1997, 146; also see Scholl 2013).

Historical Origins of Cooperative Extension

It is a common misperception that agricultural instruction began after passage of the Smith-Lever Act. In fact, informal education about agriculture started in the late eighteenth century. After the American Revolution, wealthy farmers organized groups to sponsor educational meetings to disseminate useful farming information (Apps 2010; Bliss 1960; Rasmussen 1989). By the 1850s, colleges in New England began holding "farmers institutes," public meetings where lecturers discussed new farming insights, an idea that spread to the Midwest (Holt 1995). George Washington Carver of the Tuskegee Institute developed the "moveable school," a mule-drawn wagon loaded with items to demonstrate improved methods to farmers in 1899, and other agricultural colleges adapted this concept by outfitting train cars for their demonstrations (Rasmussen 1989). In the early 1900s, advocates for improving the lives of rural women insisted that the farmers institutes also provide sessions for farmers' wives (Holt 1995; Montgomery 2006; Scholl 2013). Home economics educators at the University of North Carolina installed a kitchen in a train car, creating the "first domestic science car" in 1909, and other states adopted this model (Elias 2008, 69, 298). Martha Van Rensselaer launched her Farmers' Wives Reading Course in 1901 (Scholl 2008). President Theodore Roosevelt in a 1907 address to Congress urged major educational reform that would provide agricultural education in rural areas and industrial education in urban centers (Cochrane 1993). Roosevelt's Commission on Country Life (1908–1909) also brought to public attention the economic and social problems of farming (Babbitt 1997).

Aware of these developments during the first decade of the 1900s, Seaman Knapp and other early innovators envisioned what is now known as Cooperative Extension. At that time, outreach from the USDA was part of the Bureau of Plant Industry, principally in the Office of Cooperative Demonstration Work, established in 1904, and in the Office of Farm Management, established in 1906 (Rasmussen 1989). With support from the USDA and philanthropists, several land-grant colleges established out-of-school educational programs to aid men and women in applying accepted practices for improving their farms, homes, and communities (Bliss 1960; Montgomery 2006; Rasmussen 1989; Rieff 2006; Scholl 2013). But progress was slow.

Frustrated by the failure of most farmers to adopt the recommended farming practices, Knapp organized boys' corn clubs, from which developed calf, pig, and potato clubs. After hearing about the corn clubs, a South Carolina school teacher, Marie Cromer, organized a tomato-growing and -canning club for girls in 1910 (Rasmussen 1989). The program quickly expanded to include women and was replicated in other states (Holt 1995; Scholl 2013). Often referred to as the "Father of Extension," Knapp was convinced that demonstrations carried out by farmers and homemakers themselves under the guidance of trained personnel were the most effective way to disseminate scientific information about farming and home improvement.

In 1900 only 3 percent of women in the United States attended college (Bliss 1960; Danbom 2006), but by 1920, 7.6 percent of women eighteen to twenty-one years of age were enrolled in institutions of higher education (Gordon 1990). Some of these women were students in domestic science, especially at the land-grant colleges. Before the Smith-Lever Act, women with domestic science (home economics) degrees, often from normal schools that focused on teacher training, were employed by the land-grant colleges to work with rural girls and women (Goldstein 2012; Montgomery 2006), but passage of the Smith-Lever Act opened even more opportunities for the employment of home economics graduates (Babbitt 1997; Holt 1995).

The Home Economics Domain:
Cooperative Extension Work with Women

The Smith-Lever Act led to the consolidation of all extension work into the State Relations Service of the USDA, organized by region (Schwieder 1993). Plans were implemented to ensure the rapid growth of programs, known as "women's work," targeted specifically to women and their perceived domestic needs (USDA 1951). Home economics county agents, rather than farm agents, delivered these programs in keeping with the gender attitudes of the time (Babbitt 1997). In three years (1914–1917), "27,000 women attended 450 home economics extension schools throughout the forty-eight states," an unprecedented contact with U.S. homemakers (Goldstein 2012, 36).

In the early twentieth century, the lives of rural women were tied to house, farm, and children, and endless domestic work, with little opportunity for outside contact or variety of experience. Most rural women, whether in landowning or tenant families, were an integral part of the farming operation, performing seasonal, if not unrelenting daily, farm work. The goals of Cooperative Extension home economics were to improve rural living standards and modernize homemaking (Harris 1997; Holt 1995; Rieff 2006). Agents offered instruction on how to prepare nutritious low-cost meals; improve water quality and sanitation; practice safe food preservation; sew clothes for the family; provide home nursing care; make the home more convenient and attractive; and budget monetary resources (Elias 2008; Hill 2012). Agents organized home demonstration clubs to more effectively deliver programs and to foster adoption of their recommendations. The clubs also encouraged socializing among the otherwise isolated women (Rieff 1994).

Home economics was a new field of study in 1914 with a relatively limited body of research, except in nutrition, upon which to base its recommendations (Babbitt 1997). Consequently, much of the early home economics programming was skills oriented. Furthermore, Bradford Knapp, who replaced his father as the head of extension work in the South, mandated a task-centered approach in the programs for women, although they might incidentally learn the underlying scientific principles (Hilton 1994). Following the establishment of the Bureau of Home Economics in the USDA in 1923, the results of research in food, nutrition, clothing, housing, and household expenditures were soon available to support the home economics programs in Cooperative Extension (Betters 1930; Goldstein 2012).

The role of Cooperative Extension expanded during World War I. The U.S. government needed to feed the armed forces and provide food for millions of displaced Europeans. Because of the need for food, the federal government appropriated an additional $11.3 million to the USDA, much of which was allocated to extension to mobilize citizens for the war effort. Nationally, the number of home economics agents more than tripled during the war years (Holt 1995). Home economics extension agents were integral to domestic food conservation programs, promoting dietary substitutes for meat and wheat (Elias 2008). They also were the liaisons between rural and urban groups on the "clean milk campaign," which advocated that milk producers regularly test herds for tuberculosis (Olmstead and Rhode 2004).

In 1928, the Capper-Ketchum Act authorized additional funds for Cooperative Extension, especially for the salaries of agriculture, home economics, and 4-H agents (Rasmussen 1989). But any celebration was short-lived as the onslaught of the Great Depression of the 1930s stretched extension's resources. Home economics agents worked with relief efforts, such as community canning centers and soup kitchens, and collaborated with other governmental and volunteer organizations helping families to get by. In Augusta County, Virginia, fifty rural women organized a curb market through their extension's Home Economics Council to sell farm produce and home-baked goods, thus securing much-needed income for their families (McCleary 2006). In Alabama home economics county agents worked with the Agricultural Adjustment Administration on a mattress-making program that used surplus cotton and provided employment for local women (Rieff 1994). Hazel Reed (1997, 183), a New York extension home economist, recalled her Depression era work with women who had time but little money: "if you taught them how, they could go to the attic and find something to make over and make do."

Race and gender attitudes hindered Cooperative Extension programs' availability and effectiveness for many southern rural women (Harris 1997; Hilton 1994; Montgomery 2006; Rieff 1994, 2006). Babbitt (1997) and Osterud (2012) described the resistance of women in the New York countryside to early extension home economics programs. While acknowledging the challenges, Montgomery (2006, 140) summarized the benefit of Cooperative Extension home economics: "The homemaking clubs, canning clubs, and Go-to-College Funds improved the standard of living in [Georgia's] rural households . . . in spite of formidable barriers of gender, class, and race." Despite enormous inequities, African American Cooperative Extension home economics personnel in South Carolina emerged as leaders in their communities (Harris

PHOTO 2.1. Display of fruits and vegetables canned by people on relief, directed primarily by Home Demonstration Club women, Durham County, North Carolina, 1933. Item number UA023.009.041. Special Collections Research Center, North Carolina State University Libraries, Raleigh.

1997). Schwieder (1993) observed that rural women in other parts of the country who had little access to educational opportunities or to the progressive thinking of the day benefited from new information and ideas delivered by extension home economists.

World War II challenged agriculture to again increase farm production. Home economics extension agents promoted gardening and food preservation, thrift, homemade clothing, and repairs. Victory gardens planted by nearly 20 million households during World War II produced up to 40 percent of all vegetables consumed domestically. One goal was to lower the price of vegetables needed by the U.S. War Department to feed troops, thus saving money that the military could spend elsewhere (Bliss 1960). Cooperative Extension homemaker clubs were powerful supporters of these efforts (USDA 1951).

Following the war, the United States experienced a housing boom, and U.S. industry produced an array of household appliances and products. Cooperative Extension home economists taught about housing, home furnishings, and kitchen design; and they gave more attention to personal relationships, parenting, and youth development in the family-focused era of the 1950s (Rasmussen 1989). In the 1960s, consumer education became an important area in response to questions about consumer issues, credit, and financial planning.

Between 1960 and 1980, major changes occurred in U.S. culture, family composition and roles, residential patterns, and public awareness of pre-

PHOTO 2.2. Nutrition educator Diana Romano (*left*), Oklahoma County Extension, teaches a family about nutritionally sound, economical food choices. Photograph by Todd Johnson, courtesy Oklahoma Cooperative Extension.

viously hidden family matters, such as domestic violence, teen pregnancy, and poverty. Cooperative Extension home economics broadened its focus with more attention to parenting, disadvantaged rural and urban youth and adults, displaced homemakers, and other quality-of-living programs while maintaining its emphasis on nutrition (Rasmussen 1989). The Expanded Food and Nutrition Education Program (EFNEP) was established in 1968 to address the problem of hunger by teaching low-income participants about food preparation, nutrition, and resource management. The EFNEP became a model for employing paraprofessionals from the target community and reporting measurable behavior change (USDA 2012).

Through the end of the twentieth century Cooperative Extension home economics addressed issues such as the energy crisis, food insecurity, and aging; adapted program delivery to adjust to changes in its audience; and adopted new technologies to extend the reach of its information. As a result of the 2008 Farm Bill legislation, the USDA's Cooperative State Research, Education, and Extension Service became the National Institute of Food and Agriculture (NIFA). This reorganization was intended to elevate the science of agriculture and related disciplines and to emphasize the priorities focused on food, agriculture, natural resources, and human resources.

Twenty-First-Century Cooperative Extension Family and Consumer Sciences

Today, Cooperative Extension family and consumer sciences has a strong presence at the USDA and in the states and local communities. Place-based engagement continues as the norm in these partnerships, although some states reorganized their extension offices into county clusters or regions to address the impact of the changing economy of the early twenty-first century, which brought decreases in state and local funding. Yet, the Cooperative Extension Service is still the largest informal educational system in the United States.

Cooperative Extension family and consumer sciences continues to address the needs of citizens in every geographic area of the United States and is also present in international settings. Within the USDA, NIFA, and the Institute of Youth, Family, and Community, the Division of Family and Consumer Sciences applies the knowledge and practice of home economics as an integrative, multidisciplinary field of science. The focus is on relationships among humans and their environments with the mission to help individuals become more effective critical thinkers and problem solvers, to improve the quality of life, to strengthen communities, and to achieve a healthy and sustainable world. Program areas include child and family development; nutrition, health, and wellness; family and consumer economics; housing and community living; community resources and rural economic development; sustainable farm enterprises; and risk management education. These programs expand traditional home economics activities by addressing the current issues of living in a complex world, such as childhood and adult obesity, household indebtedness, early childhood development, and family relationships across the lifespan and in various household configurations.

With administrative oversight from NIFA and strategic leadership by the Extension Committee on Organization and Policy (ECOP), Cooperative Extension works through 106 land-grant universities and has a presence in more than three thousand U.S. counties and parishes. A comprehensive study conducted in 2008 indicated that trust in and support of Cooperative Extension is exceptionally high among users of family and consumer sciences programs with 90 percent of respondents rating the programs "excellent" or "very good" (Copernicus Marketing, Consulting, and Research 2009). Yet the research confirmed that the stock comment that Cooperative Extension is the nation's "best-kept secret" was entirely correct—general public awareness of Cooperative Extension family and consumer sciences is low. Thus, a branding initiative was launched in 2012 for use nationwide, with the summary statement

PHOTO 2.3. Barbara O'Neill, an extension specialist in financial resource management and a Distinguished Professor at Rutgers University Cooperative Extension, develops educational programs and materials to deliver financial literacy education to the public. Photograph courtesy Dr. Barbara O'Neill.

"Cooperative Extension provides education you can trust, to help people, business, and communities solve problems, develop skills, and build a better future" (National Extension Branding Initiative 2012).

Cooperative Extension family and consumer sciences focuses on "strategic opportunities" where expertise and advances in physical and behavioral sciences are needed to address identified needs (ECOP 2007, 2012). Several key words are good descriptors of the resulting programs: partnership, entrepreneurship, interdisciplinary, engagement, impacts, high touch and high tech, urban, and global. The legacy of place-based, local education continues while programs address rapid demographic, economic, sociological, and technological shifts that require innovation to solve vexing problems.

Today, the focus is on the complex issues faced by individuals, families, businesses, and communities and on working with colleagues across disciplines and often at different universities. For example, "Small Steps to Health and Wealth" promotes daily behavioral changes in nutrition, health, spending, and savings; it is available online (O'Neill and Ensle 2010). Addressing issues of at-risk youth brings together resources from human development, educational psychology, sociology, and nutrition (USDA–NIFA 2009). Decreasing obesity in a community, another priority in the USDA–NIFA, requires expertise from nutrition, health, kinesiology, and community planning, necessitating an interdisciplinary knowledge base and approach.

Cooperative Extension family and consumer sciences emphasizes outcomes, asking: How are behaviors changed as a result of Cooperative Extension programs? Going from bean counting (e.g., number of publications, workshop attendance, website hits) to describing outcomes (e.g., how personal debt has decreased, or family communications have improved, or community health is better) is much more difficult, but these results are essential to track and report. Showing returns on dollars invested, both public and private, has taken on such significance that ECOP has launched a website (www.excellenceinextension.org) to collect impact statements that report program outcomes for target audiences and in terms of "public value," which is the value of a program beyond those who directly benefit (Kalambokidis 2011). For example, parenting education reduces child neglect, which results in less demand on child protective agencies; and EFNEP's nutrition and food preparation instruction leads to better individual food choices, which reduces the costs of nutrition-related disease in the population.

While federal, state, and county tax dollars provide the core funding for Cooperative Extension programs, the fiscal crisis that began around 2007–2008 has eroded these resources. Funding has not kept pace with the demand for programming. Contemporary advocacy endeavors make the case that continued reductions are equal to "eating our seed corn" (APLU 2013). Family and consumer sciences personnel now have a responsibility to obtain funds via gifts and competitive processes in the public, private, nonprofit, and foundation sectors, and they also use entrepreneurship tools to generate resources. At local, state, and national levels, Cooperative Extension family and consumer sciences professionals often link with public, nonprofit, or private agencies. While information exchange is standard practice, partnerships operate at a higher level of collaboration: partners plan programs together; pool resources, both in-kind and monetary; and share credit for results. Some of the time and expertise formerly spent in the educational process now is devoted to grant writing and the management of funded projects.

Cooperative Extension programs are known for place-based education to address individual and local needs. This "high-touch," hands-on, experiential learning sets Cooperative Extension apart from many other informal educational entities. At the same time, the exponential expansion of electronic technology requires the twenty-first-century extension to be technologically astute. The place-based model is still alive and well, but now, in many states, mobile devices and the internet, not printed bulletins or newsletters, are used to connect learners with information twenty-four hours a day. Adopting this high-tech approach at the turn of the twenty-first century, www.extension.org was created. This "learn anytime, anywhere" tool has more than seventy-five communities of practice (subject areas) that contribute content and an ask-an-expert function that fields more than 4,500 questions monthly.

Volunteers also are an important part of Cooperative Extension education design, delivery, and evaluation, often using the "master" approach perfected in the master gardener program. Family and consumer sciences programming on such topics as managing household money or a farm business, sewing, mentoring teens or new parents, or improving household energy efficiency starts with an extension professional teaching "master" volunteers, who then offer their knowledge to audiences. For example, the master clothing volunteer program in Texas provides additional training to individuals with previous sewing skills, and expects at least fifty hours annually returned to the community (Brown 2003). Texas master clothing volunteers, both women and men, provided nearly fifty-two thousand hours, worth an estimated $675,350 in 2001, enabling some participants to start home-based businesses and others to save money by sewing for their families.

The iconic Norman Rockwell painting of the expert agriculture extension agent examining the daughter's 4-H heifer project while the rest of the family looks on reflects the assumption that extension focuses on rural communities exclusively. While the painting may create nostalgia for 1948 ideal farm life, today that is not where most users of Cooperative Extension family and consumer sciences live. The 2013 biannual National Urban Extension Conference reinforced the fact that individuals and families in urban centers are in dire need of the knowledge base of family and consumer sciences to improve their nutrition, health, financial literacy, resource management, child and family resiliency, housing, home safety, and energy efficiency (K-State Research and Extension 2013). Cooperative Extension family and consumer sciences meets people where they are, providing situation-appropriate programming for rural, suburban, and urban target audiences.

Future Challenges and Opportunities

A multitude of challenges face Cooperative Extension family and consumer sciences programs. Finding adequate fiscal resources and keeping pace with changing technology loom large and have been discussed above. Other challenges include the rapidly changing demographics of the United States, recruiting sufficient numbers of personnel with family and consumer sciences expertise, responding to crises and emerging issues, globalization, and the need for social capital in communities. Family and consumer sciences extension professionals operate from the belief that in every challenge there is an opportunity.

The "big three" in the changing demographic profile of the United States are that the population is increasing, getting older, and becoming more diverse (Shrestha and Heisler 2011). Half the country's population increase in 2011–2012 occurred in just 46 of the 3,143 counties and parishes, and there are now 52 metropolitan areas with more than a million residents (Population Connection 2013). Fifty-one percent of the population growth between 2000 and 2010 occurred in southern states (Johnson and Kasarda 2011). In 1950, people sixty-five and older represented 8 percent of the total population; in 2000 older people were 12 percent; and they are projected to be 18 percent in 2025 (Shrestha and Heisler 2011). Hispanics are now the nation's largest minority. While other ethnic and racial groups (Asian and Black) are projected to increase as a proportion of the population, the proportion of White citizens will decline during the coming decades. These trends have implications for Cooperative Extension programs' emphasis, expertise, location of personnel, and methods of delivery.

Changes in U.S. households have consequences for the availability of economic resources and everyday support systems for individuals, and these changes also affect community vitality or malaise. Of the 116.7 million households, 66 percent are "family households," while 27 percent are persons living alone (the others live with non-relatives only) (U.S. Census Bureau 2012). Women head 19 percent of family households, and 7 percent are headed by single fathers (Pew Research 2013). Thirty-five percent of children reside in single-parent families (Annie E. Casey Foundation 2013). The economic recession of 2007–2010 contributed to a sharp increase in the number of children being raised by grandparents, about one in ten in 2008 (Pew Research 2013), and more adult children returning to live in their parents' homes. The number of U.S. children living in families in poverty increased from 19 percent in 2005 to 23 percent in 2011 (Annie E. Casey Foundation 2013). Mothers of children of all ages worked outside the home and were significant contributors to household income (Johnson and Kasarda 2011). The income disparity between the well-to-do and those who are poor is growing wider (Edelman 2012). These statistics only scratch the surface of the plethora of personal and intergenerational relationships and the economic, health, and housing aspects of living in the twenty-first century. It is evident that Cooperative Extension family and consumer sciences will never run out of opportunities for engaging with the public to discover ways to achieve and sustain a quality of life worth pursuing.

However, Cooperative Extension family and consumer sciences could face a crisis in human resources. This challenge was addressed by the Extension Committee on Organization and Policy (ECOP 2012) to the academic administrators of family and consumer sciences departments and colleges with a simple message: More family and consumer sciences graduates are needed in extension to meet the demands of an increasingly diverse population. The National Coalition for Family and Consumer Sciences Education also has identified the shortage of teaching professionals with appropriate degrees. Given the broad scope of topics for which many Cooperative Extension family and consumer sciences personnel are responsible, a generalist degree typical of traditional home economics education majors is needed. Although few of these programs still are offered, some U.S. colleges and universities have re-instituted this major. In recent decades most students have specialized in a subject area within home economics. Personnel with specialized areas also are needed, but they would benefit from coursework related to adult learning and program development and, more important, from the integrative frame-work characteristic of home economics.

The creation of an innovative, online master's degree program by the Great Plains Interactive Distance Education Alliance in 1994 continues to enable place-bound individuals to earn degrees (Great Plains IDEA n.d.). In other cases, personnel with degrees closely allied with family and consumer sciences have been hired in specialized roles and particular areas of expertise. Providing college students with personally rewarding practicum and internship experiences in Cooperative Extension is an effective recruitment strategy. Attention to increasing the diversity among family and consumer sciences extension personnel is essential for future effectiveness.

Balancing ongoing programming with the ability to respond to crises, changing public concerns, and emerging trends is a challenge for any large institutional system. Cooperative Extension family and consumer sciences keeps in close contact with the changes that affect the basic life skills of families and consumers, and it is increasingly nimble in responding to major challenges. Examples are abundant. The complex issues facing military families, including the impacts of frequent deployment on marriages and children, traumatic injuries, and financial stress, are being addressed through comprehensive programs combining the research and engagement expertise of both faculty and extension agents (Huebner et al. 2009; Institute for the Health and Security of Military Families n.d.). Encouraging the adoption of "green living" in response to environmental concerns is another example. Oklahoma and Kansas are highly prone to tornadoes, and turning these disasters into an opportunity for sustainable green building takes visionary planning, which the Cooperative Extension family and consumer sciences personnel in these states have undertaken as they expand their emergency preparedness programming (St. Pierre et al. 2012). Renewed public interest in environmental issues, mostly dormant since the 1970s, provides opportunities to address behavioral change from the perspective of housing, health, financial, and environmental sustainability (Koonce, Turner, and Chapman 2011) and clothing (also see Ordon, this volume).

Federal Smith-Lever, state, and local government funds for Cooperative Extension are intended for domestic programs, but the rapidly changing demographics and economy of the United States require a global perspective. Staff development to understand multiculturalism and to respond locally to immigration, cultural diversity, economic globalization, and inclusive community decision making has become a part of Cooperative Extension family and consumer sciences. While there are many examples of how family and consumer sciences extension personnel have worked effectively with local citizens and new residents, more remains to be done. Furthermore, opportunities to affiliate with international networks are expanding.

Cooperative Extension's historical foundation included community betterment. Today, issues from bullying among children, to changes in health care policies, to family resiliency in the face of disaster, to regional economic viability, to water quality are challenges for communities large and small. These and other challenges that will emerge in the future are opportunities for Cooperative Extension family and consumer sciences to bring the human dimension to helping solve problems. An emphasis on social capital (e.g., social networks and norms of reciprocity and trustworthiness, which enable people and institutions to communicate, advance their interests, and benefit their communities) characterizes the leadership role of family and consumer sciences both in the United States and internationally (Nickols et al. 2010). Building social capital is increasingly important in a fractious world. Cooperative Extension family and consumer sciences agents work from the time-honored philosophy of helping people help themselves, and they have the expertise to facilitate groups in addressing the community issues affecting quality of life.

Cooperative Extension celebrated its centennial in 2014. The present is a pivotal time for the nation's premier informal education system as it plans for the future. In order to weather unprecedented fiscal challenges, stay connected to a high-tech world, be relevant in a rapidly changing demographic milieu, and continue to be trusted educators in both rural and urban places, innovative leadership and dedicated educators are critical. However, the responsibility for continuity is not entirely on Cooperative Extension personnel. Family and consumer sciences knowledge and skills have both personal and public value; therefore, the direct beneficiaries and the advocates who understand that knowledge benefiting individuals and families can also strengthen communities and the nation must spread that message. The values that undergird Cooperative Extension family and consumer sciences professionals, and that keep them committed to their work, include a sincere belief in people and education, and the paramount belief that Cooperative Extension is the link between the people and the people's universities.

ACKNOWLEDGMENTS

We thank Nick T. Place, the dean and director of the University of Florida extension, for the development of some key concepts in the section on twenty-first-century family and consumer sciences Cooperative Extension; Shane Ball, USDA–NIFA, for his extensive research on the history of family and consumer sciences at the federal level; and Sharon Y. Nickols for contributing information about studies of rural women and Cooperative Extension and facilitating the development of this chapter.

REFERENCES

Annie E. Casey Foundation. 2013. *2013 Kids Count Book*, http://www.aecf.org/resources/the-2013-kids-count-data-book (accessed August 6, 2013).

APLU (Association of Public and Land Grant Universities). 2013. "FY 2014 Appropriations Request, National Institute of Food and Agriculture, Smith-Lever," http://www.land-grant.org/docs/FY2014/SL-14.pdf (accessed May 2013).

Apps, Jerry. 2010. *Horse-Drawn Days: A Century of Farming with Horses*. Madison: Wisconsin Historical Society Press.

Babbitt, Kathleen R. 1997. "Legitimizing Nutrition Education: The Impact of The Great Depression." In *Rethinking Home Economics: Women and the History of a Profession*, edited by Sarah Stage and Virginia B. Vincenti, 145–162. Ithaca, N.Y.: Cornell University Press.

Betters, Paul V. 1930. *The Bureau of Home Economics: Its History, Activities, and Organization*. Washington, D.C.: Brookings Institution.

Bliss, Ralph K. 1960. *History of Cooperative Agriculture and Home Extension in Iowa: The First Fifty Years*. Ames: Iowa State University Press.

Brown, Pamela J. 2003. "Texas Sewing Program Helps Economy, Community." *Journal of Family and Consumer Sciences* 95(3): 61–62.

Cochrane, Willard W. 1993. *The Development of American Agriculture: A Historical Analysis*, 2nd ed. Minneapolis: University of Minnesota Press.

Copernicus Marketing, Consulting, and Research. 2009. "Cooperative Extension Brand Value Research," http://www.aplu.org/NetCommunity/Document. Doc?id=1480 (accessed May 13, 2013).

Danbom, David B. 2006. *Born in the Country: A History of Rural America*, 2nd ed. Baltimore, Md.: Johns Hopkins University Press.

ECOP (Extension Committee on Organization and Policy), Strategic Priorities Task Force. 2007. "Cooperative Extension Strategic Opportunities," http://www.aplu.org/NetCommunity/Document.Doc?id=369 (accessed May 13, 2013).

———. 2012. "Cooperative Extension Strategic Opportunities," http://www.aplu.org/document.doc?id=4096 (accessed May 13, 2013).

Edelman, Peter. 2012. *So Rich, So Poor: Why It's So Hard to End Poverty in America*. New York: New Press.

Elias, Megan J. 2008. *Stir It Up: Home Economics in American Culture*. Philadelphia: University of Pennsylvania Press.

Eppright, Ercel Sherman, and Elizabeth Storm Ferguson. 1971. *A Century of Home Economics at Iowa State University: A Proud Past, a Lively Present, and a Future Promise*. Ames: Iowa State University, Home Economics Alumni Association.

Goldstein, Carolyn M. 2012. *Creating Consumers: Home Economists in Twentieth-Century America*. Chapel Hill: University of North Carolina Press.

Gordon, Lynn D. 1990. *Gender and Higher Education in the Progressive Era*. New Haven, Conn.: Yale University Press.

Great Plains IDEA (Interactive Distance Education Alliance). N.d. *Family and Consumer Sciences Education*, http://www.hsidea.org/programs/fcsed (accessed May 13, 2013).

Harris, Carmen. 1997. "Grace Under Pressure: The Black Home Extension Service in South Carolina, 1919–1966." In *Rethinking Home Economics: Women and the History of a Profession*, edited by Sarah Stage and Virginia B. Vincenti, 203–228. Ithaca, N.Y.: Cornell University Press.

Hill, Elizabeth G. 2012. *A Splendid Piece of Work, 1912–2012: One Hundred Years of Arkansas' Home Demonstration and Extension Homemakers Clubs*. Lexington, Ky.: CreateSpace.

Hilton, Kathleen C. 1994. "'Both in the Field, Each with a Plow': Race and Gender in USDA Policy, 1907–1929." In *Hidden Histories of Women in the New South*, edited by Virginia Bernhard, Betty Brandon, Elizabeth Fox-Genovese, Theda Perdue, and Elizabeth H. Turner, 114–133. Columbia: University of Missouri Press.

Holt, Marilyn I. 1995. *Linoleum, Better Babies, and the Modern Farm Woman, 1890–1930*. Albuquerque: University of New Mexico Press.

Huebner, Angela J., Jay A. Mancini, Gary L. Bowen, and Dennis K. Orthner. 2009. "Shadowed by War: Building Community Capacity to Support Military Families." *Family Relations* 58(2): 216–228.

Hurt, Douglas R. 2002. *American Agriculture: A Brief History*, 2nd ed. West Lafayette, Ind.: Purdue University Press.

Institute for the Health and Security of Military Families. N.d. www.militaryfamilies.k-state.edu (accessed August 5, 2013).

Johnson, James H., and John D. Kasarda. 2011. *Six Disruptive Demographic Trends: What Census 2011 Will Reveal*. Chapel Hill: University of North Carolina, Kenan Institute.

Kalambokidis, Laura. 2011. "Spreading the Word About Extension's Public Value." *Journal of Extension*, http://www.joe.org/joe/2011april/a1.php (accessed May 13, 2013).

Koonce, Joan, Pamela R. Turner, and Sue W. Chapman. 2011. "Greening Your Life." *Journal of Family and Consumer Sciences* 103(3): 47–51.

K-State Research and Extension. 2013. "National Urban Extension Conference: Relevant, Reliable, Responsive and Remarkable," http://www.dce.k-state.edu/conf/urban-extension (accessed May 20, 2013).

McCleary, Ann E. 2006. "'Seizing the Opportunity': Home Demonstration Club

Markets in Virginia." In *Work, Family, and Faith: Rural Southern Women in the Twentieth Century*, edited by Melissa Walker and Rebecca Sharpless, 97–134. Columbia: University of Missouri Press.

Montgomery, Rebecca S. 2006. *The Politics of Education in the Rural South: Women and Reform in Georgia, 1890–1930*. Baton Rouge: Louisiana State University Press.

National Extension Branding Initiative. 2012. "Cooperative Extension Brand Value Toolkit," http://create.extension.org/node/92257 (accessed May 13, 2013).

Nickols, Sharon Y., Kaija Turkii, Gertraud Pichler, Leena Kirjavainen, Jorge H. Atiles, and Francille M. Firebaugh. 2010. "Sustaining Families, Communities, and Natural Environments by Building Social Capital." *Journal of Family and Consumer Sciences* 102(4): 10–16.

Olmstead, Alan L., and Paul W. Rhode. 2004. "The 'Tuberculosis Cattle Trust': Disease Contagion in an Era of Regulatory Uncertainty." *Journal of Economic History* 64(4): 929–963.

O'Neill, Barbara, and Karen Ensle. 2010. "The Online Small Steps to Health and Wealth Challenge: A Model for Interdisciplinary FCS Programs." *Journal of Family and Consumer Sciences* 102(4): 52–55.

Osterud, Grey. 2012. *Putting the Barn Before the House: Women and Family Farming in Early Twentieth-Century New York*. Ithaca, N.Y.: Cornell University Press.

Pew Research. 2013. "Household and Family Structure." *Social and Demographic Trends*, www.pewsocialtrends.org/topics/househod-and-family-structure (accessed August 5, 2013).

Population Connection. 2013. "U.S. Census Data, 2011–2012." *Reporter* 45(2): 4–5.

Rasmussen, Wayne D. 1989. *Taking the University to the People: Seventy-Five Years of Cooperative Extension*. Ames: Iowa State University Press.

Reed, Hazel. 1997. "Reminiscences." In *Rethinking Home Economics: Women and the History of a Profession*, edited by Sarah Stage and Virginia B. Vincenti, 181–184. Ithaca, N.Y.: Cornell University Press.

Rieff, Lynn A. 1994. "'Go Ahead and Do All You Can': Southern Progressives and Alabama Home Demonstration Clubs, 1914–1940." In *Hidden Histories of Women in the New South*, edited by Virginia Bernhard, Betty Brandon, Elizabeth Fox-Genovese, Theda Perdue, and Elizabeth H. Turner, 134–149. Columbia: University of Missouri Press.

———. 2006. "Revitalizing Southern Homes: Rural Women, the Professionalization of Home Demonstration Work, and the Limits of Reform, 1917–1945." In *Work, Family, and Faith: Rural Southern Women in the Twentieth Century*, edited by Melissa Walker and Rebecca Sharpless, 135–165. Columbia: University of Missouri Press.

Scholl, Jan. 2008. "Early FCS Extension Specialist: Martha Van Rensselaer." *Family and Consumer Sciences Research Journal* 37(2):149–156.

———. 2013. "Extension Family and Consumer Sciences: Why It Was Included in the Smith-Lever Act of 1914." *Journal of Family and Consumer Sciences*, 105(4): 8–16.

Schwieder, Dorothy. 1993. *75 Years of Service: Cooperative Extension in Iowa*. Ames: Iowa State University Press.

Shrestha, Laura B., and Elayne J. Heisler. 2011. *The Changing Demographic Profile of the United States*. Washington, D.C.: Congressional Research Service.

St. Pierre, Eileen, Lani Vasconcellos, Pamela Muntz, and Gina Peek. 2012. "Preparing Communities for Disaster Recovery and Green Rebuilding." *Journal of Family and Consumer Sciences* 104(3): 41–43.

U.S. Census Bureau. 2012. *Households and Families: 2010*, www.census.gov/prod/cen2010/briefs/c2010br-14.pdf (accessed August 5, 2013).

USDA (U.S. Department of Agriculture). 1951. "The Home Demonstration Agent." Agriculture Information Bulletin AID-38. Washington, D.C.: U.S. Government Printing Office.

———. 2012. "EFNEP Impact Report," http://www.nifa.usda.gov/nea/food/efnep/pdf/impact_data_report_2012.pdf (accessed May 20, 2013).

USDA–NIFA. 2009. "Children, Youth, and Families at Risk Philosophy," http://www.csrees.usda.gov/nea/family/cyfar/philosophy.html (accessed August 5, 2013).

3. Home Economics in the Twentieth Century

A Case of Lost Identity?

RIMA D. APPLE

The history of home economics can be studied from many different perspectives: the evolution of the discipline; the theories seeking to explain its ideology and pedagogical bases; the growth of vocational training; evolving careers; and its leaders. The discipline's various aspects loosely coalesced in the domestic realm in the early 1900s, but it did not have any universally accepted form. Despite this diversity, home economics emerged imbued with one essential characteristic: social justice—a relatively coherent objective shaped by the hopes and ideals of the Progressive movement. Over the century since its inception the field lost much of its sense of social responsibility, however, and its organizational structure underwent many changes. An analysis of the field's transformation can point the way toward redefinition and revitalization.

Many of us who passed through home economics classes in the mid-twentieth century remember learning how to boil an egg and insert a zipper in a skirt. Those who took more recent classes may remember studying the food pyramid and how to read the care label on a garment. Though these admittedly limited memories do not do justice to the breadth of the many classes offered over the past century, they do suggest why the public commonly defines home economics as merely cooking and sewing. They also highlight the profound gulf between the hopes of early leaders and the status of the field today. Home economics was and is a highly varied field. Based on my reviews of historical records, syllabi, textbooks, and standards and guidelines for coursework, this chapter traces major shifts in home economics over the century and identifies trends that have shaped the modern field.

As urbanization, industrialization, and massive new immigration dramatically altered life in the United States in the late nineteenth and early twentieth centuries, many social commentators worried that society was decaying. Home economists promoted education, particularly science education, believing it would create a better future. The founders of the field asserted that the solution to the perceived problem of social upheaval lay in the home, the foundation of society, under the direction of educated women.

The gendered nature of home economics was its strength in the early twentieth century. Most women were not employed outside the home; women did not yet have the vote. However, women wielded power in the home and spent many long hours laboring there. The founders of home economics and other Progressives believed that educated women would produce strong families, strong children, strong communities, and a strong nation. Ellen Richards (1911, 122) declared that the purpose of scientific home economics was "nothing less than an effort to save our social fabric from what seems inevitable disintegration." As a response to social problems, home economics was rooted in the home, yet intended to reach beyond its walls into the wider society.

Though she is not as well known today as Richards, Caroline L. Hunt is a paradigmatic example of the early home economist. She was born in 1865 in Chicago, and she lived most of her formative years in the boom and bustle of that city, which was fueled by commerce and immigration (East 1982). She began her career teaching science in public high schools. She earned an undergraduate degree from Northwestern University and attended the University of Chicago where she studied with Marion Talbot (Apple and Coleman 2003). Hunt lived part-time at Hull House, the settlement house established by Jane Addams in Chicago. For the U.S. Department of Agriculture (USDA) experiment stations, she interviewed over a thousand families in the crowded Chicago immigrant neighborhoods, collecting dietary histories and social indicator data in the late 1890s. From 1896 to 1902 Hunt was an instructor in "domestic economy" at the Lewis Institute in Chicago, and in 1903 she was appointed the first professor of home economics at the University of Wisconsin, Madison (Apple 2003; East 1982).

Hunt, a close friend of Richards, attended most of the Lake Placid Conferences (except the first and seventh). She prepared some of the most definitive statements about the ideals and purposes of home economics. Her statement "Revaluations" was delivered at the third conference and concluded, "The final test of the teaching of home economics is freedom. If we have unnecessarily complicated a single life by perpetuating useless conventions . . . just so far have we failed. If we have simplified one life and released in it energy for its own expression, just so far have we succeeded" (Hunt 1901, 89; also see East 1982).

Hunt served with Isabel Bevier and Alice P. Norton on the Standing Committee on Home Economics in Higher Education. She believed that social justice was an integral part of home economics education. Hunt insisted at the ninth Lake Placid Conference:

> [Women's] knowledge of the dangers which lurk in food materials prepared by modern processes brings with it the knowledge that the best methods of preparation in the home can not make wholly safe those foods which have been adulterated before reaching the consumer which have been handled by careless or uncleanly methods. Their understanding of the dangers which lurk in bad air shows that proper street cleaning may be as large a factor as ventilation in securing pure air in their homes. . . . For these reasons intelligent educated women are entering upon public work, not as a substitute for that work which is done in the interest of home life, but as a necessary means under present conditions of realizing those ideals for which the home stands. (1907, 12)

Hunt also enumerated the things for which Progressive women were advocating:

> for enactment and enforcement of efficient food laws, for pure milk, for clean markets, for better methods of collecting garbage and other kinds of waste, for the passing and enforcing of smoke ordinances, for the protection of the trees and other natural beauties, for the abolishment of billboards, for public school art, for public playgrounds, for better conditions of work for women, and for a public opinion and for legislation which shall assure to all the sons and daughters of the republic, the poor as well as the rich, the right to childhood—the right to protection for body, mind, and soul, and the right to training for useful citizenship. (ibid., 15)

Home economics education should lead a woman to understand the connections between her home and the wider world, using this knowledge to affect the public sphere as well as her family. In its formative years, home economics shared much the same philosophy as "social maternalism" and "municipal housekeeping," two very active campaigns of the period (Muncy 1991; Stage 1997; Weigley 1974). In their homes, women were responsible for the health and well-being of their husbands and children, and the health of the family was connected directly to the health of the nation. An inattentive homemaker risked maladjusted children and spouse, but women needed education to be prepared for that responsibility (Apple 2006; Lindenmeyer 1997). Hunt encouraged home economics–trained women to be ethical consumers. She expected them to investigate the conditions of production and then avoid those items produced under poor labor conditions. In this way, she argued, women could help improve the working and living situations of those with less power.

At the University of Wisconsin, Madison, where she was hired in 1903 to establish a home economics program, Hunt envisioned a rigorous course of study incorporating the scientific and social philosophy of the early home economists. She argued that the function of such university study "should be to teach women the social significance of the control which they have over wealth, of the fact that they can determine to a large extent what shall be made and under what condition it shall be made" (Hunt 1908). Furthermore, she said, "I see no place for cooking and sewing in such courses except as they give an understanding of materials and processes."

Relatively few women could attend college in the early twentieth century; consequently, home economists sought other venues for advocating their social justice philosophy. Beginning in 1905, Hunt established a series of "housekeepers conferences," outreach short courses offered in conjunction with the farmers course in the University of Wisconsin's College of Agriculture. The 1908 conference signaled Hunt's belief in the power of home economics through educated women to improve society. Its lectures covered "dressing for health," the "campaign for pure milk," the "preparation of milk for infant feeding," the "pollution and inspection of the water of the state," and an illustrated talk on "life in Japan" (Apple 2003). Women's short courses were popular adjuncts of the farmers institutes of many land-grant colleges and were offered across the country.

Pressure from the University of Wisconsin administration to emphasize domesticity and manual skills clashed with Hunt's academic rigor and activist philosophy. Her leadership at the university ended in 1908 (Apple and Coleman 2003). She continued her commitment to home economics through twenty years of employment in the federal Bureau of Home Economics where she wrote numerous food and nutrition bulletins (East 1982). Personal correspondence with a friend in 1909 and 1913 indicated that Hunt was active in the movement for women's suffrage (cited in East 1982). At the request of colleagues, she wrote "the definitive biography" of Ellen H. Richards (Hunt 1912).

Other early home economists looked to an even broader audience, namely girls in primary and secondary public schools. At the 1901 Lake Placid Conference, the Committee on Public School Education instructed high school home economics teachers to include in their curriculum a section on municipal housekeeping, described as the "share of [a] homemaker in insuring honest building, clean streets, pure water, effective disposal of waste" ("Report of Special Committee" 1901). Abby Marlatt, like many leaders of the movement in its first decades, began her career in public schools. As a teacher of domestic science at the Manual Training High School of Providence, Rhode Island, she explained to the attendees of the 1903 Lake Placid Conference the importance

of "hand work": handcrafts and sewing. She did not equate home economics in a vocational school with vocational training. She contended that such
instruction would "fit [the students] to grapple with the complex problems
of modern life and master them" (Marlatt 1903, 19). Specifically, she expected
that studying "sewing, millinery, dressmaking may teach the girl the value of
such labor and make her an intelligent consumer, an enemy to sweatshop labor" (ibid.). Marlatt continued, "Respect for labor, realization of the value of
time, greater interest in the esthetic value of our industrial products, broadened judgment, sympathetic insight gained thru hand labor in our high school
courses for girls are arguments enough, even if there were not the economic
side, which demands that the woman of today be an intelligent producer as
well as a wise consumer" (ibid., 19–20). To be a "wise consumer" meant more
than finding a good buy; it meant recognizing the quality of the goods and the
conditions of their production and sale. Marlatt's words contained a stirring
commitment to the ideal of social justice that underlay the impetus for the
home economics movement.

In 1913, the Committee on Nomenclature and Syllabus of the AHEA (1913),
composed of leaders such as Isabel Bevier, Abby Marlatt, and Flora Rose,
produced the defining syllabus for the evolving field. The publication reinforced the political intentions of the movement: home economics education
taught girls to be interested in improving their communities and bettering
society. As the primary consumers of food, clothing, and household products
and as guardians of their families' health, women must be actively involved.
Throughout the publication, the authors consistently emphasized the interdependence of individual, family, and community responsibility. Articles by
and for home economics teachers in education journals also connected public school home economics courses with the themes of social responsibility
and training for good citizenship, as did the textbooks on the "household
arts" (Cooley et al. 1918; Kinne and Cooley 1915, 1916; Norton 1900; "Why Teach
Domestic Science?" 1911).

Early home economists considered the overtly Progressive orientation of
their field to be its distinguishing characteristic. Their subject area dealt with
a wide variety of issues, such as foods, textiles, sanitation, and housing. They
expected that students would study biology, physiology, chemistry, sociology,
and other topics because these subjects underpinned the study of home economics. The uniqueness and significance of the field lay in its political stance
and its insistence that girls would learn to recognize and women would
have the power to ameliorate social ills through their education in home
economics.

Over the decades, however, the sense of social responsibility disappeared.
The objective continued to be to educate girls and women, and more recently

boys and men, to be good consumers, but it was consumerism for the benefit of self and family. In responding to changing social and political conditions, the discipline replaced the emphasis on social justice with an emphasis on vocational preparation, which splintered the field into specialized subjects. Financial and pedagogical factors modified the direction of home economics after the first generation of home economics leaders. First, the Smith-Lever Act of 1914 authorized funds for the Cooperative Extension Service, which provided instruction and practical demonstrations in agriculture and home economics through land-grant universities. Then, the Smith-Hughes Act of 1917, commonly called the Vocational Education Act, funded teacher training in specific vocational, not academic, areas (Apple 1997; Powers 1992). These new financial streams for home economics departments both advanced and inhibited the field. On the positive side, these resources expanded the employment potential for the increasing numbers of women with college degrees in home economics. On the negative side, they even more closely entwined home economics with domestic and occupational arenas that were gendered female. By concentrating attention on preparing Cooperative Extension personnel and teachers for public schools, the vocational aspects of home economics gradually dominated the field.

In the same period, educationalists heatedly debated curriculum reform in the United States. Though Progressive leaders tended to embrace a "social reconstructionist" model, those in schools were inclined to be more "eclectic," to use the terms of historian Herbert M. Kliebard. As he explained, school administrators "were a mixed lot politically and only sporadically responded to the vision of a new social order that the social reconstructionists were advancing. Eclecticism, on the other hand, was not nearly as politically sensitive, and the public appeal of a curriculum tied directly to the needs of children as well as the duties of life made it a much safer course for school administrators to follow" (2004, 186). Stressing the "duties of life" also fostered a greater emphasis on skills training.

Home economics literature reflected the gradual shift away from "social responsibility" as the goals of home economics were modified. The "educated consumer" continued to be the objective of instruction, but now that term referred to education for the improvement of the life of the student and her family, and it often lacked a more extensive social context. Two circulars distributed by the U.S. Bureau of Education in 1918 marked the beginning of this redefinition. The introduction to *Home Economics Teaching in Small High Schools* promoted a far-reaching view of the field: giving girls "the principles that underlie the building of the home" and "a sense of responsibility in the life of the community" (Bureau of Education 1918a, 2). However, the courses of study described in the circular dealt basically with knowledge of textiles and foods and skills in these areas. The foods section included an analysis of foods and meal planning, followed by "table service" and "practical work-cooking." The "ethics of shopping" appeared under "clothing study" with no elucidation. The circular *Current Problems in Home Economics* presented what teachers thought a girl should learn in home economics before she graduated eighth grade: basic skills such as "practical cooking; ... how to make a bed properly; ... [how to] make a washable dress" (Bureau of Education 1918b, 7).

The rationale was that girls needed home economics training in order to raise their families and run their households. However, not all girls would marry. Explaining that home economics courses were important even for a single girl, Calvert (1925, 3) declared, "Study home economics to learn how to take care of your own health; how to select your food and clothing; how to save money; how to be a more efficient wage earner and useful citizen." The focus was on the benefits for the individual; a useful citizen was one who knew her duty and fulfilled it. The social efficiency curriculum model—preparing individuals for the role they would play as adult members of the social order—was popular earlier in the century and increasingly influenced home economics curricula from the 1930s onward (Kliebard 2004).

Further reports reinforced this limited definition of home economics. When Trilling and her colleagues (1920) surveyed home economics curricula and textbooks, they found that the subject had been reduced to published recipes and commercial clothing patterns. Counts (1926) investigated progressive high schools, those that would appear to have a natural affinity to the political and social goals of home economics, but he found that at least 85 percent of the home economics courses offered were cooking and sewing. When the sociologists Robert Lynd and Helen Lynd (1929) studied Muncie, Indiana, they found that home economics courses were designed for girls who were expected to be homemakers with classes concentrated on food, clothing, and house planning. Students could choose more advanced courses in the higher grades, including dressmaking, millinery, hygiene, home nursing, household management, and food and clothing selection (also see Apple 1994). Clearly the cooking and sewing cliché was already well established by the third decade of the century.

Typical home economics textbooks and articles on teaching in the 1930s exalted the individual, individual decision making, and a person's role in the family (Kaufman 1930; Spafford 1938; Trilling, Williams, and Reeves 1931). Ivor Spafford, one of the foremost home economics leaders of the period, declared, "It is not enough to learn about the family in society, the relation of health and juvenile delinquency to housing, to apply art principles to house furnishings. In the long run, the individual wants to know how to select a house, to meet his family's needs, to feed the members of his particular family with its income and its likes and dislikes, to build a satisfying life under the individual conditions which affect him" (1938, 28).

Despite the fact that in the 1930s the overwhelming enrollment in home economics was female, Spafford used the conventional masculine pronoun in her article. The core of home economics had become "home living," which made it a unique and worthwhile course of study as women learned to carry out their familial responsibilities (Spafford, Albright, and Blach 1939). The emphasis on family living became even stronger in the post–World War II period.

In the decades following World War II, economic, technological, scientific, and political events, such as the civil rights movement, women's movement, dissemination of devices such as television and the microwave, spread of the suburbs, increasing entry of women into the paid workforce, enrollment of boys in public school home economics classes, and recognition of a new stage-of-life category, the teenager, radically remolded the United States. Social and cultural demands altered home economics instruction. For instance, the content of cooking classes recognized the growth of prepared and convenience foods and new kitchen equipment. Home décor played a larger role in the home economics curriculum. Books and chapters on interpersonal relationships, particularly on suitable dating behavior, and lessons on correct babysitting were prevalent. Textbooks on family living, such as *Our Home and Family* (Baxter, Justin, and Rust 1952) and *Living in Families* (Smart and Smart 1958), were tailored for high school students and went through several editions.

As various cultural changes played out during the next decades, home economics curricula diverged further from the original Progressive objectives of the field. For example, the Oregon Department of Education released *Home Economics for Oregon Schools: Nutrition and Foods* (1978). The program sought "to strengthen home and family life" with material on meal planning and preparation and the "rights and responsibilities" of the consumer. These included the right of consumers to be informed of deceptive practices and the responsibility of consumers to inform themselves. Students learned how to complain, but not how to investigate and not how to go beyond their individual needs. No mention was made that perhaps they should look at the broader social and economic context. Other state curriculum standards documented a similar concentration. The 1999 Texas nutrition and food science program expected students to "demonstrate safety and sanitation practices with handling, storing, preparing, and serving food" (Hays 1999, 92–94). Teachers were to direct students to research and discuss food-borne illnesses, such as salmonella and *E. coli*, so that they could "identify potential safety and sanitation hazards." Little attention was paid to what the consumer can or should do outside the home to protect the food supply of the community. Nutrition standards in other states also concentrated on home and consumer skills ("Food and Nutrition Curriculum Update" 1984; Life Skills Center 1994; N.C. State Department of Public Instruction 1988; Office of Career, Technical, and Adult Education 2008).

Some state curriculum standards did resonate with the principles of the home economics pioneers. Wisconsin's 1997 guide listed standards such as "explain what it means to assume personal and social responsibility as a family member and citizen" and "develop, implement, and assess an individual, family, or community action plan designed to reach specific goals" (Nikolay et al. 1997). The guide included a plan to learn more about the effects of domestic abuse on children and to volunteer in a shelter with goals that included developing skills for working with children and promoting awareness of signs of abuse. These goals evoked some of the objectives described for home economics nearly a century earlier. To what extent teachers were prepared to implement, or actually implemented, these standards in their classrooms is an open question.

Late in the twentieth century, home economics was renamed family and consumer sciences, but the programs in schools did not become homogeneous in content, and they generally lacked the original underlying social justice rationale. Family and consumer sciences varies across states, with different course requirements and curriculum standards. There are school districts with no family and consumer sciences classes, due to lack of demand or lack of funding; and there are others with extensive kitchens and sewing machines in which teachers emphasize cooking and sewing. In 2002–2003, an estimated 5.5 million students were enrolled in family and consumer sciences classes in the United States, enrollment figures that had not changed much since 1959 as a proportion (25 percent) of the total secondary school population (Werhan and Way 2006). Family and consumer sciences courses continue today in some form in all fifty states; however, the most recent survey of enrollment indicated a decline over the previous ten years to approximately 3.4 million students (Werhan 2013). The drop in enrollment has been exacerbated by a shortage of family and consumer sciences teachers, the closing of family and consumer sciences teacher preparation programs in colleges, and decisions to focus on "core" academic courses in local schools (ibid.).

In many states, the goal of the discipline has become vocational preparation, influenced by national recommendations that students be introduced to careers in middle school and have more specialized courses in high school. Furthermore, what is taught differs from classroom to classroom, depending on the teacher, the teacher's training, the equipment, and the commitment of school officials. Not surprisingly, then, many define home economics according to their personal experiences in the classroom, not the pronouncements of academic and professional leaders or their carefully developed curricula. This disconnect was and continues to be a problem. As long as people define the field by the cliché of cooking and sewing, they are blinded to the larger possibilities that could, and do, engage and energize many in the field.

Lacking an underlying connective rationale, the heterogeneity of family and consumer sciences has led to other threats to the field. For example, nutrition, foods, and food study represented one of the strongest, if not *the* strongest, components in early home economics. Since the 1966 Child Nutrition Act, and especially in the twenty-first century with increasing anxiety over childhood obesity, public schools have paid more attention to nutrition education. This concern could provide a basis for reestablishing the pivotal position of home economics in the elementary and secondary school curricula. Yet, contemporary nutrition education has further destabilized family and consumer sciences. In 1996, nutrition education was "concentrated in the health curriculum, science classes, and school health programs" (National Center for Education Statistics 1996). The report also claimed that in 93 percent of the secondary schools studied, nutrition was included in the health curriculum, and in 92 percent nutrition was in the home economics curriculum. However, the researchers did not report the number of students enrolled, the depth of study, nor if nutrition was a required course. A more focused study (Murimi, Sample, and Hunt 2008) explored nutrition education in the seventh grade, discovering that over one-quarter of those teaching nutrition did not have a background in family and consumer sciences education. A second-grade class in East Harlem enjoyed a nutrition class called CookShop, brought to their school by a nonprofit advocacy group, the Food Resource Center (Bird 2002). Other schoolchildren received nutrition education in physical education classes (Katz et al. 2011). Carter and her colleagues (2007) presented an interdisciplinary curriculum, Planet Health, in which nutrition instruction was embedded in language arts, mathematics, science, social studies, and physical education classes. But such instruction commonly dealt with food knowledge, meal planning, and eating behavior, thus remaining narrowly focused on the individual and the family. Only a few courses delved into problems like world hunger, food scarcity, and the need to protect our food sources. It is difficult to evaluate the status or content of nutrition education in public school curricula. What is obvious, however, is that there is no distinct or unambiguous placement.

Today, individuals outside the profession are promoting the reinsertion of home economics in the school curriculum. "Bring Back Home Economics Education," a commentary in the *Journal of the American Medical Association* (Lichtenstein and Ludwig 2010, 1857), argued that "instruction in basic food

preparation and meal planning skills needs to be part of any long-term solution" to the growing concern over childhood obesity. The authors suggested
incorporating topics such as food safety, sources of food, nutrient information, and the like into courses such as science and economics, leaving home
economics classes with only "hands-on cooking and field trips" (see Jackson
2010 for a response). An opinion piece in the *New York Times*, "Time to Revive
Home Ec," proposed a home economics that focused on "teaching cooking"
(Veit 2011), and an article in *Parenting New Hampshire* discussed the breadth
of life skills taught in "the new Home Ec" (Plenda 2014). That all these authors
asserted this home economics cliché indicates the potential power of name
recognition, but also the problems of defining the field.

To those who have studied the history of home economics, particularly
recent theoretical models of the discipline, this argument may not be totally
new. Article after article and conference after conference have addressed the
fragmentation of the discipline and the pull between skills-oriented instruction, a content-based disciplinary approach, and a "critical science" perspective that recognizes the power relations of society. Yet, when these discussions
occur, as they have with increasing frequency in the past four decades, they
have tended to remain in limited sectors of the profession, only to be revisited again without resolution. Articles such as those in *JAMA* and the *New York
Times* reveal huge gulfs between what professionals debate and what happens
in classrooms, but more important, what the broader public expects home
economics or family and consumer sciences to be. It is this last group, which
is often missing from the discussions, that must be convinced of the importance of family and consumer sciences education.

Over recent decades, a sense of social responsibility has reinvigorated elements of the field. Individual faculty members and teachers have worked on
projects directly involving their communities, and service-learning courses
have returned students to this earlier commitment. Brown and Paolucci's
(1979) work on critical science often forms the basis of this revitalization. For
example, the Family and Consumer Sciences Department at Ball State University offers service-learning experiences because they provide "an outstanding
opportunity for FCS professionals to collaborate with community agencies by
providing a needed service while bringing relevance to the traditional text-
based approach to learning" (Friesen, Whitaker, and Piotrowicz 2004; also see
Paulins 1999). Not surprisingly then, Banerjee and Hausafus (2007) found that
60 percent of family and consumer sciences faculty employed some form of
service learning in their courses.

Yet, service learning is not unique to the discipline of home economics.
Toward the end of the twentieth century, many in education insisted that
schools at all levels were responsible for developing educated and engaged

citizens. The most often acknowledged proponent of these innovations was Ernest Boyer (1966), whose "scholarship of engagement" is frequently cited. Service learning today creates a conundrum for family and consumer sciences. Its basic principles well reflect the ideals of the home economics pioneers, but service learning is now so scattered through the curricula of various departments that it has no one disciplinary home.

By the end of the twentieth century, 32 percent of public schools and over half of high schools had incorporated some aspect of service learning across their curricula (Celio, Durlak, and Dymnicki 2011). In one instance, middle school students in San Francisco learned about the situation of the homeless through projects developed in their social studies and language arts classes (Hershey and Reilly 2009). In higher education, professional schools (e.g., pharmacy and business), liberal arts programs (e.g., art), and social sciences courses (e.g., environmental studies) all utilize service learning as important parts of their curricula (Boulay and Lynch 2012; Braunsberger and Flamm 2013; Kearney 2004; Wyner 2013; Youder 2013). Most telling, a metastudy designed to evaluate the impact of service learning on students in elementary schools through higher education collected its data from studies published in journals ranging from the *American Journal of Community Psychology* to the *Journal of Adolescence*, but did not undertake a systematic search of the *Journal of Family and Consumer Sciences* (Celio, Durlak, and Dymnicki 2011).

The home economics profession has provided a template for service learning, though the term would mean little to Caroline Hunt. As with the example of nutrition, successful pedagogical and philosophical innovations in home economics have been adopted by a diverse range of other fields. This could indicate that home economics as a discipline has once again lost its uniqueness. Yet research has suggested that at least in the primary and secondary grades, there is an evident decline in the number of courses providing service-learning opportunities (David 2009). This gap affords home economics the opportunity to develop pivotal service-learning programs and the opportunity to reclaim its niche in the curriculum.

As in the early years of the twentieth century, commentators inside and outside of education are invoking home economics as the solution to social concerns. What is missing from today's call is a coherent, commonly accepted definition of this malleable field and the mission that drove the pioneers to persevere. It is crucial that we find the energy of the early moments of the history of home economics in order to undertake the revitalization that is needed. Furthermore, we must remember that home economics accomplishes the most when it positions itself as a crucial response to social concerns. Most critically, this position, which demands recognition of the power and the possibilities of a field that addresses individual, family, and community life with a sense of social justice, needs to be communicated to a larger audience, outside of the home economics community.

REFERENCES

AHEA (American Home Economics Association). 1913. *Syllabus of Home Economics.* Baltimore, Md.: AHEA.

Apple, Rima D. 1994. "The Science of Homemaking: A History of Middle School Home Economics to 1970." In *The Education of Early Adolescents: Home Economics in the Middle School,* edited by Frances M. Smith and Cheryl O. Hausafus, 30–48. Washington, D.C.: American Home Economics Association, Teacher Education Section.

———. 1997. "Liberal Arts or Vocational Training? Home Economics Education for Girls." In *Rethinking Home Economics: Women and the History of a Profession,* edited by Sarah Stage and Virginia Vincenti, 79–95. Ithaca, N.Y.: Cornell University Press.

———. 2003. *The Challenge of Constantly Changing Times: From Home Economics to Human Ecology at the University of Wisconsin-Madison, 1903–2003.* Madison, Wis.: Parallel Press.

———. 2006. *Perfect Motherhood: Science and Childrearing in America.* New Brunswick, N.J.: Rutgers University Press.

Apple, Rima D., and Joyce Coleman. 2003. "'As Members of the Social Whole': A History of Social Reform as a Focus of Home Economics, 1895–1940." *Family and Consumer Sciences Research Journal* 32(2): 104–126.

Banerjee, Madhumita, and Cheryl O. Hausafus. 2007. "Faculty Use of Service-Learning: Perceptions, Motivations, and Impediments for the Human Sciences." *Michigan Journal of Community and Service Learning* 14(1): 32–45.

Baxter, Laura, Margaret Justin, and Lucile O. Rust. 1952. *Our Home and Family.* Chicago: Lippincott.

Bird, Laura. 2002. "Schools Teach Kids to Give Peas a Chance." *Wall Street Journal* (eastern ed.), June 14, B1.

Boulay, Margaret C., and Kathryn A. Lynch. 2012. "Fostering Environmental Stewardship Through Creative Expression: Incorporating Art into Service-Learning." *Interdisciplinary Humanities* 29(3): 102–114.

Boyer, Ernest L. 1966. "The Scholarship of Engagement." *Journal of Public Service and Outreach* 1(1): 11–20.

Braunsberger, Karin, and Richard O. Flamm. 2013. "A Mission of Civic Engagement: Undergraduate Students Working with Nonprofit Organizations and Public Sector Agencies to Enhance Societal Wellbeing." *Voluntas* 24: 1–31.

Brown, Marjorie, and Beatrice Paolucci. 1979. *Home Economics: A Definition.* Alexandria, Va.: American Home Economics Association.

Bureau of Education, U.S. Department of the Interior. 1918a. *Home Economics Teaching in Small High Schools.* Washington, D.C.: U.S. Government Printing Office.

———. 1918b. *Current Problems in Home Economics.* Circular No. 2. Washington, D.C.: U.S. Government Printing Office.

Calvert, Maude Richman. 1925. *First Course in Home Making*. Atlanta, Ga.: Turner E. Smith.

Carter, Jill, Jean L. Wiecha, Karen E. Peterson, Suzanne Nobrega, and Steven L. Gortmaker. 2007. *Planet Health: An Interdisciplinary Curriculum for Teaching Middle School Nutrition and Physical Activity*, 2nd ed. Champaign, Ill.: Human Kinetics.

Celio, Christine I., Joseph Durlak, and Allison Dymnicki. 2011. "A Meta-Analysis of the Impact of Service-Learning on Students." *Journal of Experiential Education* 34(2): 164–181.

Cooley, Anna M., Cora M. Winchell, Wilhelmina Spoor, and Josephine A. Marshall. 1918. "Home Economics Studies in Grades Seven to Twelve." *Teachers College Record* 19(2): 119–130.

Counts, George S. 1926. *The Senior High School Curriculum*. Chicago: University of Chicago Press.

David, Jane L. 2009. "Service-Learning and Civic Participation." *Educational Leadership* 66(8): 83–84.

East, Marjorie. 1982. *Caroline Hunt: Philosopher for Home Economics*. State College: Pennsylvania State University, College of Education.

"Food and Nutrition Curriculum Update: A State-by-State Survey." 1984. *Forecast for Home Economics* (May): 36–43.

Friesen, Carol A., Sue H. Whitaker, and Kay Piotrowicz. 2004. "Service Learning in an FCS Core Curriculum: A Community-Campus Collaboration." *Journal of Family and Consumer Sciences* 96(3): 12–15.

Hays, Tricia. 1999. *Nutrition and Food Science: Teacher's Instructional Guide*. Lubbock: Texas Tech University, Home Economics Curriculum Center/Texas Education Agency, Division of Career and Technology Education.

Hershey, Sarah, and Veronica Reilly. 2009. "'Hobo' Is Not a Respectful Word." *Educational Leadership* 66(8): 64–67.

Hunt, Caroline L. 1901. "Revaluations." In *Proceedings of the First, Second and Third Conferences*, 79–89. Lake Placid, N.Y.: n.p.

———. 1907. "Woman's Public Work for the Home." In Lake Placid Conference on Home Economics, *Proceedings of the Ninth Conference*, 10–16. Lake Placid, N.Y.: n.p.

———. 1908. Letter to Charles Van Hise. Papers of President Charles Van Hise, University of Wisconsin-Madison Archives, ser. 4/10/1, box 3.

———. 1912. *The Life of Ellen H. Richards, 1842–1911*. Washington, D.C.: American Home Economics Association.

Jackson, Carolyn W. 2010. "JAMA Article Supports FCS in War on Obesity." *Journal of Family and Consumer Sciences* 102(2): 5.

Katz, David L., Catherine S. Katz, Judith A. Treu, Jesse Reynolds, Valentine Njike, Jennifer Walker, Erica Smith, and Jennifer Michael. 2011. "Teaching Healthful Food Choices to Elementary School Students and Their Parents: The Nutrition Detectives." *Journal of School Health* 81(1): 1–28.

Kaufman, Treva E. 1930. *Teaching Problems in Home Economics*. Philadephia: Lippincott.

Kearney, Kevin R. 2004. "Service-Learning in Pharmacy Education." *American Journal of Pharmaceutical Education* 68(10): 1

Kinne, Helen, and Anna M. Cooley. 1915. *Shelter and Clothing: A Textbook of the Household Arts*. New York: Macmillan.

———. 1916. *Foods and Household Management: A Textbook of the Household Arts*. New York: Macmillan.

Kliebard, Herbert M. 2004. *The Struggle for the American Curriculum*, 3rd ed. New York: Routledge Falmer.

Lichtenstein, Alice H., and David S. Ludwig. 2010. "Bring Back Home Economics Education." *Journal of the American Medical Association* 303(18): 1857–1858.

Life Skills Center. 1994. *Potentials and Possibilities: Home Economics High School Competency Based Curriculum Guide*. Upper Montclair, N.J.: Montclair State College.

Lindenmeyer, Kriste. 1997. *"A Right to Childhood": The U.S. Children's Bureau and Child Welfare, 1912–1946*. Urbana: University of Illinois Press.

Lynd, Robert S., and Helen Merrell Lynd. 1929. *Middletown, a Study in Contemporary American Culture*. New York: Harcourt, Brace.

Marlatt, Abby L. 1903. "Hand Work for High School Girls." In Lake Placid Conference on Home Economics, *Proceedings of the Fifth Conference*, 16–21. Lake Placid, N.Y.: n.p.

Murimi, Mary W., Alicia Sample, and Alice Hunt. 2008. "Nutrition Instruction in Seventh Grade: A Comparison of Teachers with and without FCS Background." *Journal of Family and Consumer Sciences* 100(3): 22-27.

Muncy, Robyn. 1991. *Creating Female Dominion in American Reform, 1890–1935*. New York: Oxford University Press.

National Center for Education Statistics. 1996. *Nutrition Education in Public and Elementary Schools*, http://nces.ed.gov/pubsearch/pubsinfo.asp?pubid=96852 (accessed October 28, 2011).

N.C. State Department of Public Instruction. 1988. *North Carolina Foods and Nutrition Guide*. Raleigh: North Carolina State Department of Public Instruction.

Nikolay, Pauli, Susan Grady, Thomas Stefonek, and Sharon Strom. 1997. *Wisconsin's Model Academic Standards for Family and Consumer Sciences Education*. Madison: Wisconsin Department of Public Instruction.

Norton, Alice P. 1900. "Home Economics." *Elementary School Teacher* 1(3): 207–210.

Office of Career, Technical, and Adult Education. 2008. *State Skill Standards: Foods and Nutrition*. Carson City: Nevada State Department of Education.

Oregon DOE (Department of Education). 1978. *Home Economics for Oregon Schools: Nutrition and Foods*. Salem: Oregon DOE.

Paulins, V. Ann. 1999. "Service Learning and Civic Responsibility: The Consumer in American Society." *Journal of Family and Consumer Sciences* 91(2): 66-72.

Plenda, Melanie. 2014. "Home Economics Classes Are Not What They Used to Be: Today's Family and Consumer Science Classes Are Teaching Kids Real-Life Skills." *Parenting New Hampshire*, www.parentingnh.com (accessed May 16, 2014).

Powers, Jane Bernard. 1992. *The "Girl Question" in Education: Vocational Education for Young Women in the Progressive Era.* Washington, D.C.: Falmer.

"Report of Special Committee on Home Economics in Elementary and Secondary Schools." 1901. In *Proceedings of the First, Second, and Third Conferences.* Lake Placid, N.Y.: n.p.

Richards, Ellen. 1911. "The Social Significance of the Home Economics Movement." *Journal of Home Economics* 3(2): 117–125.

Smart, Mollie Stevens, and Russell C. Smart. 1958. *Living in Families.* Boston: Houghton Mifflin.

Spafford, Ivor. 1938. "Education for Home Living in the Secondary Schools." *Education Digest* 3(8): 26–28.

Spafford, Ivor, Norma Albright, and Sara Blach. 1939. *A Tentative Statement Concerning Home Economics in General Education at the Secondary Level.* Minneapolis, Minn.: Burgess.

Stage, Sarah. 1997. "Ellen Richards and the Social Significance of the Home Economics Movement." In *Rethinking Home Economics: Women and the History of a Profession,* edited by Sarah Stage and Virginia Vincenti, 17–33. Ithaca, N.Y.: Cornell University Press.

Trilling, Mabel Barbara, Ethelwyn Miller, Leonora Florence Bowman, Florence Willliams, Clara Blance Knapp, Viola Maria Bell, Bertha Miller Rugg, and Harold Ordway Rugg. 1920. *Home Economics in American Schools.* Chicago: University of Chicago Press.

Trillling, Mabel Barbara, Florence Williams, and Grace G. Reeves. 1931. *A Girl's Problems in Home Economics: Clothing, Home, Food, Family.* Chicago: Lippincott.

Veit, Helen Zoe. 2011. "Time to Revive Home Ec." *New York Times,* September 5, A30.

Weigley, Emma Seifrit. 1974. "It Might Have Been Euthenics: The Lake Placid Conferences and the Home Economics Movement." *American Quarterly* 26(1): 79–96.

Werhan, Carol R. 2013. "Family and Consumer Sciences Secondary School Programs: National Survey Shows Continued Demand for FCS Teachers." *Journal of Family and Consumer Sciences* 105(4): 41–45.

Werhan, Carol, and Wendy L. Way. 2006. "Family and Consumer Sciences Programs in Secondary Schools: Results of a National Survey." *Journal of Family and Consumer Sciences* 98(1): 19–25.

"Why Teach Domestic Science?" 1911. *Journal of Education* 73(8): 206.

Wyner, Yael. 2013. "A Case Study: Using Authentic Scientific Data for Teaching and Learning Ecology." *Journal of College Science Teaching* 42(5): 54–60.

Youder, Stephen A. 2013. "Responding to Disaster with a Service Learning Project for Honors Students." *Honors in Practice* 9: 113–128.

II. Achieving Well-Being
Through Food and Clothing

While asserting that cooking and sewing are not all there was, or is, to home economics, understanding and enabling individuals and families to meet these basic human needs are core functions of the profession. Food and clothing issues occupy a large segment of public discourse and popular culture. The five chapters in this part are devoted to these topics.

In chapter 4, "Our Own Food: From Canning Clubs to Community Gardens," Elizabeth L. Andress and Susan F. Clark recount how home economists worked with government agencies and local communities to facilitate food security through canning clubs and victory gardens during periods of crisis in the twentieth century. The resurgence of interest in locally grown food has brought home economists, horticulturalists, and community organizers together with citizens to address issues of food quality and availability.

Weight has been a weighty concern in the United States for many decades. Rachel Louise Moran in chapter 5, "Weighing in About Weight: Advisory Power in the Bureau of Home Economics," describes the work of home economics researchers in the U.S. Department of Agriculture's Bureau of Home Economics in the early 1900s in response to women's concerns about weight. This chapter illustrates the inseparability of the work performed by home economists and the home economists themselves. Moran recounts the importance of communication between the bureau personnel and their constituency of women to the mission and advisory role of the bureau.

In chapter 6, "From the War on Hunger to the Fight Against Obesity," Richard D. Lewis, Emma M. Laing, and Stephanie M. Foss explore some initiatives of gov-

ernmental agencies in the mid-twentieth century to combat hunger and nutritional deficiencies among at-risk populations in the United States. Home economists served in a variety of roles, including public policy advising and education.
The authors recount how obesity became an overriding concern of the twenty-
first century.

Two chapters juxtapose home economists' attention to clothing in the early
twentieth century and in the twenty-first. In chapter 7, "How Home Economists
Taught American Women to Dress, 1910–1950," Linda Przybyszewski explains that
during the 1920s through the 1940s, home economists provided instruction to
middle-class rural women and working-class urban women about appropriate
dress, including standards for attractive, healthful, and affordable apparel. In
college home economics courses, students were introduced to the principles of
art as applied to apparel as their instructors emphasized artistic, democratic, and
practical modernity.

In chapter 8, "New Patterns for Women's Clothing: Consumption versus Sustainability," Margarete Ordon tackles the exploitation of natural and human resources in twenty-first-century clothing production. Through interviews with
women about their acquisition, maintenance, and care of clothing, and through
examining the broader issues of the clothing life cycle, Ordon explores the relationship between U.S. women's wardrobe abundance and international and domestic temporal, economic, and marketing influences. Her work illustrates the
interdisciplinary nature of home economics research and theory development,
and advocates for new patterns of clothing consumption based on an ethic of
sustainability.

4. Our Own Food

From Canning Clubs to Community Gardens

ELIZABETH L. ANDRESS *and* SUSAN F. CLARK

In 1914, girls canning club members and their supervising home economists in fifteen southern states canned 6 million pounds of tomatoes and other vegetables from their one-tenth-acre gardens. The result was over 1.9 million cans or jars worth approximately $284,880, yielding nearly $200,000 profit. That year, about 7,800 members participated, but the next year nearly 50,000 girls enrolled with four hundred supervising agents (Martin and Creswell 1915). Their goal was to increase the food security of their families. A century later Shannon Hayes (2010, 1) reported the activities of twenty-first-century "tomato-canning feminists" who embraced the traditions of homemaking, and Kelly Coyne and Erik Knutzen (2010) provided guidance for people interested in reviving the "old home arts" in order to create a life of ecological sustainability.

Community gardens have long been present in American history, often related to the social, economic, and environmental context of the times, such as war and economic crisis (Bassett 1981; Lawson 2005). Pingree's Potato Patches, pioneered in Detroit in 1893 as a vacant-lot garden providing land to the poor to raise food, is purported to be the first community garden in the United States (Lawson 2005). The first children's school garden was established at the Putnam School in Boston in 1890 and remained vibrant for thirty years. Teachers and school administrators supported gardening because they believed it addressed needed educational reform, as well as social, moral, recreational, and environmental issues (ibid.). The early community gardens augmented people's food supplies through subsequent food preservation and often provided a means for the unemployed to grow their own food. A food-growing renaissance, including a wide spectrum of activities from community gardens to farmers markets to community-supported agriculture, has occurred in the twenty-first century.

What circumstances and events account for household needs and desires to grow and preserve "our own food"? This chapter addresses the role of home economics, Cooperative Extension, and the U.S. Department of Agriculture (USDA) in providing education and support services for families seeking food security and better food quality at various points during the twentieth and twenty-first centuries. Gardening and food preservation are at the center of these activities.

Home Economics, Tomato Clubs, and Food Preservation

Federal funds in the early twentieth century were used to take the food and nutrition expertise of home economists into communities in many agriculture-related endeavors. Federal support for farm demonstration programs began in 1903 under the leadership of Dr. Seaman Knapp, who was appointed to be the special agent for the promotion of agriculture in the South by the USDA (Extension Service, USDA 1953). Knapp brought educator O. B. Martin from South Carolina to USDA headquarters in Washington, D.C., to assist in the development of boys' corn clubs for practical agricultural instruction (Martin 1953). Soon a demand for a comparable girls' activity surfaced to enable them to carry out skillful home-related work. Consequently, girls' tomato clubs were organized in South Carolina and Virginia in 1910 (Creswell 1916). This was the beginning of the career of home demonstration agent within home economics, working with those first forty-seven girls growing tomatoes in their home gardens and canning them (Martin and Powell 1921).

By the fall of 1916, demonstration work with women and girls under the instruction of home economics agents was operational in 420 counties in the southern states. One of the objectives was the development of skills leading to the "economic independence of girls and women in the country," thus reinforcing the view of farm homes as producing centers and not just consuming households (Knapp and Creswell 1916). Cooperative Extension specialists at the land-grant colleges, who contributed skill and knowledge in home economics as well as in horticulture, dairy, and poultry subjects, aided the county home demonstration agents. Rapid expansion into every state was assisted first with funds from the General Education Board and then with federal appropriations through the Smith-Lever Act of 1914, which supported agriculture and home economics demonstration work (Creswell 1916; also see Atiles, Crocoll, and Schuchardt, this volume). Referred to as either girls' canning clubs (Creswell 1916) or mother-daughter home canning clubs (Benson 1917), the groups were an opportunity to teach home economics in rural areas. Canning club directors were educated as home economists and they taught various concepts for improving life in the farm home ("Girls' Canning Clubs" 1915).

Canning and other types of food preservation (or conservation) have been an integral part of home economics since the beginning of the profession. Early USDA work in support of home economics included research in food chemistry and nutrition. The Office of Home Economics was established in 1915 under the leadership of C. F. Langworthy to expand the nutrition research formerly housed in the Office of Experiment Stations and to initiate new programs in improving living conditions in homes and communities (Swanson 1965). The office was elevated in status and renamed the Bureau of Home Economics in 1923 (Betters 1930). Several USDA Farmers' Bulletins on home canning were published between 1910 and 1919 (Andress and Kuhn 1983). During these years, more attention was given to the operation of equipment and the methodology of canning than to the theory behind the sterilization of foods; however, in 1917 a Farmers' Bulletin was issued that provided more education about microbiology, spoilage, and the goals of processing versus sterilization (Andress and Kuhn 1983; Creswell and Powell 1917).

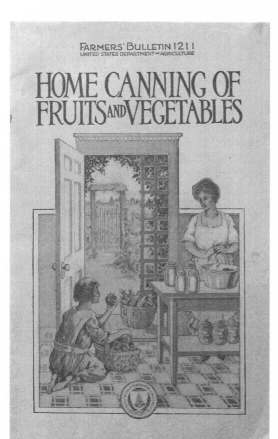

PHOTO 4.1. Farmers' Bulletin No. 1211, issued by the U.S. Department of Agriculture in 1921, was the first canning guide to incorporate the results of bacteriology and heat penetration tests in canned foods, which were conducted by the Office of Home Economics. Photograph by Cal Powell, Elizabeth Andress personal collection.

The USDA and the state colleges enthusiastically reported on the size of girls' canning clubs, the work of women's home demonstration clubs, and the volume of food raised and canned (Martin and Creswell 1915). During the early twentieth century, the *Journal of Home Economics* carried many reports of home canning and preservation experiences, studies being conducted by home economists, and progress reports on canning clubs and home demonstration work (HEARTH 1914–1921).

Gardening and Food Preservation in Times of Scarcity and War

The role of home economists and Cooperative Extension was prominent in food security during the two world wars. During World War I, the U.S. Food Administration coordinated domestic food security efforts. Food production decreased in the United States as agricultural workers went to serve in the military forces. State supervisors of Cooperative Extension's home demonstration programs were appointed as directors for the Food Administration. One of the advantages of enlisting home economists in the work of the Food Administration was that they were tied into the fairly new national Cooperative Extension Service infrastructure and thus were a great help in reaching rural Americans (Goldstein 2012). The home economists promoted food conservation at home to eliminate waste and stabilize prices through a variety of strategies for controlling food use, especially meat, sugar, and wheat. Reducing food consumption and increasing conservation were considered to be patriotic duties ("Work of the Food Administration" 1917).

With the slogan "Food Will Win the War," the state specialists in nutrition, food preservation, and horticulture, along with the county agents, helped families to plant gardens and can food (Rieff 2006). With the formation of the National War Garden Commission, terms such as "victory gardens," "liberty gardens," and "food gardens for defense" became part of the national vocabulary. Private as well as public lands were seen as candidates for gardens of any size. Canning was prominent in the campaign as represented in the slogan "Can Vegetables, Fruit, and the Kaiser Too" (NWGC 1919). Canning and drying methods were explained in many federal government publications and taught to the public by the networks of home economists throughout the states.

Even though the end of World War I brought about some relief from the need to conserve food, the period 1920–1940 still had crises that affected the food supply and food security—the Great Depression and the drought of the 1930s (McIntosh 1995). Prices for farm products declined dramatically and remained low throughout the 1920s, and many families lost their farms. Still, home canning research and education continued as an emphasis for the home economics program at the USDA. Although no research reports appear to have been issued between 1927 and 1930, by 1930 questions were arising over the safety of some home canning methods (Tanner 1935; USDA 1944). Many families and communities continued growing and preserving their own food supply through the Great Depression, 1929–1939 (Lawson 2005). During this period there was a surge of interest in and renewed organization of community canning centers.

With the onset of World War II gardening and preserving food were again considered to be patriotic duties. Victory gardens were brought back, and the War Food Administration launched a national Victory Garden Program with five stated goals, including promoting food availability, decreasing the materials needed for food processing and distribution, increasing citizens' morale, preserving fruits and vegetables in the event that shortages worsened, and easing the burden on railroads, which were needed to transport war munitions, by reducing the need to ship produce (Bassett 1981). The USDA estimated that over 20 million garden plots were planted in 1944 (War Food Administration 1944). The amount of fruits and vegetables canned in home kitchens and community canneries was estimated at 3.5 billion quarts, which were preserved by about 25 million families. Home canned vegetables represented about half of the 1944 civilian supply and home canned fruits about two-thirds (Stiebeling 1945).

Even 4-H youth programs and club projects emphasized wartime food production and preservation. For example, 1,778 community 4-H clubs existed in Georgia in 1942. They engaged 26,717 girls and 8,688 boys in garden projects. Food and nutrition projects in total attracted over 38,000 girls, who canned 677,000 quarts of fruit and 697,000 quarts of vegetables, dried 471,000 pounds of food products, and brined 13,800 gallons of food (Sutton et al. 1942).

Community Canning Centers

The commercial canning industry developed in the United States in the mid-1800s (McIntosh 1995). During the Great Depression many localities developed community canning centers to assist families in having enough food throughout the year. Generally, a community agency provided the facilities and the equipment and families shared their labor in order to can large batches of food. During periods of food insecurity, interest in the canning centers surged. At the end of World War II there were over 3,800 centers in the United States. During wartime the canneries were subsidized, but this ceased after the war (Coffey and Sternberg 1977). It could be said that the early girls' canning clubs in rural areas were the precursor to the community canning centers.

In post–World War I Georgia, community canning facilities were developed through schools and the Department of Vocational Agriculture (Wheeler 1948). The first was built in 1926 in Franklin County and processed nine thousand cans of food that year. In Hart County, the vocational agriculture teacher started teaching canning in 1926 by going farm to farm, and in 1927 he set up a small facility with a processing retort and steam boiler, which were later transferred to the school. By 1941, a food preservation plant or vocational building played a major role in the large rural schools of Georgia. The program and building often consisted of classrooms for home economics and agriculture as well as the food plant. Boys and girls were taught food preservation, and whole families were brought into the school activities around food production, preservation, and conservation.

The popularity of these centers grew, and by 1942 there were 383 community canning units operating in connection with vocational agriculture programs in Georgia, producing 10.5 million cans of food (Wheeler 1948). Several schools also built cold storage, meat curing, and/or freezing plants for the preservation of meat and fruit, and some communities installed community freezer lockers. In 1942, four dehydrating demonstration plants were installed and operated in cooperation with the Tennessee Valley Authority (ibid.).

Recognizing that community food preservation was a time-honored activity that brought neighborhoods together, the USDA published detailed guidance for community food preservation centers as part of the national defense program in 1941 (Bureau of Home Economics 1941). The guide outlined all the government agencies and administrations available to help, operating principles, the equipment needed, and processing instructions for canned foods. The publication acknowledged that community food preservation centers already in existence included homes with backyard operations, churches and other community kitchens, home economics laboratories, and formal commercial canning and freezing plants operated by the community. Additional guidance was published throughout the war years in cooperation with the War Food Administration. Although community canning centers declined throughout the country after the 1950s, there has been renewed interest and several centers operate in the United States today (Andress and Hamlin 2012; Geering 2012).

Research: Foundation for Best Practices

During the years 1944–1946, the USDA's Bureau of Human Nutrition and Home Economics undertook what has become the landmark research for most of the low-acid home canning recommendations still offered today (Stiebeling 1946; Toepfer et al. 1946). Until then, many home canning procedures were adaptations of commercial processes. Because of differences in home methods, safety margins were added, but these caused concern about the over-processing of foods and loss of nutritional value (Stiebeling 1944). Congress provided funding for the bureau to undertake research to study home canning processes. The work was conducted in federal laboratories and also involved cooperative projects with state agricultural experiment stations (ibid.).

The bureau also conducted research on other methods of home preservation in addition to canning. In the wartime years, to assist families lacking pressure canners for preserving their garden produce, research on the proper equipment and methods for drying foods, as well as the storage of home-dried foods, was begun (Sherman 1943). It is worth noting that through the 1940s, the bureau also was involved in processed food research that aided the food industry, including studies of the palatability of dehydrated eggs and meats (ibid.; Stiebeling 1945). The USDA home economists expected that the freezing of foods at home was the preservation method most likely to expand after the war, so they began to study the effects of freezing methods on the retention of nutrients and preservation of quality (Stiebeling 1944, 1945).

As expected, food freezer ownership increased in the 1950s. Home food preservation now meant that beyond processing fruits, vegetables, meats, and fish for preservation, baked goods and complete meal dishes could be preserved (Hooker 1981; McIntosh 1995). Home economics food preservation research turned away from canning and toward recommendations for the home freezing of foods. A variety of studies were conducted and reported in the *Journal of Home Economics* and elsewhere, including whether to blanch vegetables before freezing (Noble and Winter 1952); the effects of blanching, freezing, and freezer storage on ascorbic acid retention (Gordon and Noble 1959); and a comparison of the home processing of apples by freezing or canning (Dawson et al. 1953).

Home Food Production and Preservation, 1960–2000

The arrival of refrigerator-freezers in most U.S. households and the presence of suburban supermarkets made the mass consumption of commercially processed frozen foods possible (Hamilton 2003). Tappan introduced the household microwave oven in the 1950s (Treisch 1955), and U.S. market saturation occurred in the 1970s. The changing economics of households and the availability of and improvements in both the freezer and the microwave contributed to widespread interest in convenience foods for household consumption.

Despite increased food security and the easy availability of convenience foods in the 1960s and 1970s for much of the U.S. population, concerns continued about areas of poverty and about those with limited access to the exploding commercially processed food supplies. Home food gardening and preservation remained important activities although not for the majority of households. A national survey conducted by the USDA found that about one of three households canned fruits and/or vegetables in 1975 with the majority canning a hundred quarts of food or less (Davis and Page 1979).

An issue related to home food preservation in the 1970s for those still canning was the energy crisis. Some efforts were undertaken to explore ways to reduce energy consumption through using less water or smaller pressure canners (Harris and Davis 1976; Walsh and Bates 1978). None of the research studies at the time or to date have yielded acceptable changes that maintain food safety. Both atmospheric steam canning and the use of small pressure saucepans for canning are still greatly debated and the subject of sporadic research (National Center for Home Food Preservation 2006, 2011).

Another issue that received extensive attention in the 1970s was the natural acidity level in fresh tomatoes. The first directives to home canners to add citric acid to home-canned tomatoes and to follow other specific canning criteria resulted from a joint meeting of scientists from the Centers for Disease Control and Prevention, the National Canners Association, the Food and Drug Administration, and the USDA in 1974 (Powers 1976). Research regarding acidification levels and palatability was conducted by the USDA's Eastern Regional Research Laboratory as well as by home economists at land-grant universities (Sapers et al. 1978; Skelton and Craig 1978; Skelton and Marr 1978; Zimmerman et al. 1978).

In the early 1980s, USDA Home Economics and Human Nutrition established the Center for Excellence in Home Food Preservation through a contract with Pennsylvania State University's Department of Food Science (Andress and Kuhn 1983). Because of continuing botulism concerns about some tomato and vegetable canning issues since the 1970s, a primary objective of the center was to review the research foundations for the then-current USDA home canning recommendations (Andress and Kuhn 1983). The center developed new tomato-canning processes and issued recommendations in a new format, the *Complete Guide to Home Canning* (USDA 1988–2009). This guide contains the current USDA recommendations for home canning, pickling, and jelly making. The most recent edition was published in 2009 and is available online (http://nchfp.uga.edu/publications/publications_usda.html).

The 1970s brought a rebirth of community gardening as a response to a growing population, inflation, an emerging environmental ethic, and a desire to build neighborly connections. Initiatives related to local food production and preservation were organized on a continuum from informal (neighborly cooperation) to highly formal and federally governed. Examples of these community-based garden initiatives that remain operational today include the New York City Green Guerillas, Seattle P-Patch, Boston Urban Gardeners, and Philadelphia Green (Lawson 2005). Although common themes of food production, income generation, recreation, education, and beautification still provide a strong rationale for gardening, their focus has been on rebuilding social networks and the infrastructure of blighted urban communities. In the twenty-first century, the resurgence in interest around food preservation and community gardening is a consumer and community quest for a local food system that promotes the health of people as well as the environment (Click and Ridberg 2010).

Civic Agriculture:
A Contemporary Local Food Concept

The groundswell for a local food culture in the early twenty-first century has included interests in gardening, meeting health and nutrition goals, enjoying fresh food in both home and restaurant meals, and preserving food for future consumption in the family or for economic benefit through home- and community-based businesses. The local food movement has gained traction and moved into mainstream culture and practice, thus presenting new opportunities for home economists.

Sustainable food systems are an innovative model of "civic agriculture," a term first used in 1988 by Thomas Lyson (2004) to designate an organized system of agriculture and food production that reconnects farm, food, and community. It embodies a commitment to developing and strengthening economically, environmentally, and socially sustainable agricultural and food systems through building community capacity, using local resources, and serving local markets and citizens. Civic agriculture encourages thinking in terms of collective need, mutual cooperation, and the responsibilities to shared ecologies around food production. As DeLind (2002, 217) emphasized, civic agriculture is "a tool and a venue . . . for nurturing a sense of belonging to a place and an organic sense of citizenship." Farmers markets, community-supported agriculture, and community gardens are forms of civic agriculture in action.

This raises the question: Could civic agriculture be the new twenty-first-century home economics? By definition, home economics is the profession or practice that deals with the economics and management of the household in the context of community. Civic agriculture addresses comparable issues about local and regional food production, economic security, and social capital. As an educational concept, it mirrors the attributes of home economics education, practice, and professional leadership. The term "civic agriculture" encompasses key tenets of home economics, including relationships between human ecology and the natural environment; nutrition, food, and health promotion; producers, consumers, and food security in the community; social and economic development; local identity, history, values, and culture; civic engagement, public policy, democracy, and community problem solving; preserving, processing, retailing, and other food-related industries; storage, distribution, and waste infrastructure; and the quality of life in both rural and urban environments.

The contemporary interdisciplinary nature of education about, research on, and organization of foods and nutrition systems is evident in the wide range of academic fields involved. Scholarship on the benefits of community gardens in relation to the broader food system has emerged in diverse journals, including those focused on family and consumer sciences, geography, horticulture, sociology, and health and nutrition. Civic agriculture is a promising force for reclaiming a healthier food system, and it reintroduces the need for home economics education.

Community Food Engagement

Examples of civic agriculture in action abound. The most familiar are farmers markets (FMs), community-supported agriculture (CSA), community and school gardens, "U-pick" operations, food and producer co-operatives or food hubs, chefs' collaboratives, and community kitchens and canning centers.

COMMUNITY GARDENS

The twenty-first-century gardening renaissance has been further validated by high-profile examples of gardening, such as First Lady Michelle Obama's oversight and participation in a vegetable garden at the White House, reminiscent of Eleanor Roosevelt's victory garden during World War II. Plots can be small or large, yet a common theme of these gardens is that they are part of a social network created and maintained by members of the community. The American Community Gardening Association conducts periodic surveys of active community gardens in the United States, which were estimated at 18,000–20,000 in 2008 (Kirby and Peters 2008). Although the numbers fluctuate annually, community gardens are present in all fifty states (Lawson, Drake, and the American Community Gardening Association 2013), and they operate on municipal land, land trusts, and private property. They are collectively organized by a few to many gardeners interested in bringing communities together and supplying healthy food. The majority of groups operating community gardens are nonprofit organizations, including cultural and neighborhood groups, schools, faith-based organizations, hospitals, jails, women's and senior centers, and housing complexes (Guitart, Pickering, and Byrne 2012).

FARMERS MARKETS

Farmers markets are specific physical spaces where farmers and others bring their produce, canned goods, and prepared foods to sell directly to the

PHOTO 4.2. Shoppers select locally grown produce at the Athens Farmers Market, Athens, Georgia. Photograph by Stephanie Schupska, courtesy University of Georgia, College of Agriculture and Environmental Sciences.

public. A central theme is that the food sold should be from "local" producers, as defined by the respective markets. FMs are good for local economies, farmers, consumers, and the environment (Litt et al. 2011). The USDA in 1994 began publishing the National Directory of Farmers Markets, which lists direct-to-consumer markets known to operate in the United States; annual updates have been published since 2008. FMs have steadily increased from 1,755 in 1994 to 7,814 in 2012 (USDA 2012). Strong consumer interest in purchasing locally produced foods is apparent in both rural and urban areas.

COMMUNITY-SUPPORTED AGRICULTURE

The success of CSA models has contributed to the groundswell of the local food movement. A CSA consists of a community of individuals who pledge at the beginning of a season to financially support or engage in work equity in a specific farm's operations in exchange for shares of the farm's food production. Members become shareholders and assume the benefits and risks of farming. This direct sales model provides the farmer with advance working capital and, ultimately, financial security. In 1986, two small farms in western Massachusetts adopted the CSA concept, and today there are approximately 6,500 farms in the United States marketing products through CSA arrangements (Galt 2011). Given the popularity of CSAs, it is apparent that consumers are ready to share agricultural risks and responsibilities with local farmers.

Most CSAs provide a weekly distribution of seasonal vegetables and fruits; however, a growing number of CSAs offer a larger array of farm produce, including shares in eggs, meat, milk, and baked goods. Consumers who join a CSA are seeking fresh produce grown in a sustainable manner by someone they know and trust. The CSA farmer typically uses organic or sustainable agricultural farming methods as they strive to provide fresh, high-quality foods to match consumer demand (Groh and McFadden 1990). Many CSAs are also tapping into other markets in specific and tailored ways (e.g., hospital and school partnerships) to connect with their communities and to extend production and revenues. Searchable databases for the country's CSAs are a valuable resource connecting farmers/producers to consumers (ATTRA 2011).

The local food movement has contributed to the growth of direct farm-to-consumer sales and the rise in the number of small- to medium-size farms in the United States (less than $50,000 in gross annual sales, and between $50,000 and $250,000 gross annual sales, respectively). The USDA's Economic Research Service reported that 40 percent of all vegetable, fruit, and nut farms (~110,000) in the United States sell their products in local and regional markets (Low and Vogel 2011). In 2008, small-scale farms averaged $7,800 in local food sales via FMs or roadside stands, whereas medium-size farms averaged $70,000. Large farms (gross annual sales of $250,000 or more) averaged $770,000 in local food sales using direct-to-consumer and other distribution avenues (Low and Vogel 2011).

A revolution in women-run farm operations has coincided with the local food movement. The USDA reported in 2009 that women accounted for nearly one-third of U.S. farmers, double the number of women-owned farms reported twenty-five years earlier (Nickerson and Hand 2009). An estimated three hundred thousand women operate farms in the United States, the largest minority group in agriculture (Hansen 2011; Martinez et al. 2010). Historically, women have always been involved in agriculture as co-owners and managers of family farms, yet they were without acknowledgment in the USDA census reports. Contemporary women farmers express the desire to build a community food system that is healthy, just, and sustainable (Costa 2010). Engaging in local food systems both facilitates and demonstrates women farmers' desire to produce better-tasting, better-quality food that is healthier for the consumer and the environment.

Creating Food Democracy Through Education and Action

Food-based education is a significant component of the various civic agriculture models. Many FMs use a "market school" concept, featuring people from the community who share their knowledge with others, from dietary considerations to how to use vermiculture to enhance a garden. Cooperative Extension specialists, including home economists and horticulturalists, work in tandem with farmers, citizens, and colleagues in other disciplines to design programs that engage or connect farm, food, and community. Such food-based curricula or programs typically include teaching a sense of seasonality through food demonstrations and recipe sharing. Cooking demonstrations and sampling unfamiliar or healthier foods are designed to enhance consumers' skills when preparing fresh food. Some school-based programs also include lessons on food preservation.

Facilitating the affordability of locally sourced foods is an example of food democracy. Many FMs and CSAs accept subsidized food assistance plan payments (SNAP, WIC), which provide low-income patrons with access to the healthier food options. These civic agriculture examples are catalysts for social change around food systems.

The emergence of community gardening networks is a return to the commons, that central place in a city or town where people gathered to plant fruits and vegetables (Linn 2009). The American Community Gardening Association and the nonprofit National Gardening Association (Payne and Fryman 2001) encourage programs that emphasize plant-based education, health and wellness, environmental stewardship, community development, and responsible community or home gardening. The GardenABCs (2013) network includes the School Garden Education Programs, which offer teaching resources and community funding. Cooperative Extension local food programs provide expertise and leadership training through the master gardeners (adult) and junior master gardeners (youth) curricula.

Challenges for Community Gardening and Home Food Preservation

The motivations for community gardening (e.g., access to fresh food, cultural or spiritual practices, education, saving money, socializing) are altruistic. Yet challenges remain, including the legal aspects of land tenure for gardens, high construction costs, poor-quality or contaminated soil, and site locations in high vandalism areas (Ferris, Norman, and Sempik 2001). The Environmental Protection Agency (EPA 2011a, 2011b) published interim guidelines for safe gardening practices, including the remediation of property to safely remove, cap, or contain soil contaminants. Community initiatives across the nation are integrating urban agriculture and community gardens for neighborhood revitalization (APA 2007). Many are reclaiming industrial brownfields for such purposes. Despite the challenges of reclaiming potentially contaminated properties, communities are overcoming them through creative efforts, partnerships, and organizing for collective impact (Hanleybrown, Kania, and Kramer 2011).

Although serving as the historical standard-bearer for home canning and food preservation research and education, USDA agencies, including Cooperative Extension, have been coping with drastic budget cuts since the mid-1990s. The number of home economics educators at both state and county levels has been greatly reduced in many states. Yet, home canning and preserving food remain popular activities in U.S. households, and the need for science-based expertise is great. With the intent of helping to meet this need and of preserving its legacy of leadership in scientifically tested, safe methods of home food preservation, the USDA established the National Center for Home Food Preservation (NCHFP) with leadership at the University of Georgia's College of Family and Consumer Sciences in 1999.

To assess the extent of home food preservation in the twenty-first century, national surveys were conducted by the NCHFP in 2000–2001 and 2005. About 26 percent of the respondents reported home canning activity in the previous season, and 98 percent reported freezing foods they grew or bought (Andress et al. 2002a, 2002b; D'Sa et al. 2007, 2008). Fourteen percent of the respondents in the 2005 survey reported drying foods at home (D'Sa et al. 2009). The surveys revealed the continuing need for food safety education for home food preservers. Friends or family members were cited as the primary sources of directions for canning or freezing in both surveys, although neither survey ascertained where those sources received their information. Despite decades of scientific evidence of food safety hazards, risky practices for canning low-acid foods, which could result in severe health consequences or even death, were practiced in more than 40 percent of surveyed households. The challenge of reaching inexperienced as well as seasoned home food preservers with education about correct canning practices looms large.

The recent development of small food business entrepreneurship and "cottage food" production again has linked home food preservation with the concept of increasing household income, which is reminiscent of the early to mid-twentieth century. Cottage food operations, which usually involve the sale of low-risk, home-produced foods in local businesses, are not subject to as many government restrictions as commercial food operations. The Association of Food and Drug Officials (2012) issued regulatory guidance for best practices for these small businesses, and as of August 2013, forty-two states allowed cottage food operations (Condra 2013). The NCHFP conducted research on the best preservation processes for several specialty food items, such as tomato and fruit salsas, relishes, and other pickled products, that are useful for other types of small business entrepreneurs; the procedures are available to the public through its website.

Virtual Communities for Gardening and Food Preservation

The internet is playing a pivotal role in developing many of the sustainable food movement's most vibrant local food initiatives. The internet and social media, including organizational and personal websites, discussion forums, how-to videos, Facebook, and personal blogs, cover issues from canning to community gardening to recipe sharing. No longer do home economists, the USDA, and Cooperative Extension have an exclusive claim to educating the public about home canning and other methods of preservation. The downside of digital technology, however, is that unsound, potentially hazardous advice can be easily shared with a wide audience.

To help maintain a scientifically sound voice from the home economics and USDA home canning legacies, the NCHFP developed a website (www.homefoodpreservation.net) in 2002, which quickly became extremely popular. In 2013 there were almost 2 million unique visitors to the website, producing 5.1 million page views, and annual traffic has continued to increase. Daily visitors in the busier summer months have reached over 290,000. Registered participants in the free, online self-study course since its 2005 debut now number in excess of 10,000 people. The participants' motivations for seeking information through this self-study include maintaining food security, economic self-sufficiency, local food culture, food safety, home gardening, and health and nutrition concerns (Andress, unpublished data).

State-level "buy local" initiatives exemplify how the internet can advocate behavioral change. In 2012, the Virginia Food System Council, which includes representatives of the local food system (producers, distributors, consumers, governmental agencies, health organizations, anti-hunger efforts, environmental and conservation groups, schools), launched a campaign to encourage consumers to spend $10 per week on local foods. Its intent was to educate Virginians about the benefits and the barriers to buying Virginia-grown food. Research by Cooperative Extension personnel had predicted that if each Virginia household spent just $10 of its total weekly food budget on local food and farm products, $1.65 billion would be generated annually (Benson and Bendfeldt 2007), a significant boost to local economies.

Thoughts on Remaking Home Economics

Have we come full circle? The victory garden campaigns of the two world wars centered on citizens' duty. In the early twentieth century and during the Great Depression gardens and food preservation provided a means to counteract the local manifestations of economic downturn. Mid-century gardening underwent a transition toward recreation or personal hobby as new housing options expanded backyard space for gardening. Those without garden access turned toward the concept of community gardening. Perhaps today the radical shift in home economics educational inquiry is better illustrated and accepted through the study of civic agriculture. Regardless of what it is called, initiatives for food security, nutrition, and health will require academic leadership grounded in home economics concepts and practices. Today, a re-purposing of home economics education is emerging, thanks in part to the local food movement's interest in the social, cultural, economic, and environmental impacts of how food is grown, accessed, processed, and distributed.

Who better to navigate this local food renaissance than home economists? Advocates, including medical practitioners and educators, have called for a mandatory home economics curriculum, including basic cooking, nutrition, and consumer economics, in public schools as a way to help mitigate the chronic diseases associated with diet and nutrition, particularly obesity (Lichtenstein and Ludwig 2010). The Academy of Nutrition and Dietetics' latest professional performance expectations for registered dietitian nutritionists include standards of competency for sustainable, healthy food and water systems (Tagtow et al. 2014). Interdisciplinary and collaborative approaches involving agriculture and home economics educators offer a means to meet this need. Research has shown that civic agriculture models like FMs, CSAs, and community gardens have the potential to increase access to safely produced fruits and vegetables (McCormack et al. 2010). The consumption of locally grown foods promotes positive dietary changes, which may in turn result in improved weight status and lower risk for chronic disease (Hamm 2008; Hoffman et al. 2012).

Leading the charge in these local foods initiatives are individuals from all walks of life and disciplinary backgrounds, but some of these people lack sustainable agriculture or home economics education. Thus, opportunities abound for universities and communities to engage them with interdisciplinary, experiential-based curricula in both formal and informal education. The reweaving of home economics education and training in a way that holistically applies its diverse dimensions to local food systems requires leadership from home economists. Higher education is well positioned to provide innovative curricula that strengthen undergraduates' understanding of the social, cultural, economic, and environmental connections between agriculture, home, communities, and food (Wright 2006). The land-grant universities continue to be distinguished by their research, academic programs, and Cooperative Extension, which delivers practical education to benefit the ways people work and live. In primary and secondary schools, extending the experiences of a school garden through the reframing of home economics classes offers opportunities to reimage and revitalize the home economics field.

Moving forward, it is paramount that education reflect the complex relationships in human ecology—the social, economic, and environmental dimensions of cultivating healthier community food systems and lifestyles. It is incumbent upon those professionals identified with home economics to educate youth and adults about community resilience, including local food system practices. Leading the way, these professionals can positively influence, transform, and sustain the revival of home economics education for the twenty-first century to ensure safe food, healthy food, and enough food for all.

REFERENCES

Andress, Elizabeth L., Elaine M. D'Sa, Mark A. Harrison, William L. Kerr, Judy A. Harrison, and Brian A. Nummer. 2002a. "A Survey of Practices in Freezing Foods at Home in the U.S." Paper 46B-2 presented at the Institute of Food Technologists annual meeting, Anaheim, Calif.

———. 2002b. "Current Home Canning Practices in the U.S." Paper 46B-3 presented at the Institute of Food Technologists annual meeting, Anaheim, Calif.

Andress, Elizabeth L., and Teri Hamlin. 2012. "Agriculture Education Food Processing Centers of Georgia," http://www.fcs.uga.edu/ext/food/docs/2012_Agriculture_Education_Food_Processing_Facilities.pdf (accessed August 1, 2013).

Andress, Elizabeth L., and Gerald D. Kuhn. 1983. "Critical Review of Home Preservation Literature and Current Research." University Park, Pa.: USDA and Penn State University. Cooperative agreement no. 12-05-300-553, http://www.uga.edu/nchfp/publications/usda/review/report.html (accessed August 1, 2013).

APA (American Planning Association). 2007. "Policy Guide on Community and Regional Food Planning," http://planning.org/policy/guides/adopted/food.htm (accessed May 10, 2013).

Association of Food and Drug Officials. 2012. "Regulatory Guidance for Best Practices Cottage Foods." http://www.afdo.org/resources/temp/Cottage_Foods_013.pdf (accessed August 1, 2013).

ATTRA. 2011. "Local Food Directories." *National Sustainable Agriculture Information Service*, http://attra.ncat.org/attra-pub/local_food/search.php (accessed July 8, 2013).

Bassett, Thomas J. 1981. "Reaping on the Margins: A Century of Community Gardening in America." *Landscape* 25(2): 1–8.

Benson, Matthew, and Eric Bendfeldt. 2007. *Annual Community Food Dollars Generated if Each Household in Virginia Spent $10/Week of Their Total Food Dollars on Fresh Local Produce and Farm-Based Virginia Products*. Blacksburg: Virginia Cooperative Extension.

Benson, O. H. 1917. "The Mother-Daughter Home Canning Club." *Journal of Home Economics* 9(6): 251–256.

Betters, Paul V. 1930. *The Bureau of Home Economics: Its History, Activities, and Organization*. Washington, D.C.: Brookings Institution.

Bureau of Home Economics. 1941. "Community Food Preservation Centers."

Miscellaneous Publication No. 472. Washington, D.C.: U.S. Department of Agriculture.

Click, Melissa A., and Ronit Ridberg. 2010. "Saving Food: Food Preservation as Alternative Food Activism." *Environmental Communication* 4(3): 301–317.

Coffey, Aline F., and Roger Sternberg. 1977. "Resurgence of Community Canneries." In *Yearbook of the Department of Agriculture*, 372–377. Washington, D.C.: U.S. Department of Agriculture, http://naldc.nal.usda.gov/download/IND79001209/PDF (accessed August 1, 2013).

Condra, Alli. 2013. "Cottage Food Laws in the United States." *Harvard Food Law and Policy Clinic Report*, http://blogs.law.harvard.edu/foodpolicyinitiative/files/2013/08/FINAL_Cottage-Food-Laws-Report_2013.pdf (accessed August 1, 2013).

Costa, Temra. 2010. *Farmer Jane: Women Changing the Way We Eat*. Layton, Utah: Gibbs Smith.

Coyne, Kelly, and Erik Knutzen. 2010. *Making It: Radical Home Ec for a Post-Consumer World*. New York: Rodale.

Creswell, Mary E. 1916. "The Home Demonstration Work." *Annals of the American Academy of Political and Social Science* 67: 241–249.

Creswell, Mary E., and Ola Powell. 1917. *Home Canning of Fruits and Vegetables, as Taught to Canning Club Members in the Southern States*. Farmers' Bulletin No. 853. Washington, D.C.: U.S. Department of Agriculture.

Davis, Carole A., and Louise Page. 1979. *Practices Used for Home Canning of Fruits and Vegetables*. USDA Home Economics Research Report No. 43. Washington, D.C.: U.S. Department of Agriculture.

Dawson, Elsie H., Olivia A. Hammerle, and Mary Smith. 1953. "Home Processing of Frozen and Canned Apple Slices." *Journal of Home Economics* 45(9): 663–667.

DeLind, L. B. 2002. "Place, Work, and Civic Agriculture: Common Fields for Cultivation." *Agriculture and Human Values* 19(3): 217–224.

D'Sa, Elaine M., Elizabeth L. Andress, Judy A. Harrison, and Mark A. Harrison. 2007. "Survey of Home Canning Practices and Safety Issues in the U.S." Paper 005-04 presented at the Institute of Food Technologists annual meeting, Chicago, Ill.

———. 2008. "Survey of Home Freezing Practices in the U.S." Paper 005-01 presented at the Institute of Food Technologists annual meeting, New Orleans, La.

———. 2009. "Survey of Home Food Dehydration and Vacuum Packaging Practices in the U.S." Paper 122-03 presented at the Institute of Food Technologists annual meeting, Anaheim, Calif.

EPA (Environmental Protection Agency). 2011a. *Brownfields and Urban Agriculture: Interim Guidelines for Safe Gardening Practices*. Washington, D.C.: EPA.

———. 2011b. *Reusing Potentially Contaminated Landscapes: Growing Gardens in Urban Soils*. Washington, D.C.: EPA.

Extension Service, USDA. 1953. *Significant Dates in the History of Cooperative Extension Work*. Washington, D.C.: USDA. American Association of Family and Consumer Sciences Records, 1899–2008, Division of Rare and Manuscript Collections, Cornell University Library, collection 6578, box 35.

Ferris, John, Carol Norman, and Joe Sempik. 2001. "People, Land and Sustainability: Community Gardens and the Social Dimension of Sustainable Development." *Social Policy and Administration* 5: 559–568.

Galt, Ryan E. 2011. "Counting and Mapping Community Supported Agriculture in the United States and California: Contributions from Critical Cartography/GIS." *ACME: An International E-Journal for Critical Geographies* 10(2): 131–162, http://www.acme-journal.org/Home.html (accessed October 16, 2014).

GardenABCs. 2013. "The School Garden Share Site," http://gardenabcs.com/Home_Page.html (accessed May 12, 2013).

Geering, Deborah. 2012. "Communities That Can." *Georgia Magazine* 68(7): 32b–39b.

"Girls' Canning Clubs." 1915. *Journal of Home Economics* 7(6): 316.

Goldstein, Carolyn M. 2012. *Creating Consumers: Home Economists in Twentieth-Century America.* Chapel Hill: University of North Carolina Press.

Gordon, Joan, and Isabel Noble. 1959. "Effects of Blanching, Freezing, Freezing-Storage, and Cooking on Ascorbic Acid Retention in Vegetables." *Journal of Home Economics* 51(10): 867–870.

Groh, Trauger M., and Steven S. H. McFadden. 1990. *Farms of Tomorrow: Community Supported Farms, Farm Supported Communities.* Kimberton, Pa.: Bio-Dynamic Farming and Gardening Association.

Guitart, Daniela, Catherine Pickering, and Jason Byrne. 2012. "Past Results and Future Directions in Urban Community Gardens Research." *Urban Forestry and Urban Greening* 11(4): 351–478.

Hamilton, Shane. 2003. "The Economies and Conveniences of Modern-Day Living: Frozen Foods and Mass Marketing, 1945–1965." *Business History Review* 77(1): 33–60.

Hamm, Michael W. 2008. "Linking Sustainable Agriculture and Public Health: Opportunities for Realizing Multiple Goals." *Journal of Hunger and Environmental Nutrition* 3(2–3): 169–185.

Hanleybrown, Fay, John Kania, and Mark Kramer. 2011. "Channeling Change: Making Collective Impact Work." *Stanford Social Innovation Review* (Winter): 36–41. http://www.ssireview.org/pdf/2011_WI_Feature_Kania.pdf (accessed August 1, 2013).

Hansen, Liane. 2011. "Women Farmers Grow Strong." *Weekend Edition Sunday*, National Public Radio, http://www.npr.org/2011/01/16/132975254/Women-Farmers-Grow-Strong (accessed August 1, 2013).

Harris, Hubert, and Lynn M. Davis. 1976. *Use of Low Water Level in Boiling Water Bath Canning.* Agricultural Experiment Station Circular 226. Auburn, Ala.: Auburn University.

Hayes, Shannon. 2010. *Radical Homemakers: Reclaiming Domesticity from a Consumer Culture.* Richmondville, N.Y.: Left to Write Press.

HEARTH. 1914–1921. *Journal of Home Economics.* http://hearth.library.cornell.edu/h/hearth/browse/title/4732504.html#1914.

Hoffman, Jessica A., Tara Agrawal, Catherine Wirth, Campbell Watts, Ganiyat Adeduntan, Lucy Myles, and Carmen Castaneda-Sceppa. 2012. "Farm to Family: Increasing Access to Affordable Fruits and Vegetables Among Urban Head Start Families." *Journal of Hunger and Environmental Nutrition* 7: 165–177.

Hooker, Richard James. 1981. *Food and Drink in America: A History.* Indianapolis, Ind.: Bobbs-Merrill.

Kirby, Ellen, and Elizabeth Peters. 2008. *Community Gardening.* New York: Brooklyn Botanic Gardens.

Knapp, Bradford, and Mary E. Creswell. 1916. "The Effect of Home Demonstration Work on the Community and the County in the South." In *Yearbook of the Department of Agriculture, 1916,* 251–266. Washington, D.C.: U.S. Department of Agriculture.

Lawson, Laura. 2005. *City Bountiful: A Century of Community Gardening in America.* Berkeley: University of California Press.

Lawson, Laura, Luke Drake, and the American Community Gardening Association. 2013. "2012 Community Gardening Organization Survey." *Community Greening Review* 18: 20-41.

Lichtenstein, Alice H., and David S. Ludwig. 2010. "Bring Back Home Economics Education." *Journal of the American Medical Association* 303(18): 1857–1858.

Linn, Karl. 2009. *Community Revitalization: Reclaiming the Sacred Commons.* Oakland, Calif.: New Village Press.

Litt, Jill S., Mah-J Soobader, Mark S. Turbin, James W. Hale, Michael Buchenau, and Julie A. Marshall. 2011. "The Influence of Social Involvement, Neighborhood Aesthetics, and Community Garden Participation on Fruit and Vegetable Consumption." *American Journal of Public Health* 101(8): 1466–1473. http://dx.doi.org/10.2105/AJPH.2010.300111.

Low, Sarah A., and Stephen Vogel. 2011. *Direct and Intermediated Marketing of Local Foods in the United States.* Report No. err-128, Washington, D.C.: U.S. Department of Agriculture, Economic Research Service.

Lyson, Thomas A. 2004. *Civic Agriculture: Reconnecting Farm, Food, and Community.* Medford, Mass.: Tufts University Press.

Martin, O. B. 1953. "The Fighting Prophet of the Demonstration . . . O.B. Martin." *Extension Service Review* 24(2): 20.

Martin, O. B., and Mary E. Creswell. 1915. "Canning Club and Home Demonstration Work." Cooperative Extension Work in Agriculture and Home Economics No. "A" 82. Washington, D.C.: U.S. Department of Agriculture, States Relations Service.

Martin, O. B., and Ola Powell. 1921. "Home Demonstration Bears Fruit in the South." In *Yearbook of the Department of Agriculture, 1920,* 111–126. Washington, D.C.: U.S. Department of Agriculture.

Martinez, Stephen, et al. 2010. *Local Food Systems: Concepts, Impacts, and Issues.* Research Report No. ERR-97. Washington, D.C.: U.S. Department of Agriculture, Economic Research Service.

McCormack, Lacy A., Melissa Nelson Laska, Nicole I. Larson, and Mary Story. 2010. "Review of the Nutritional Implications of Farmers' Markets and Community Gardens: A Call for Evaluation and Research Efforts." *Journal of the American Dietetic Association* 110(3): 399–408. http://dx.doi.org/10.1016/j.jada.2009.11.023.

McIntosh, Elaine N. 1995. *American Food Habits in Historical Perspective.* Westport, Conn.: Praeger.

National Center for Home Food Preservation. 2006. "Burning Issue: Canning in Pressure Cookers," http://nchfp.uga.edu/publications/nchfp/factsheets/pressurecookers.html (accessed August 1, 2013).

———. 2011. "Projects of the Center 2011–2014," http://nchfp.uga.edu/projects.html (accessed August 1, 2013).

Nickerson, Cynthia, and Michael S. Hand. 2009. *Participation in Conservation Programs by Targeted Farmers: Beginning, Limited-Resource, and Socially Disadvantaged Operators' Enrollment Trends*. Report No. EIB-62. Washington, D.C.: U.S. Department of Agriculture, Economic Research Service, http://www.ers.usda.gov/Publications/EIB62.pdf (accessed July 3, 2013).

Noble, Isabel, and J. D. Winter. 1952. "Is Blanching Necessary when Vegetables Are to Be Kept in Frozen Storage a Month or Less?" *Journal of Home Economics* 44(1): 33–35.

NWGC (National War Garden Commission). 1919. *Home Canning and Drying of Fruits and Vegetables*. Washington, D.C.: NWGC.

Payne, Karen, and Deborah Fryman. 2001. "Cultivating Community: Principles and Practices for Community Gardening as a Community-Building Tool." *American Community Gardening Association*, http://www.communitygarden.org/learn/resources/publications.php (accessed May 10, 2013).

Powers, John J. 1976. "Effect of Acidification of Canned Tomatoes on Quality and Shelf Life." *CRC Critical Reviews in Food Science and Nutrition* 7(4): 371–396.

Rieff, Lynne A. 2006. "Revitalizing Southern Homes: Rural Women, the Professionalization of Home Demonstration Work, and the Limits of Reform, 1917–1945." In *Work, Family, and Faith: Rural Southern Women in the Twentieth Century*, edited by Melissa Walker and Rebecca Sharpless, 135–165. Columbia: University of Missouri Press.

Sapers, G. M., J. G. Phillips, F. B. Talley, O. Panasiuk, and J. Carre. 1978. "Acidulation of Home Canned Tomatoes." *Journal of Food Science* 43(4): 1049–1052.

Sherman, Henry C. 1943. "Report of the Chief of the Bureau of Human Nutrition and Home Economics, Agricultural Research Administration." In *Annual Reports of Department of Agriculture* (Washington, DC: U.S. Government Printing Office), 6–8.

Skelton, Marilyn M., and J. A. Craig. 1978. "Ascorbic Acid Content, pH and Flavor Characteristics of Acidified Home Canned Tomatoes." *Journal of Food Science* 43(4): 1043–1045.

Skelton, Marilyn M., and Charles W. Marr. 1978. "Ascorbic Acid Content, pH and Acceptability of Tomatoes Processed by Different Home Canning Methods." *Home Economics Research Journal* 6(4): 305–311.

Stiebeling, Hazel K. 1944. "Report of the Chief of the Bureau of Human Nutrition and Home Economics, Agricultural Research Administration." In *Annual Reports of Department of Agriculture* (Washington, DC: U.S. Government Printing Office), 3–4.

———. 1945. "Report of the Chief of the Bureau of Human Nutrition and Home Economics, Agricultural Research Administration." In *Annual Reports of Department of Agriculture* (Washington, DC: U.S. Government Printing Office), 7–9.

———. 1946. "Report of the Chief of the Bureau of Human Nutrition and Home

Economics, Agricultural Research Administration." In *Annual Reports of Department of Agriculture* (Washington, DC: U.S. Government Printing Office), 5–9.

Sutton, W. A., Jr., E. Nelson, and L. W. Eberhardt Jr. 1942. "Special 4-H Club Report—Georgia, 1942." Georgia Cooperative Extension, typewritten report, 3 pp. Elizabeth Andress personal collection.

Swanson, Pearl. 1965. "Charles Ford Langworthy, 1864–1932." *Journal of Nutrition* 86(1): 1–16.

Tagtow, Angie, et al. 2014. "Academy of Nutrition and Dietetics: Standards of Professional Performance for Registered Dietitian Nutritionists (Competent, Proficient, and Expert) in Sustainable, Resilient, and Healthy Food and Water Systems." *Journal of the Academy of Nutrition and Dietetics* 114(3). http://dx.doi.org/10.1016/j.jand.2013.11.011.

Tanner, Fred W. 1935. "Home Canning and Public Health." *American Journal of Public Health* 25(3): 201–313.

Toepfer, Edward W., Howard Reynolds, Gladys L. Gilpin, and Katherine Taube. 1946. *Home Canning Processes for Low-Acid Foods*. Technical Bulletin No. 930. Washington, D.C.: U.S. Department of Agriculture.

Treisch, Pauline. 1955. "Research and Developments in Household Equipment: Gas and Electric Ranges." *Journal of Home Economics* 47(10): 743–745.

USDA (U.S. Department of Agriculture). 1944. *History of Home Economics Work in the U.S. Department of Agriculture on Home Canning*. Unpublished report in author's possession (Andress).

———. 1988–2009. *Complete Guide to Home Canning*. Agriculture Information Bulletin No. 539. Washington, D.C.: Extension Service, USDA.

———. 2012. "Farmers Markets and Local Food Marketing: 1994–2012." *Agricultural Marketing Service*, http://www.ams.usda.gov/AMSv1.0/ams.fetchTemplateData.do?template=TemplateS&leftNav=WholesaleandFarmersMarkets&page=WfmFarmersMarketGrowth&description=Farmers%20Market%20Growth (accessed May 3, 2013).

Walsh, B. H., and R. P. Bates. 1978. "Safety of Home Canning Procedures for Low-Acid Foods." *Journal of Food Science* 43(2): 439–443.

War Food Administration, Extension Service. 1944. *Report to the National Victory Garden Conference*. Washington, D.C.: U.S. Department of Agriculture, http://naldc.nal.usda.gov/download/CAT31030569/PDF (accessed August 1, 2013).

Wheeler, John Taylor. 1948. *Two Hundred Years of Agricultural Education in Georgia*. Danville, Ill.: Interstate. http://babel.hathitrust.org/cgi/pt?id=uc1.b3900559;view=1up;seq=251 (accessed August 1, 2013).

"Work of the Food Administration." 1917. *Journal of Home Economics* 9(9): 419–420.

Wright, D. Wynne. 2006. "Civic Engagement Through Civic Agriculture: Using Food to Link Classroom and Community." *Teaching Sociology* 34(3): 224–235.

Zimmerman, C. A., J. A. Phillips, C. B. Wood, and N. L. Marable. 1978. "Home-Canned Tomatoes: A Comparison of the Effects of Varying Time and Temperature Combinations During Processing." *Home Economics Research Journal* 7(2): 108–115.

5. Weighing in About Weight

Advisory Power in the Bureau of Home Economics

RACHEL LOUISE MORAN

In 1928, a mother in Virginia wrote to the federal government, "What will reduce the flesh or fat on my little girl? . . . She is only 11 years and she is getting
so fat" (Clopton 1928). The letter was sent to the Children's Bureau, which for-
warded such letters to the Bureau of Home Economics, where a home economist finessed a response that focused on the nutritional quality of the girl's
food intake and all but ignored the mother's question about weight (Haines
1928). This chapter examines how the home economics researchers in the Bureau of Home Economics approached the public's increasing obsession with
weight in the 1920s and 1930s. Torn between their commitment to scientific
studies of nutrition, on the one hand, and the necessity to serve the public interest and address real women's concerns, on the other, the bureau eventually
began to address issues of weight, but not without substantial caveats and attempts to keep the focus on good nutrition.

In 1923, the U.S. Department of Agriculture (USDA) upgraded the Office of
Home Economics to bureau status. Charles F. Langworthy, who had headed
the office, insisted that a female home economist take over the new bureau as
part of the project of better orienting it toward its female audience. Dr. Louise
Stanley became the first woman to head an agency in the USDA, and she was
the highest-paid woman in the USDA throughout her twenty years as chief of
the Bureau of Home Economics (BHE) (Baker 1976; Goldstein 2012).

The BHE was organized into three sections: food and nutrition, textiles, and
household economics. The centrality of nutrition on the agenda of the bureau
was clear from the beginning. Stanley herself initially served both as chief of
the BHE and as head of the Food and Nutrition Division. The Office of Home
Economics had played a critical role in translating federal research on calories and food values into consumable knowledge. The BHE would continue

this mission of both researching and translating the increasingly complex science of nutrition, now on a much larger scale.

When the BHE became a federal bureau, it divided its resources among four nutrition projects: food composition studies, vitamin studies, dietary studies and standards, and cooking experiments (Betters 1930). Above all else, professional home economists of the late 1920s and 1930s, especially those working in the federal government, considered themselves scientific experts. While some historians have argued that turning their elite chemistry and biology degrees toward home economics represented the miserable "women's work" of science, more recent considerations of the subject have argued that many home economists were not sidelined, but were actually happy to apply their research skills to the practical problems of home economics (Apple 2003; Elias 2008; Rossiter 1980). These home economists also fiercely defended their status as scientific professionals.

It is impossible to ignore, though, that the woman-run and heavily female-staffed bureau was created with different expectations than the male-dominated units in the USDA. The BHE owed far more to its audience than did most other federal agencies. In a reception held in 1948 to honor twenty-five years of the BHE, Hazel Stiebeling (Stanley's successor) explained the importance of American women outside of government to the agency. "The fact that the Bureau of Human Nutrition and Home Economics exists," she explained, "is due in no small measure to the . . . women of the country." She said the BHE "was established because you kept asking the Department of Agriculture and the State Colleges for information which could come only from research. And today [the BHE] is the only federal agency given full time to research on problems of direct concern to women as homemakers and to the family as a consuming unit" (Stiebeling 1948). At the same event, Secretary of Agriculture Charles F. Brannan (1948) asserted, "I don't think, of all our agencies, there is any one that's closer to the people that we serve than you folks in this Bureau."

Indeed, the home economists in the bureau had responsibilities beyond those of other federal agencies. Like the other major female-led agencies created in the first decades of the twentieth century, the Children's Bureau and the Women's Bureau, the BHE existed not simply to research but to make that research relevant. This meant turning nutrition studies into easily understood and often substantially simplified bulletins and diet plans. Disseminating materials designed to make American women's lives more efficient, organized, and rationally planned was the purpose of the organization. Without public agreement that the BHE was meeting these goals, the agency would lose its legitimacy.

The relationship between the bureau and the women it served was an unusual one. Like the Children's Bureau, created in 1912 in the Department of Commerce and Labor, the BHE was part of the "advisory state" (Moran 2013). The advisory state is conceptualized as a repertoire of governing tools with subtle techniques and sizable impacts. Advisory state tools are political projects instituted through neither force nor coercion. Rather, they include federal research with explicit social aims, an expectation that persons and groups will voluntarily do the work asked of them by the government, and the use of persuasive discourses like quantification and advertising to compel what cannot be legislated. The BHE had been designed with an enormous mission (fix America's health, homes, budgets, and consumption habits) and only moderate financial resources at its disposal. More constraining still, the BHE was a federal agency with almost no legislative sway or enforcement authority.

The BHE was specifically charged with research and with developing materials that translated that research for the average woman (Betters 1930). The BHE did not have any power to demand that women use BHE nutrition advice, or the funds to ensure that women even noticed that advice. The agency, instead, needed to make its work so compelling that its audience would voluntarily take up its advice. Bureau personnel largely relied on their expertise and the persuasive language of science. To retain its legitimacy, however, the communication between the bureau and its audience could not remain one-sided. While the main charge of the agency was to disseminate the health information that it deemed important, it also found it necessary to respond to pressing questions from its audience. Thus, the BHE home economists eventually found themselves weighing in about weight.

Although often overlooked in studies of the development of government during the early twentieth century, American women, especially middle-class women, were accustomed to voluntary participation in government goals. They sought and used advice from government agencies about standards for a variety of matters and attended voluntary classes and clinics. This voluntary participation was at times almost mandatory, however, when goals were framed in the language of proper mothering or patriotism during wartime (Capozzola 2008; Goldstein 2012; Leavitt 2002). While the BHE had no legislative authority, it played a prominent role in the national politics of physique through its advisory function. The BHE produced materials with advice and information on nutrition, and from the 1920s through the 1930s encouraged nonprofessional women, mothers, teachers, and home economics Cooperative Extension agents to turn this information into active education and programming, thus intervening authoritatively in the public improvement of national health. Women were asked to monitor the physiques of their children, husbands, and communities. Access to simplified yet scientific language and ideas from the BHE helped authorize these interventions. It was through this structure of information and volunteerism that the agency had its impact.

The Vitamin or the Scale

Through its nutrition research the Bureau of Home Economics worked to understand the role of vitamins and minerals in good health, but in the 1920s and 1930s many women in the United States were encountering nutrition information from a different perspective. In this era, female thinness came into vogue. Everywhere, the slender female body was promoted. Women's magazines and advertising started incorporating images of the thin ideal (Fangman et al. 2004). By the 1920s silent film starlets displayed increasingly svelte figures, while the "flapper" image celebrated a single body type, slender and nearly curveless. The new styles also showed more of the body than previous styles had, and women's bodies increasingly were understood as public rather than private sites (Brumberg 1988, 1997). Fashionable clothes were mass produced and sold "off the rack" rather than tailored to specific bodies. The development of off-the-rack clothes necessitated size and measurement standards. People whose body proportions did not fit in standard sizing now began to register their difference as inferiority (Schwartz 1986). Eventually, the new physical regime displaced images of women with different—especially larger—body types, and separated those older models of womanhood from the new ideal.

As the ideal body shape and type for women changed, so too did the popular attitude toward women with larger-than-ideal frames. Men and women were newly described as having "over-adiposity" or "the unlovely condition of corpulence" (Foxcroft 2011, iv). In response to changing interests and ideals, a commercial weight loss culture was born. Tobacco companies advertised that their products would decrease women's appetites to help them lose weight. Some advice encouraged women to take laxatives or to eat foods with laxative effects. Lulu Hunt Peters wrote a bestselling diet book in 1918, in which she persuaded women to diet as a religious activity: to "repent" when they "sinned" by consuming excess calories (Brumberg 1988, 238–240). By the mid-1920s, dieting had become common enough among upper-middle-class girls to merit its discussion in the handbooks of women's colleges like Mount Holyoke and Smith. While the official handbooks encouraged "rational methods" of watching one's weight, the condemnation of "crazy diets" indicated the widespread prevalence of fad dieting among those women (Lowe 2003, 143–144). Weight loss pills, powders, chewing gums, soaps, and creams filled shelves; diet advice filled book and magazine pages (Yager 2010). This new

PHOTO 5.1. Mary Logan, a nutrition worker in the U.S. Department of Agriculture, records the weight of a rat living on an adequate diet, 1941. Photograph N-1224, NARA II, College Park, Md., RG 16-G, Records of the Office of the Secretary of Agriculture, Historical File, 1900–1959, box 213, folder: Health–Nutrition.

culture of weight obsession and fad diets concerned nutritionists and health experts. Above all, it concerned male physicians, who saw the trend toward thin, androgynous female figures as a rejection of fertility and thus of women's prescribed social role (Brooks 1929; Phillips 1929).

While home economists in the BHE avoided discussing weight, they accepted a related area as a critical part of nutrition research: growth. Public health and Children's Bureau officials of the 1920s also believed that children's growth was an important way of measuring children's health; however, the Children's Bureau measured growth primarily through height and weight, and they relied on these measurements much more heavily than the BHE ever would. In the 1920s and 1930s, the BHE understood references to growth as a reliable teaching tool and used growth narratives as a method of communication for illustrating the importance of specific nutrients in a general way (i.e., they "promote growth"), rather than as a way of measuring existing health.

Growth was, above all, *evidence* to the BHE. It illustrated some of the research that the bureau already had conducted on vitamins and minerals, but it was not treated as a scientific discussion in and of itself. The BHE frequently distributed pamphlets, posters, and teaching materials that included photos of rats, mice, or guinea pigs showing an animal before and after exposure to a vitamin, or one control animal next to an animal that had been either exposed to or deprived of some nutrient (Stanley 1925). The images were stark and the message was simple: include this vitamin in your meals. The distributed materials were meant to make discussions of vitamins appealing and convincing to the public whom bureau personnel wanted to convince of various nutrition facts. Indeed, for a number of years the bureau even provided home economics clubs and classrooms with guinea pigs so that these groups could conduct their own growth experiments.

The BHE refused to address growth by using human subjects in dietary studies. Hazel E. Munsell (1927), a nutrition expert for the bureau, explained that "no pictures of human beings are included" because there are too many complicated variables in human growth. There could be no easy "control" human beings, Munsell continued. Because human growth involved many variables, the BHE worried that it could not produce good science with human subjects. Furthermore, in the bureau's view, human weight represented a messy and unscientific way of assessing health.

The Bureau's Struggle with Weight

The public's obsession with weight in the 1920s and early 1930s contributed to the BHE being regularly confronted with questions about weight and diets from the women it served. Women who had come to rely on the agency for health advice expected that it could assist them as they tried to find reliable information about managing both their own and their children's weight among the confusing images and claims in popular culture. The bureau scientists were not unaware; they kept a voluminous file of weight reduction and fad diet materials.

The BHE received letter after letter on weight. Questions like "is a diet of eggs and tomatoes good for reducing weight?" were "not unusual" (Stanley 1926). Some women requested information on fad diets. Some sought to gain weight, such as Nita Hatcher, a 112-pound, thirty-two-year-old woman in Illinois, who requested that the bureau "send me your bulletins on increasing weight" (Hatcher 1929). Women simply assumed that the BHE was prepared to help with such requests. After all, weight was everywhere in popular culture. But excluding those discussing good nutrition, which usually had no explicit reference to weight, the BHE had no such publications at the time.

BHE home economists consistently responded with advice on their main interests: vitamins and food groups. They advised women to focus on meeting all their daily dietary needs before attempting to change their weight, especially before dieting or "reducing." In response to Nita Hatcher, the woman trying to gain weight, Stanley explained that the bulletin on good proportions in the diet could substitute for information directly on weight. "In any diet," Stanley wrote, "it is necessary first of all to meet the needs of the body for protein, minerals, and vitamins, as explained in the Bulletin" (Stanley 1929). Stanley did not fully ignore Hatcher's question. She recommended milk and "plenty of rest"; however, she did not address Hatcher's questions in the terms Hatcher likely expected.

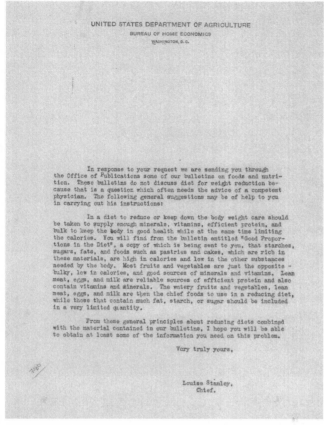

UNITED STATES DEPARTMENT OF AGRICULTURE
BUREAU OF HOME ECONOMICS
WASHINGTON, D. C.

In response to your request we are sending you through
the Office of Publications some of our bulletins on foods and nutrition. These bulletins do not discuss diet for weight reduction because that is a question which often needs the advice of a competent
physician. The following general suggestions may be of help to you
in carrying out his instructions:

In a diet to reduce or keep down the body weight care should
be taken to supply enough minerals, vitamins, efficient protein, and
bulk to keep the body in good health while at the same time limiting
the calories. You will find from the bulletin entitled "Good Proportions in the Diet", a copy of which is being sent to you, that starches,
sugars, fats, and foods such as pastries and cakes, which are rich in
these materials, are high in calories and low in the other substances
needed by the body. Most fruits and vegetables are just the opposite -
bulky, low in calories, and good sources of minerals and vitamins. Lean
meat, eggs, and milk are reliable sources of efficient protein and also
contain vitamins and minerals. The watery fruits and vegetables, lean
meat, eggs, and milk are then the chief foods to use in a reducing diet,
while those that contain much fat, starch, or sugar should be included
in a very limited quantity.

From these general principles about reducing diets combined
with the material contained in our bulletins, I hope you will be able
to obtain at least some of the information you need on this problem.

Very truly yours,

Louise Stanley,
Chief.

PHOTO 5.2. A form letter from Louise Stanley, the chief of the Bureau of Home Economics, used to reply to inquiries regarding weight management, early 1930s. Records of the Bureau of Human Nutrition and Home Economics, Department of Agriculture, Bureau of Home Economics, Subject Correspondence, 1917–1937, RG 176, entry NC 68-2, National Archives at Kansas City.

By 1931 the frequency of letters on weight and physique had grown to the point that Stanley and her aides composed form letters for quick responses. The responses emphasized that "care should be taken to supply enough minerals, vitamins, efficient protein, and bulk to keep the body in good health while at the same time limiting the calories" (BHE n.d.). Fruits and vegetables were good for weight loss, the form letter addressing weight reduction explained, while sugars and starches were of no help to dieters. Typically, a pamphlet about food groups, designed to help women figure out what to feed themselves and their families, was included. The home economists' discomfort about even suggesting a link between weight and health was evident in the BHE letters.

A second form letter responding to questions about physique (e.g., weight gain, weight loss, worries about children's heights) encouraged deference to medical authorities. "Before any person starts to make a radical change in weight in either direction, it is wise to obtain the advice of a competent physician," said the bureau writers (BHE n.d.). By the 1930s, the expanding role of professional pediatricians and the well-child visit had chipped away at the authority of women's role in family health care (Apple 2006). The fact that physicians relied less heavily on weight charts than did public health officials or Children's Bureau volunteers was a plus for the stubbornly science-minded home economists in the BHE (Brosco 2001). While declining to help the letter writers through a pound-by-pound weight loss program, the BHE hoped to contribute to their general health.

Cooperative Extension Fills the Gap

While the BHE offered women limited information about weight gain and loss, other home economists outside the BHE were positioned to more directly address the explicitly weight-based concerns that constituents brought to them. Cooperative Extension–based home economists proved especially adept at making home economics information directly serve, rather than shape, the interests of the women they were assisting. Tied to land-grant research universities, extension home economists (like their male counterparts working in agricultural extension) were charged with making research useful to the public.

County-based extension home economists instituted weight-based programs (some for gaining, more for reducing, and many with a combined mission) in the 1920s and early 1930s. Classes like "Watchful Weighing" held in Tompkins County, New York, focused on decreasing the calories in meals and introduced a simple regime of calorie counting. Program success was reported in quantifiable measures: "One woman whose weight has been reduced from 265 to 245 pounds says she feels better than she had in months. Another woman lost 10 pounds herself and had given diet suggestions to another woman who had lost 20 pounds" (*Annual Report of County Extension Workers* 1932–1933). As with many early weight loss programs instituted by government agencies, the Cooperative Extension Service saw its actions as responding to a public desire rather than imposing a program on its rural constituencies. The decision to increase the number of these weight loss programs was based not on stated beliefs that county residents were overweight, but instead on the large attendance at lectures on the subject and the enthusiasm of the women who participated.

Weight also played a major role in Cooperative Extension's youth program,

4-H. Beginning in the mid-1920s, 4-H held "health contests" for its young members. Adult programming tended to emphasize weight reduction, but youth programs focused on healthy weight gain, using children's weights as a shortcut for assessing health. Although the contest forms also asked for an assessment of everything from children's gums to their bowel movements, the seemingly objective and straightforward measurement of weight made for an easy-to-use health estimate and was the primary tool for judging (Birdseye [1925?]). Whereas the BHE carefully separated the concepts of health and weight, those working directly with women's groups and 4-H found weight to be a useful shortcut.

Contestants in the 4-H programs were measured, weighed, and inspected in a general fashion by physicians. Promotional materials explained, "the hundred percent boy or girl will have . . . steady growth / firm, well-developed muscles / average weight for height, or above" (Birdseye [1925?]). While the purpose was theoretically instructional, monetary prizes, small trophies, and ribbons were distributed to the boys and girls who scored "healthiest" out of the available 100 points. The best of the best from the states were sent to the 4-H national congress for a more involved physical examination. Winners of that contest received even better prizes. In 1927 the male winners were given silver trophies, and the female winners were given silver flatware (Sixth Annual National Boys and Girls 4-H Club Congress 1927). The 4-H judges conflated health with height-weight measurements and used these measurements as their primary mode of communicating appropriate physique.

Some home economics professors at major land-grant universities began to address public concern about adult and child weight in the 1920s. Professors at Cornell University taught about height-weight charts and children's weight gain as a part of their nutrition instruction. The willingness of professors like Flora Rose and Mary Henry to engage in this less scientifically approved discourse likely reflects the close relationships between campus-based faculty (Rose) and nearby extension personnel (Henry, who was a home demonstration agent in Chenango, New York). Moreover, this was a historical moment in which diet fervor had turned into trendy but dangerous fad diets, especially among the sort of young women enrolled in their Cornell courses.

Rose and Henry authored chapters with weight advice for the American Medical Association in *Your Weight and How to Control It* (1927). They emphasized the importance of milk consumption, vitamins, and following federal nutrition advice. They remained conservative about just what weight could indicate healthwise. Still, they were more comfortable with giving advice about weight and about quantified standards in assessing health than were their federal peers. They even reproduced the 1915 Life Extension Institute's height-weight tables, developed by the insurance industry. These home economists argued that body build was important, that quality of bodily mass was more important than actual poundage, and that weight slightly beyond the standard was acceptable if the individual was otherwise healthy. Children might be better off weighing more than the standards, they added, giving them a physical advantage akin to "a tadpole's tail" (Rose and Henry 1927, 147). While Rose and Henry modeled compromise, the BHE was avoiding the topic of body weight in the 1920s and early 1930s.

The Bureau of Home Economics Makes Adjustments

Form letters and referrals to medical authorities did not cap the flow of inquiries about weight to the BHE. The bureau staked its reputation on its responsiveness to citizen concerns; consequently, it could not simply ignore the stream of letters asking for more specific advice about "reducing" and weight guidelines. Influenced by their constituent women, who were living in an increasingly weight-conscious society, and following the lead of home economists outside the agency, BHE staff realized that the bureau would need to adjust.

In the early 1930s, the BHE developed a pamphlet called *Consider Your Weight: Fatter, Thinner, or "As Is."* The 1933 version did not include a height-weight table nor any specifically quantitative discussion of the size at which one should or should not diet. "If you weigh decidedly more or less than the average weight for your height and age," the pamphlet explained, "it's up to you either to do something about it, or to prove that you are in your best health 'as is'" (BHE 1933, 1). Compared to the charts of the American Medical Association and the specific over- and underweight percentiles used by social workers and physicians, the vague discussion of averages speaks to the continued reluctance on the part of the BHE writers to invest too heavily in weight statistics.

In an attempt to counter the popular magazine and movie emphasis on female dieting, the pamphlet mentioned that overweight people might not "look or feel as well as when [they] were more slender," and then focused primarily on diseases of the liver and kidneys, as well as physical inefficiency, which might accompany extreme overweight (BHE 1933, 1). For those who were underweight, the message ignored aesthetics entirely, and focused on health concerns like fatigue, nervousness, and susceptibility to tuberculosis. The focus on medical concerns, including the requisite advice that women contact their doctors, distinguished the home economics response from that of other popular sources, such as magazines, and organizations like the American Medical Association and the Children's Bureau. Even for those who determined themselves over- or underweight, the BHE writers sought to discourage dieting. "REMEMBER," they concluded, "the only safe way to change body weight is to modify a WELL BALANCED DIET" (BHE 1933, 8). The fact that the professionally trained BHE leaders paid any attention to reducing and gaining weight, despite a belief that dieting was scientifically unsound, illustrates the influence of women outside of government on this federal bureau. Having received many letters and observing an increase in fad diets and quack solutions, the BHE appears to have been compelled to offer what its home economists perceived as a better perspective on the issue.

In the 1934 revisions to the weight pamphlet, the BHE was more invested in weight and also appeared more comfortable with promoting a stricter set of standards and a harder line against weight that fell outside the bodily norms. Moreover, rather than portraying dieting as something to be done only if truly necessary, the revised pamphlet acknowledged that more women should diet. Statements such as "There are, you know, boundary lines above and below which we should not go if our weight is to be desirable for our build at any age" appeared throughout this version (Carpenter and Stiebeling 1934).

Rowena Carpenter and Hazel Stiebeling, the bureau agents who wrote this piece, still did not include a height-weight table nor name any specific source of such tables, but they did emphasize the increased role played by insurance companies in defining physical standards. They assumed that women already had access to or were familiar with some set of standards. Reluctantly agreeing that they were the "best guides we now have," the BHE advised its audience to adjust the existing charts slightly based on body build and age. "Weight *isn't* just a matter of personal vanity," the authors counseled. "It is really an indication of how things are going inside of us" (Carpenter and Stiebeling 1934, 1). Despite the BHE's slow movement toward accepting the quantitative measurements and health implications of physique that its female audience already embraced, the 1934 pamphlet went over well. The supply of *Consider Your Weight* quickly ran out, and it was reprinted in 1935 (Parkinson 1935).

Techniques of the Advisory State

The Bureau of Home Economics would come to incorporate weight into most of its discussions of nutrition by the late 1930s and into the early 1940s, although weight never became a primary discourse for the BHE the way it had for the Children's Bureau in the 1920s. Still, the BHE's increasing attention to weight came with an increasing acceptance of weight as a useful measurement of an individual's broader health.

The BHE had avoided such a message during the 1920s and very early 1930s, primarily because it was at odds with bureau scientists' strict definitions of the scientific work they were producing. The BHE spread its nutritional message by relying on voluntary networks to encourage and even gently coerce adoption of the agency's nutrition guidelines. As homemakers, teachers, and extension agents around the country came to understand the BHE as their source for nutrition advice, they also expected that the bureau would address *their* concerns. The BHE's power to convince and persuade only came through its ability to connect with the women who were its constituents, so it slowly had to adjust to the expectation that weight had a simple, causal relationship with nutrition and health.

The ability of nonprofessional women to pressure a federal agency to pay attention to their interests is an incredible story of agency from below. In this case, however, the story is messier because of the tensions between the mandate of the researchers and the pressures of the popular culture. While the science produced by the BHE continued to reflect its intense interest in vitamins, food composition, and dietary standards, the Bureau of Home Economics scientists began to take weight into account as a research variable. Responding to its constituents thus maintained the underresourced agency's legitimacy and extended its relevance to its audience.

ACKNOWLEDGMENTS

I wish to acknowledge the Emerging Scholar Fellowship I received for the multidisciplinary conference "Home Economics: Classroom, Corporate, and Cultural Interpretations Revisited.

REFERENCES

Annual Report of County Extension Workers. 1932–1933. Tompkins County, N.Y.: Extension Service. Cornell University Special Collections Library, RG 4282, box 1, folder 8.

Apple, Rima D. 2003. *The Challenge of Constantly Changing Times: From Home Economics to Human Ecology at the University of Wisconsin-Madison, 1903–2003.* Madison, Wis.: Parallel Press.

———. 2006. *Perfect Motherhood: Science and Childrearing in America.* New Brunswick, N.J.: Rutgers University Press.

Baker, Gladys L. 1976. "Women in the U.S. Department of Agriculture." *Agricultural History* 50(1): 190–201.

Betters, Paul V. 1930. *The Bureau of Home Economics: Its History, Activities, and Organization.* Washington, D.C.: Brookings Institution.

BHE (Bureau of Home Economics). 1933. *Consider Your Weight: Fatter, Thinner, or "As Is."* Washington, D.C.: U.S. Department of Agriculture. Records of the Bureau of Human Nutrition and Home Economics, NARA II, College Park, Md., RG 176, entry 2, box 541, folder: Mimeographed Materials.

———. N.d. Form Letter on Weight. Records of the Bureau of Human Nutrition and

Home Economics, NARA II, College Park, Md., RG 176, entry 2, box 541, folder:
Mimeographed Materials.

Birdseye, Miriam. "What Is an Optimal Child?" [1925?]. Manuscript Records of the
Bureau of Home Economics and Human Nutrition, NARA II, College Park, Md., RG
176, entry 4, box 583, folder: Miriam Birdseye.

Brannan, Charles F. 1948. Untitled speech notes, June 2. National Agricultural
Library Archives, Beltsville, Md., RG 176, Bureau of Human Nutrition and Home
Economics, folder: 25th Anniversary of the Bureau of Human Nutrition and Home
Economics, 1923–1948.

Brooks, Harlow. 1929. "The Price of a Boyish Form." In *Your Weight and How to Control
It: A Scientific Guide by Medical Specialists and Dieticians*, edited by Morris
Fishbein, 31–35. New York: Doran.

Brosco, Jeffery P. 2001. "Weight Charts and Well-Child Care: How the Pediatrician
Became the Expert on Child Health." *Pediatrics and Adolescent Medicine* 155:
1385–1389.

Brumberg, Joan Jacobs. 1988. *Fasting Girls: The History of Anorexia Nervosa*. New York:
Vintage.

———. 1997. *The Body Project: An Intimate History of American Girls*. New York: Random
House.

Capozzola, Christopher. 2008. *Uncle Sam Wants You: World War I and the Making of the
Modern American Citizen*. New York: Oxford University Press.

Carpenter, Rowena Schmidt, and Hazel K. Stiebeling. 1934. *Consider Your Weight*.
Washington, D.C.: U.S. Department of Agriculture. Bureau of Home Economics,
NARA II, College Park, Md., RG 176, entry 2, box 541, folder: Mimeographed
Materials.

Clopton, T. C. 1928. Letter to Julia Lathrop, November 1. Records of the Children's
Bureau, NARA II, College Park, Md., RG 102, entry 3, box 272, folder 4-6-4-1.

Elias, Megan J. 2008. *Stir It Up: Home Economics in American Culture*. Philadelphia:
University of Pennsylvania Press.

Fangman, Tamara D., Jennifer P. Ogle, Marianne C. Bickle, and Donna Rouner. 2004.
"Promoting Female Weight Management in 1920s Print Media: An Analysis
of *Ladies Home Journal* and *Vogue* Magazines." *Family and Consumer Sciences
Research Journal* 32(3): 213–253.

Foxcroft, Louise. 2011. *Calories and Corsets: A History of Dieting over 2,000 Years*.
London: Profile.

Goldstein, Carolyn M. 2012. *Creating Consumers: Home Economists in Twentieth-
Century America*. Chapel Hill: University of North Carolina Press.

Haines, Blanche M. 1928. Letter to Mrs. T. C. Clopton, November 30. NARA II, College
Park, Md., RG 102, Records of the Children's Bureau, entry 3, box 272, folder: 4-6-4-1.

Hatcher, Nita. 1929. Letter to Bureau of Home Economics, March 19. Bureau of Human
Nutrition and Home Economics, NARA II, College Park, Md., RG 176, entry 1, box 12,
folder: Hat–Hd.

Leavitt, Sarah A. 2002. *From Catharine Beecher to Martha Stewart: A Cultural History of
Domestic Advice*. Chapel Hill: University of North Carolina Press.

Letters to Bureau of Home Economics. Various dates. National Agricultural Library

Special Collections, Beltsville, Md., Bureau of Home Economics and Human Nutrition, box 5, folders: Bot–Bri and Bro–Bt.

Lowe, Margaret A. 2003. *Looking Good: College Women and Body Image, 1875–1930.* Baltimore, Md.: Johns Hopkins University Press.

Moran, Rachel Louise. 2013. "Body Politic: Government and Physique in Twentieth Century America." PhD diss., Pennsylvania State University.

Munsell, Hazel E. 1927. Memorandum to Sybil Smith, May 17. Experiment Station Record, Records of the Bureau of Home Economics and Human Nutrition, NARA II, College Park, Md., RG 176, entry 2, box 528.

Parkinson, V. 1935. Letter to Rowena Schmidt Carpenter, March 21. Records of the Bureau of Human Nutrition and Home Economics, NARA II, College Park, Md., RG 176, entry 2, box 558, folder: Carpenter, Rowena 1933–1937.

Phillips, Wendell C. 1929. "Introduction." In *Your Weight and How to Control It: A Scientific Guide by Medical Specialists and Dieticians,* edited by Morris Fishbein, vii–xii. New York: Doran.

Rose, Flora, and Mary Henry. 1927. "Part II: Principles of Nutrition, and Diets and Menus for Reducing and Gaining Weight." In *Your Weight and How to Control It: A Scientific Guide by Medical Specialists and Dieticians,* edited by Morris Fishbein, 139–257. New York: Doran.

Rossiter, Margaret A. 1980. "'Women at Work' in Science, 1880–1910." *Isis* 71(3): 381–398.

Schwartz, Hillel. 1986. *Never Satisfied: A Cultural History of Diets, Fantasy, and Fat.* New York: Free Press.

Sixth Annual National Boys and Girls 4-H Club Congress. 1927. Extension Service, NARA II, College Park, Md., RG 33, entry 14, box 1, folder: Club Congress Souvenir Programs, 1925–1928.

Stanley, Louise. 1925. Letter to Hazel Munsell, March 24. Records of the Bureau of Human Nutrition and Home Economics, NARA II, College Park, Md., RG 176, entry 2, box 550, folder: Hazel E. Munsell, 1924–1930.

———. 1926. "Composition of Foods." Manuscript for *1926 Agricultural Yearbook.* Bureau of Home Economics and Human Nutrition, NARA II, College Park, Md., RG 176, entry 2, box 535, folder: Composition.

———. 1929. Letter to Nita Hatcher, March 29. Bureau of Human Nutrition and Home Economics, NARA II, College Park, Md., RG 176, entry 1, box 12, folder: Hat–Hd.

Stiebeling, Hazel. 1948. "Research in the Bureau of Human Nutrition and Home Economics." First draft of speech, June 2. Bureau of Human Nutrition and Home Economics, National Agricultural Library Archives, Beltsville, Md., RG 176, folder: 25th Anniversary of the Bureau of Human Nutrition and Home Economics, 1923–1948.

Yager, Susan. 2010. *The Hundred Year Diet: America's Appetite for Losing Weight.* New York: Rodale.

6. From the War on Hunger to the Fight Against Obesity

RICHARD D. LEWIS, EMMA M. LAING,
and STEPHANIE M. FOSS

Over the last half century, there has been a significant shift in focus on foods and nutrition across the United States as efforts to alleviate micronutrient deficiencies and malnutrition have been displaced by actions targeted at obesity and chronic disease management. Home economists with expertise in the field of nutrition have been at the forefront of these issues and have spearheaded research, policy development, nutrition education, and direct nutrition care services for children and older adults. Colleges in the United States, primarily land-grant universities, have educated home economists in nutrition-related areas, offering baccalaureate and advanced degree programs in nutrition science, dietetics, consumer foods, and institutional management. Graduates of these programs are qualified for careers in school nutrition, Cooperative Extension and community outreach, clinical dietetics, the food industry, and academia.[1] The goal of this chapter is to describe the key events and policies over the past fifty years that have shaped the nation's public health approach to issues of food security, nutrition education, and obesity, and to highlight the roles of home economists in this ever-changing landscape.

Hunger and Poverty in America

Hunger in the United States was recognized as a serious issue during the Great Depression of the 1930s. Food conservation was a national theme during the war years of the 1940s. Lack of food in a significant number of U.S. households was widespread, but often hidden, in the 1960s. Officials attempted to document the extent of the problem, but assessing the prevalence of hunger posed challenges because individuals were reluctant to disclose such dire cir-

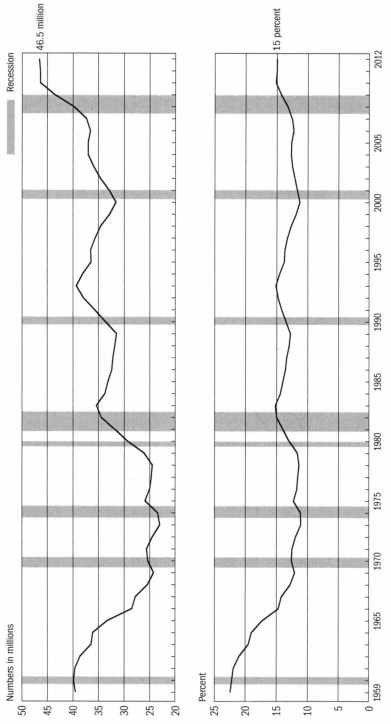

FIGURE 6.1. Number of people in Poverty and Poverty Rate, United States, 1959–2012. Source: U.S. Census Bureau, Current Population Survey, 1960 to 2013 Annual Social and Economic Supplements.

cumstances in their personal lives. However, food inadequacy and hunger are closely tied to poverty, and such statistics were recorded.

Figure 6.1 illustrates trends in the number of individuals in poverty and the poverty rates in the United States from 1959 to 2012 (U.S. Census Bureau 2013). In 1959, approximately 22 percent of the U.S. population, or 40 million Americans, fell below the poverty level. As a result of successful initiatives established during the 1960s, the poverty rate was reduced to approximately 12 percent in 1975, affecting about 26 million people. Poverty rates trended upward again in the early 1980s but remained below 15 percent for most of the next decade. The poverty rate dropped during the late 1990s and was at about 11 percent in 2000, affecting about 32 million Americans. The 2007–2009 recession contributed to an increase in the poverty rate, which stood at 15 percent between 2010 and 2012, when the number of people in poverty reached 46.5 million.

Since 1995, household food insecurity has been calculated by the U.S. Department of Agriculture (USDA) as a specific indicator (Coleman-Jensen et al. 2012; Coleman-Jensen, Nord, and Singh 2013). The incidence of food insecurity closely parallels the poverty rate. The highest rate of food insecurity recorded since 1995 was 14.9 percent in 2011.

Legislation on Hunger, Food Adequacy, and Nutrition Education

A sequence of events in the 1960s drew considerable attention to the crisis of hunger and poverty in the United States. During a campaign speech in West Virginia in 1960, presidential candidate John F. Kennedy promised to implement a program to expand food distribution (USDA 2013a). Michael Harrington published *The Other America* (1962), a powerful exposé of the extent of poverty in the United States. President Lyndon B. Johnson declared the "war on poverty" in his State of the Union speech in January 1964, and soon thereafter requested that the U.S. Congress make President Kennedy's temporary food stamp program a permanent one. This program provided individuals with enough food stamps to purchase items for a low-cost, nutritionally adequate diet. In 1967, a fact-finding trip to Mississippi by Senators Robert Kennedy and Joseph Clark documented hunger issues in the poorest areas of the United States. The senators found evidence of malnutrition and hunger, which were thought at that time to exist only in underdeveloped countries.

Several other pieces of legislation that would have dramatic public health implications were implemented in the 1960s. The Older Americans Act of 1965 provided services for older adults, including funding for congregate and home-delivered meal programs (89th U.S. Congress 1965). The Child Nutrition Act of 1966 provided funding for the implementation of the nation's school breakfast program (89th U.S. Congress 1966). The Expanded Food and Nutrition Education Program (EFNEP) was established in 1968 through the USDA and Cooperative Extension to teach low-income families with limited household resources the skills and behavior modifications needed to obtain nutritionally adequate diets and healthy lifestyle habits (NIFA 2013). Cooperative Extension home economics agents today continue to work at the local, state, and national levels to support and deliver EFNEP education.

The national focus on poverty persisted through the end of the 1960s. Nick Kotz, the author of *Let Them Eat Promises* (1969), received a Pulitzer Prize in 1968 for his reports on hunger in the United States. The CBS television documentary *Hunger in America*, narrated by Charles Kuralt, brought further attention to hunger and malnutrition throughout the nation (Carr and Davis 1968). The journal of the American Society for Nutrition, the *American Journal of Clinical Nutrition*, published an article titled "Hunger USA 1968" (Pollack 1969) in which the author examined the complex etiology of malnutrition and recommended that nutrition researchers and educators address malnutrition by examining the primary causes (i.e., inadequate food availability, poor absorption of food, increased nutritional needs, lack of knowledge about nutrition and food preparation). This article was of particular importance to the profession of home economics because it recognized that nutrition education must be an essential component of preventing hunger and malnutrition.

As the decade came to a close, President Richard Nixon convened the 1969 White House Conference on Food, Nutrition, and Health to address the nutritional needs of the nation and to devise strategies to combat hunger and malnutrition (Nixon and Mayer 1969–1971). Prior to the conference, Jean Mayer, a special consultant to the president, sent a letter requesting support from the American Home Economics Association to develop strategies to effectively provide nutrition education and to plan for food adequacy in the future (Mayer 1969). The White House Conference on Food, Nutrition, and Health recommended that federal action should be taken to expand the food stamp program, improve child nutrition and other existing nutrition programs, and provide consumer protection and information. In 1965, approximately five hundred thousand Americans were receiving food stamps; by 1971, there were 10 million participants (USDA 2013a).

Despite severe budget cuts in the late 1970s and early 1980s, nutrition education became a component of the food stamp program in 1981. Currently named SNAP-ED (Supplemental Nutrition Assistance Program–Education), it was established as an optional program for states (USDA 2012). States were eligible to apply for matching funds from the federal government in order to provide nutrition education to all individuals with an income at or below 185 percent of the federal poverty level, who may or may not be receiving food stamps. The objective was to provide nutrition education focused on preparing balanced meals and meeting the dietary guidelines, while also emphasizing how to do so on a budget. With the creation of SNAP-ED, currently available in every state, new opportunities developed for home economists to provide nutrition education. SNAP-ED programs, delivered by registered dietitian nutritionists (RDNs) and Cooperative Extension home economists, currently focus on nutrition education and obesity prevention (USDA 2014). These programs have shown effectiveness in increasing fruit and vegetable intakes, reducing rates of obesity, and improving food safety practices among participants.

Another outcome from the White House conference was that school lunches were extended to more children. In 1969, 15 percent of children who participated in school lunch received free or reduced-price lunches, and by 1972, that rate had doubled to over 32 percent. As of this writing, almost 68 percent of students participating in the school lunch program receive free or reduced-price lunches through school-based child nutrition programs (USDA 2013b). One of the primary places of employment for dietetics graduates is in school nutrition programs at the local, state, and national levels. These individuals work as educators, researchers, and directors of school nutrition programs (Academy of Nutrition and Dietetics 2013). Key responsibilities include nutrition education in home economics classes, managing school nutrition activities as part of school wellness policies, and development of menus that adhere to USDA regulations.

In 1972, the Women, Infants and Children (WIC) program was created after physicians reported that young pregnant women were entering their clinics with illnesses related to malnutrition. WIC was designed for pregnant women, women who were breastfeeding or up to six months postpartum, and children aged five years and younger. On October 7, 1975, WIC was established as a permanent program (Code of Federal Regulations 1975). The WIC program differed from other food assistance programs at the time, because in addition to the provision of specific nutritional foods needed during pregnancy, lactation, and early childhood, a nutrition education component was required. The WIC program became one of the primary employment and training opportunities for newly graduating nutrition students from colleges of home economics. This represented a shift in professional career responsibilities from more general home economics programming to a specialization in nutrition and health with an emphasis on maternal and child health. Public health WIC nutritionists today also conduct community nutrition and health education programs, often collaborating with local Cooperative Extension home economics agents.

The Food and Agriculture Act of 1977 included a federal nutrition program referred to as the Nutrition Education and Training Program (95th U.S. Congress 1977). This program provided grants to state agencies for nutritional training of food service personnel and conducting nutrition education activities in schools and childcare facilities. Many food service managers received this training during summer sessions offered by faculty at colleges of home economics. The National Food Service Management Institute (www.nfsmi. org), located at the University of Mississippi, was created in 1991 and funded by the U.S. Congress to train child nutrition and childcare professionals to provide high-quality child nutrition programs. Dietitians and home economists have been integral in creating the institute, conducting research on best practices, and developing and providing educational programs and resources. These and other programs addressing food adequacy and nutrition continued to operate through the end of the twentieth century and into the twenty-first, with moderate adjustments.

Nutrition Surveys Discover an Obesity Epidemic

Monitoring the health of the public was established by the mid-twentieth century. Such surveys enabled public health officials to detect the emergence of obesity as a threat to individual and national health in the 1990s. Currently, one of the major focus areas for home economists in nutrition is the obesity epidemic in both adults and children (Ogden et al. 2014; Skinner and Skelton 2014).

Though the USDA had conducted periodic dietary surveys since the 1930s, the U.S. Congress passed the National Health Survey Act in 1956 to authorize a continuing survey that would document illness and disability in the nation (84th U.S. Congress 1956). The first survey, the National Health Examination Survey I (NHES I), was conducted between 1959 and 1962 (USDHHS 1959–1962). These surveys included physical measurements that could be used to assess body mass index (BMI), thereby providing some of the earliest population measures of obesity.

Studies conducted by the USDA in the 1960s and 1970s, the Nationwide Food Consumption Survey and its successor, the Continuing Survey of Food Intakes by Individuals, provided information about the quality of U.S. diets and the amount of money spent on food by individuals and households (Swan 1983). While not providing information on individuals' nutritional status, these surveys provided dietary data for planning food assistance programs and developing nutrition education to meet the public's needs.

Assessment of nutritional status was not part of the NHES in 1959–1962, but among researchers, educators, and the public, nutrition was becoming linked to health and disease. A key recommendation of the 1969 White House

Conference on Food, Nutrition, and Health was to enhance the nation's nutrition surveillance. Therefore, in 1970 the National Nutrition Surveillance System (NNSS) was created to develop a mechanism to monitor the nutritional status and health of populations in the United States and to coordinate and standardize the efforts of the federal agencies conducting the surveys. Soon thereafter the NHES was merged with the NNSS, creating the National Health and Nutrition Examination Survey (NHANES). Nutrition and health surveys are currently conducted under this rubric.

The NHANES surveys provide a continuous data source to assess the nutritional status of the U.S. population (Flegal et al. 2012; Ogden and Carroll 2010; Ogden et al. 2014; Skinner and Skelton 2014). These surveys have documented the shift toward obesity among adults in the United States from 1962 to 2012, as shown in figure 6.2.[2]

Data from the NHES reported that in 1962, 31.5 percent of U.S. adults (ages twenty to seventy-four years) were overweight, and 13.4 percent were obese (USDHHS 1959–1962). The prevalence of overweight and obesity in the 1971–1974 survey (NHANES I) was slightly higher than in 1962, and in NHANES II, conducted between 1976 and 1980, the overweight and obesity percentages in adults were similar (USDHHS 1971–1974, 1976–1980).

Obesity became more prevalent in the 1980s. The Centers for Disease Control and Prevention established the Behavioral Risk Factor Surveillance System (BRFSS) in 1984 to collect data on health-related risk behaviors and chronic diseases (Public Health Surveillance 2013). Nutritionists facilitated development of the survey, which provided valuable insight into the emerging obesity epidemic. Currently, the BRFSS operates in all U.S. states and territories. Data from adults and youth are used to build and target health promotion activities to combat morbidity and mortality.

NHANES III, conducted between 1988 and 1994, reported that the percentage of overweight individuals remained basically the same as in the late 1970s, but the percentage of obese and extremely obese individuals increased from 15 percent obese and 1.4 percent extremely obese to 22.9 percent and 2.9 percent, respectively (USDHHS 1988–1994). Data from 2005–2006 showed that while the percentage of overweight was at its lowest point in three decades, the percentage of obese (34.3 percent) and extremely obese (5.9 percent) adult Americans was at the highest level ever recorded (Ogden et al. 2007). Compared to the NHANES II data, the percentage of Americans who were obese and extremely obese more than doubled and quadrupled, respectively. The most recent data from this survey (2011–2012) show that 34.9 percent of U.S. adults are obese (Ogden et al. 2014). As a result, public health officials have labeled obesity an epidemic, and the American Medical Association now recognizes obesity as a disease.

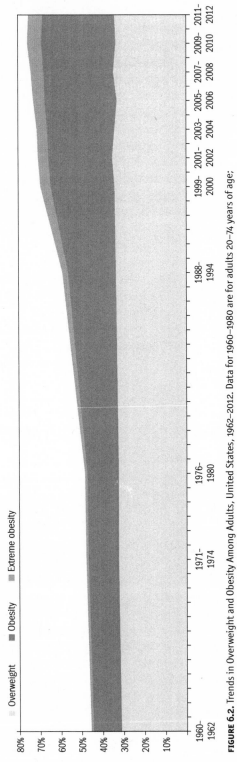

FIGURE 6.2. Trends in Overweight and Obesity Among Adults, United States, 1962–2012. Data for 1960–1980 are for adults 20–74 years of age; data for 1988–2012 are for adults 20 years and older. Sources: Ogden and Carroll 2010; Flegal et al. 2012; Ogden et al. 2014.

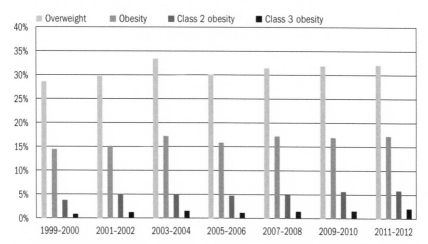

FIGURE 6.3. Prevalence of Overweight and Obesity Among Children, United States, 1999–2012. Data are for children 2–19 years of age. Sources: NHANES 1999–2012; Skinner and Skelton 2014.

The same pattern of increase in overweight and obesity has been documented in children. Since 1963, obesity has more than tripled in children six to nineteen years of age (Ogden et al. 2014; Skinner and Skelton 2014). Since 2001, over 30 percent of children ages two to nineteen years have been determined to be overweight, and, as shown in figure 6.3, since 1999 the incidence of obesity has increased. With the increasing prevalence of childhood obesity, adult-onset chronic diseases are now being diagnosed in youth.

Dietary Recommendations, Food Guides, and Prevention of Nutrition Deficiencies

In the early twentieth century, the primary focus for home economists was nutrient discovery and the prevention of nutritional deficiencies. Nutrition research pioneer W. O. Atwater, the director of the first U.S. agricultural experiment station, examined the energy and nutritive values of foods and also developed rudimentary nutrition guidelines (Atwater 1894; Carpenter 1994). The USDA employed many of the early scientists affiliated with home economics, who provided leadership in researching food and its nutrient composition (Goldstein 2012) as well as responding to constituent concerns (also see Moran, this volume). Another significant role of home economists was working with food companies on the enrichment of foods and beverages.

In 1941, the first Recommended Dietary Allowances (RDAs) were published, setting guidelines for intakes of calories, protein, iron, calcium, and vitamins A, B1 (thiamin), B2 (riboflavin), B3 (niacin), C, and D (National Research

Council 1941). Home economists had significant input to the development of the RDAs. For example, Hazel Stiebeling, a nutrition researcher and head of the section on food economics at the USDA Bureau of Home Economics, was a member of the committee that developed the guidelines. Lydia J. Roberts, a nutrition researcher and the head of the Department of Home Economics at the University of Chicago, chaired the 1941 RDA committee. "In overseeing the work of this committee, which developed the process by which the RDAs were established, Roberts made a major contribution. She emphasized throughout the necessity for a sound scientific basis for the allowances" (Harper 2003, 3701), and she also established the practice of seeking wide "democratic" input from stakeholders in the process (Jack 2009, 111).

The Basic 7 was introduced by the USDA in 1943, promoting the inclusion of (1) green and yellow vegetables, (2) oranges, tomatoes, grapefruit, (3) potatoes and other vegetables and fruits, (4) milk and milk products, (5) meat, poultry, fish, or eggs, (6) bread, flour, and cereals, and (7) butter and fortified margarine (Human Nutrition Information Service 1943). Both the RDAs and the Basic 7 were created to establish standards that would provide adequate nutrition to select groups, such as the armed forces faced with food rations during World War II. Such groups of individuals were chosen to promote nutrition principles supported by research (for example, eating citrus fruits to prevent scurvy). To ensure an adequate intake of vitamins and minerals, Americans were advised to consume foods from each category every day. Overeating was not a concern then, as evidenced by a World War II–era poster depicting the Basic 7 guidelines, which included the statement "In addition to the Basic 7, eat any other foods you want." Clearly, such a statement would not be made during a time of concern about overweight and obesity. It is also unlikely that such a statement would have prompted excessive food intake at the time because items such as meat, cheese, sugar, butter, and dried fruit were in limited supply. During this time home economists helped to ensure adequate food availability by assisting women in planting victory gardens and canning food (see Andress and Clark, this volume).

In 1956, the Basic 4 nutrition guidelines replaced the Basic 7 (Human Nutrition Information Service 1956). The Basic 4 recommended minimum amounts of (1) vegetables and fruits, (2) milk, (3) meat, and (4) cereals and breads to provide enough nutrients, but there was no guidance on the appropriate intakes for fats, sweets, and alcohol. Home economists provided nutrition education on the Basic 4 and taught women about incorporating frozen, canned, and powdered foods into meals and making one-pan dishes, such as casseroles, to decrease meal preparation time. The publication *The Basic 4* was the last set of nutrition guidelines that did not address diet, overconsumption, and chronic diseases.

Dietary Recommendations and Food Guides:
Avoiding Overconsumption

Because of the escalating rates of chronic diseases in the 1960s, the focus of public health nutrition recommendations shifted from simply preventing nutritional inadequacies to promoting health by limiting excess intakes of foods associated with chronic diseases. Scientists discovered in 1959 that polyunsaturated fats lowered serum cholesterol and in 1961 that cholesterol was linked with arteriosclerosis. Apart from diabetes, cardiovascular disease was the only chronic illness associated with a specific dietary component. The relationship between diet and cardiovascular disease prompted federal investments in policies and practices related to diet and health. (See McGinnis and Foege [1993] for a thorough discussion of the link between nutrition and chronic disease risk, and related policy developments.)

By the 1970s, research, education, and policy efforts to alleviate the health risks of excessive food intake expanded and began to highlight the health benefits of weight loss. As dietary guidelines were being developed for the nation, home economists played a pivotal role by serving on select committees helping guide the priorities of the national nutrition recommendations. *Dietary Goals for the United States* provided a new direction for home economists, nutritionists, physicians, and the food industry (U.S. Senate Select Committee on Nutrition and Human Needs 1977). The quantities of carbohydrates, proteins, fatty acids, sugar, sodium, and cholesterol that should be obtained through the diet were specified. In 1979, the USDA developed *The Hassle-Free Guide to a Better Diet* (USDA 1980), which was aligned with the messages from the *Dietary Goals*.

Healthy People: The Surgeon General's Report on Health Promotion and Disease Prevention was a landmark publication in 1979 that recognized the influence of diet on health outcomes (USDHEW 1979). This report was a key factor in the release of *Nutrition and Your Health: Dietary Guidelines for Americans* in 1980 (USDHHS 1980). Because the creation of the *Dietary Guidelines* was a joint effort by the USDA and the Department of Health, Education, and Welfare (HEW, renamed Health and Human Services [HHS] in May 1980), this document became the policy guidelines for all federal food programs. It had an important impact on industry and food labeling. In general, the guidelines emphasized that individuals should consume a varied diet to provide the essential nutrients; limit fat, saturated fat, cholesterol, and sodium intake; and maintain a healthy weight to reduce the risk of developing chronic diseases.

The 1985 edition of *Nutrition and Your Health: Dietary Guidelines for Americans* included many of the same recommendations as the original, but added information about unsafe weight loss diets, abstinence from alcoholic bever-

age consumption by pregnant women, and warnings about large-dose vitamin and mineral supplements (USDHHS 1985). These guidelines were widely
accepted and used as the basis for consumer nutrition education messages,
as well as guidance for healthy diets by consumer, industry, medical, and scientific groups. County home economics agents in Cooperative Extension and
local public health nutritionists continued to use the dietary guidelines in individual and group educational efforts.

In 1990, following reports from the surgeon general's office (USDHHS 1988)
and the National Research Council (1989), the third edition of *Nutrition and
Your Health: Dietary Guidelines for Americans* (USDHHS 1990) emphasized
weight control through enjoyable eating, moderation, and variety. This was
the first set of dietary guidelines to provide specific numerical goals for total
fat ($\leq$ 30 percent of daily calories) and saturated fat ($\leq$ 10 percent of daily calories). Following the 1990 National Nutrition Monitoring and Related Research
Act (101st U.S. Congress 1990a), the USDA and HHS were required to issue a new
edition of *Dietary Guidelines for Americans* at least every five years.

In 1992, *The Food Guide Pyramid* was developed by the USDA as a teaching tool to help consumers incorporate the dietary guidelines into daily living (USDA 1992). The graphic categorized foods that should be limited in
the diet, and provided daily ranges of foods from each category in order to
meet caloric goals. The Nutrition Labeling and Education Act of 1990 (101st
U.S. Congress 1990b) was implemented nationwide in 1994 and required the
printing of nutrition information on the majority of all processed and pack-
aged foods. Providing nutrition information was intended to help consumers
make more informed choices and meet the recommendations outlined in *The
Food Guide Pyramid*. Cooperative Extension home economists and dietitians
incorporated understanding nutrition labels into their nutrition educational
messages to the public.

The fourth and fifth editions of *Dietary Guidelines for Americans* (USDHHS
1995, 2000) were published online and addressed more directly the link between chronic diseases and obesity and the need to achieve a healthy weight.
Both documents highlighted the importance of physical activity in addition
to healthy eating. As the concern for overweight and obesity escalated in
the 1990s, many state Cooperative Extension units implemented community weight management programs. One example was the Weight Off Wisely
program delivered by county home economics agents with the University of
Georgia and Mississippi State University (Lewis and Mixon 1992). These programs recognized the interdisciplinary nature of successful weight management and went beyond dietary interventions, incorporating physical activity
and behavior modification strategies.

Federal, state, private, and public heath interest in obesity prevention heightened after the release of a report by Surgeon General David Satcher in 2001. The report addressed the drastic increase in obesity, particularly among children and adolescents, its link with chronic diseases, and the associated costs (USDHHS 2001). Dr. Satcher made an analogy between obesity and cigarette smoking to highlight the probability that future mortality and morbidity rates resulting from obesity could be very high, and are preventable.

The sixth and seventh editions of the *Dietary Guidelines for Americans* were released in 2005 and 2010, respectively (USDHHS 2005, 2010a). MyPyramid replaced the earlier *Food Guide Pyramid* in 2005, and the agency provided more extensive advice through online tools and teaching resources to help consumers conform to the dietary guidelines. MyPyramid was an abstract image of a segmented spire, which represented the importance of variety in the diet and which narrowed at the top to represent portion control. A figure climbing the MyPyramid image emphasized the importance of physical activity.

In the 2010 *Dietary Guidelines for Americans*, managing body weight throughout the life cycle, proper child nutrition, the eating environment, and reduction of salt were key recommendations that amended or added to the 2005 edition. High-profile national initiatives were launched, emphasizing multifaceted approaches. In January 2010, U.S. surgeon general Regina Benjamin and HHS secretary Kathleen Sebelius promoted the "fight against obesity" through better nutrition, regular physical activity, and community support of healthy choices, and First Lady Michelle Obama launched the "Let's Move" campaign to encourage children to become more physically active. *The Surgeon General's Vision for a Healthy and Fit Nation* stressed the need for obesity prevention in communities, home environments, childcare settings, schools, work sites, and medical facilities (USDHHS 2010b). The National Institute of Food and Agriculture (NIFA) launched a partnership with America on the Move to encourage healthy food choices and increased physical activity; and numerous land-grant universities joined the effort through their Cooperative Extension programs (NIFA 2010). Another program managed by Cooperative Extension home economists in many states promotes walking and fitness, incorporating personal and community goals and record keeping to reinforce behavioral change (e.g., "Walk Georgia," "Walk Kansas," "Walk Across Texas"). These programs include extensive collaboration among public and private agencies.

Since 2011, efforts have been made to simplify educational tools to help home economists in nutrition and health educators disseminate consistent nutrition and physical activity messages to various audiences. The USDA introduced MyPlate as the visual tool to represent the food patterns outlined in the 2010 *Dietary Guidelines for Americans*. It replaced the MyPyramid image, which had been criticized as being ambiguous and complicated (Heath and

Heath 2010). The MyPlate icon was created to serve as a simple visual representation of what a typical plate should contain at every meal. The message provided by MyPlate is the general proportions to be provided by the food groups, and the word "My" emphasizes a personalized approach to healthy eating. Larger intakes of vegetables and fruits are emphasized in the MyPlate graphic in comparison to the previous pyramid images, while grains are deemphasized. The USDA website where MyPlate can be accessed (www.choose myplate.gov) has materials for food tracking, meal planning, and nutrition, and it includes healthy lifestyle education tools for all ages and nutritional needs. There is some reason for optimism about the success of these nutrition education and fitness programs since rates of obesity in some states have leveled (Centers for Disease Control and Prevention 2013; Ogden et al. 2014).

Hunger and Obesity: Ongoing Challenges

While it would seem that hunger and obesity are mutually exclusive, opposite extremes, this is not the case. Through the last half of the twentieth and into the twenty-first century, both obesity and food insecurity rates have increased. The prevalence of obesity is now highest in low-income populations. Because the federal government invested in a coordinated national surveillance system, researchers have been able to track these trends and, using these data, contribute to developing effective interventions.

Whereas the focus of nutrition education and intervention programs has shifted from nutrient deficiencies and malnutrition toward over-nutrition and obesity, the setting for many recent initiatives is in communities with inadequate access to safe and healthy food. For example, Fulton County Cooperative Extension operates Fulton Fresh, a mobile farmers market to deliver fresh produce from area farmers to Atlanta, Georgia, residents living in communities designated as "food deserts" ("Fulton Fresh" n.d.). To be eligible for the produce, community residents attend a nutrition education and healthy cooking class aimed at reducing obesity, diabetes, and other chronic diseases. To raise public awareness about hunger in the United States, September has been named Hunger Action Month, which is promoted by the charitable organization Feeding America (2013), composed of over two hundred food banks nationwide. Many community garden organizations partner with local food banks year-round to provide fresh produce to the food banks' clientele.

Twenty-first-century national data suggest that there has been a slowing or leveling off in obesity rates among most age groups. This can be attributed, in part, to home economists at the forefront of national, state, and local efforts to address both hunger and obesity. These individuals have been involved in every aspect from research to policy development, community education, school nutrition, food service, and clinical care. Successful statewide obesity prevention programs led by home economists, such as the walking programs, show that a large number of citizens can be motivated to improve their health.

At the national level, home economists in nutrition have leveraged their efforts through collaborations with government agencies and private partners. For example, the American Society for Nutrition and the Obesity Society worked in partnership with the National Institutes of Health to develop treatment guidelines for obesity (Jensen et al. 2013), the first guidelines update in over a decade. With input from the Academy of Nutrition and Dietetics, a final rule was published in May 2014 by the Centers for Medicare and Medicaid Services to allow qualified RDNs to order therapeutic diets and nutrition-related laboratory tests in clinical settings without physician approval (Federal Register 2014). This is a significant step forward to provide more efficient multidisciplinary obesity treatment and prevention care for patients.

As a profession that has expertise working with individuals, families, communities, government agencies, and private partners, home economics professionals are part of an interdisciplinary approach in the war against hunger and the fight against obesity. Home economists will continue to make meaningful, positive differences in the health of Americans.

NOTES

1. Those eligible for professional registration and licensure may apply to the Academy of Nutrition and Dietetics, which offers credentialing as a registered dietitian or as a registered dietitian nutritionist.

2. Body mass index (BMI) was calculated using the formula [weight (kg)]/[height (m)2]. Weight classifications based on BMI were established as follows: < 18.5 is underweight, 18.5–24.9 is normal, 25.0–29.9 is overweight, and > 30.0 is defined as obese (Expert Panel 1998). The most recent guidelines were published in 2013 and include obesity classifications by severity: class I (BMI 30.0–34.9), class II (BMI 35.0–39.9), and class III (BMI ≥ 40.0) (Jensen et al. 2013).

REFERENCES

84th U.S. Congress. 1956. National Health Survey Act, report no. 2108 to accompany S. 3076. Washington, D.C.: U.S. Government Printing Office.

89th U.S. Congress. 1965. Older Americans Act of 1965. Public Law 89-73; 79 Stat. 218. Washington, D.C.: U.S. Government Printing Office.

89th U.S. Congress. 1966. Child Nutrition Act of 1966. Public Law 89-642; 80 Stat. 885. Washington, D.C.: U.S. Government Printing Office.

95th U.S. Congress. 1977. Food and Agriculture Act of 1977. Public Law 95-113; 91 Stat. 913. Washington, D.C.: U.S. Government Printing Office.

101st U.S. Congress. 1990a. National Nutrition Monitoring and Related Research Act of 1990. Public Law 101-445. Washington, D.C.: U.S. Government Printing Office.

101st U.S. Congress. 1990b. Nutrition Labeling and Education Act of 1990. Public Law 101-535; 104 Stat. 2353. Washington, D.C.: U.S. Government Printing Office.

Academy of Nutrition and Dietetics, Quality Management Committee and Scope of Practice Subcommittee. 2013. "Academy of Nutrition and Dietetics: Scope of Practice for the Registered Dietitian." *Journal of the Academy of Nutrition and Dietetics* 113(6 Suppl.): S17, S28.

Atwater, Wilbur O. 1894. *Foods: Nutritive Value and Cost.* Farmers' Bulletin No. 23. Washington, D.C.: U.S. Department of Agriculture.

Carpenter, Kenneth J. 1994. "The 1993 W. O. Atwater Centennial Memorial Lecture: The Life and Times of W. O. Atwater (1844–1907)." *Journal of Nutrition* 124(9 Suppl.): 1707S–1714S.

Carr, Martin, and Peter Davis. 1968. *Hunger In America.* CBS Reports, CBS News, Carousel Films, New York.

Centers for Disease Control and Prevention. 2013. "Vital Signs: Obesity Among Low-Income, Preschool-Aged Children—United States, 2008–2011." *Morbidity and Mortality Weekly Report* 62(31): 629–634.

Code of Federal Regulations. 1975. Part 246—Special Supplemental Nutrition Program for Women, Infants and Children (WIC), 7 CFR, ch. ii(1-1-13), sec. 246.1–28, Public Law 94-105. Washington, D.C.

Coleman-Jensen, Alisha, Mark Nord, Margaret Andrews, and Steven Carlson. 2012. *Household Food Security in the United States in 2011.* U.S. Department of Agriculture, Economic Research Service, Economic Research Report No. ERR-141. Washington, D.C.: U.S. Government Printing Office.

Coleman-Jensen, Alisha, Mark Nord, and Anita Singh. 2013. *Household Food Security in the United States in 2012.* U.S. Department of Agriculture, Economic Research Service, Economic Research Report No. ERR-155. Washington, D.C.: U.S. Government Printing Office.

Expert Panel on the Identification, Evaluation, and Treatment of Overweight in Adults. 1998. "Clinical Guidelines on the Identification, Evaluation, and Treatment of Overweight and Obesity in Adults: Executive Summary." *American Journal of Clinical Nutrition* 68(4): 899–917.

Federal Register. 2014. "Part II: Final Rule." Department of Health and Human Services, Centers for Medicare and Medicaid Services 79(91), http://www.gpo.gov/fdsys/pkg/FR-2014-05-12/pdf/2014-10687.pdf (accessed October 9, 2014).

Feeding America. 2013. "Hunger Action Month." http://feedingamerica.org/get-involved/hunger-action-month.aspx (accessed August 20, 2013).

Flegal, Katherine M., Margaret D. Carroll, Brian K. Kit, and Cynthia L. Ogden. 2012. "Prevalence of Obesity and Trends in the Distribution of Body Mass Index Among U.S. Adults, 1999–2010." *Journal of the American Medical Association* 307(5): 491–497.

"Fulton Fresh Mobile Farmer's Market to Hit the Road June 8." N.d. www.fultoncountyga.gov/latest-news/4099-fulton-fresh-mobile-farmers-market-to-hit-the-road-June8 (accessed May 20, 2014).

Goldstein, Carolyn M. 2012. *Creating Consumers: Home Economists in 20th Century America.* Chapel Hill: University of North Carolina Press.

Harper, Alfred E. 2003. "Contributions of Women Scientists in the U.S. to the Development of Recommended Dietary Allowances." *Journal of Nutrition* 133(11): 3698–3702.

Harrington, Michael. 1962. *The Other America: Poverty in the United States*. New York: Simon and Schuster.

Heath, Chip, and Dan Heath. 2010. *Switch: How to Change Things when Change Is Hard*. New York: Broadway Books.

Human Nutrition Information Service. 1943. *The Basic 7*. U.S. Department of Agriculture. Washington, D.C.: U.S. Government Printing Office.

———. 1956. *The Basic 4*. U.S. Department of Agriculture. Washington, D.C.: Agricultural Research Service.

Jack, Jordynn. 2009. "Lydia J. Roberts's Nutrition Research and the Rhetoric of 'Democratic' Science." *College Composition and Communication* 61(1): 109–129.

Jensen, Michael D., et al. 2013. "2013 AHA/ACC/TOS Guideline for the Management of Overweight and Obesity in Adults: A Report of the American College of Cardiology/American Heart Association Task Force on Practice Guidelines and the Obesity Society." *Journal of the American College of Cardiology*. http://dx.doi.org/10.1016/j.jacc.2013.11.004.

Kotz, Nick K. 1969. *Let Them Eat Promises: The Politics of Hunger in America*. Englewood Cliffs, N.J.: Prentice Hall.

Lewis, Richard D., and Melissa Mixon. 1992. *The Plan WOW: Weight Off Wisely*. Mississippi State: Mississippi State University, Cooperative Extension Service.

Mayer, Jean. 1969. "The White House Conference on Food, Nutrition, and Health." *Journal of Home Economics* 61(7): 499–502.

McGinnis, J. Michael, and William H. Foege. 1993. "Actual Causes of Death in the United States." *Journal of the American Medical Association* 270: 2207–2212.

National Research Council. 1941. *Recommended Dietary Allowances*. Washington, D.C.: Committee on Food and Nutrition, Nutrition Division, Federal Security Agency.

———. 1989. *Diet and Health: Implications for Reducing Chronic Disease Risk*. Food and Nutrition Board, Committee on Diet and Health, Commission on Life Sciences. Washington, D.C.: National Academies Press.

NIFA (National Institute of Food and Agriculture). 2010. *America on the Move and the Cooperative Extension Service: Partners for Healthy Living*, http://www.americaonthemove.org/usda (accessed September 26, 2013).

———. 2013. *Expanded Food and Nutrition Education Program Policies*, http://www.nifa.usda.gov/nea/food/efnep/pdf/program-policy.pdf (accessed August 20, 2013).

Nixon, Richard M., and Jean Mayer. 1969–1971. *White House Conference on Food, Nutrition and Health: Final Report*. Washington, D.C.: U.S. Government Printing Office.

Ogden, Cynthia L., and Margaret D. Carroll. 2010. *Prevalence of Overweight, Obesity and Extreme Obesity Among Adults: United States, Trends 1960–1962 Through 2007–2008*. Washington, D.C.: Centers for Disease Control and Prevention, Division of Health and Nutrition Examination Surveys, National Center for Health Statistics.

Ogden, Cynthia L., Margaret D. Carroll, Brian K. Kit, and Katherine M. Flegal. 2007.

Obesity Among Adults in the United States—No Statistically Significant Change Since 2003–2004. National Center for Health Statistics, Data Brief No. 1. Hyattsville, Md.: National Center for Health Statistics.

———. 2014. "Prevalence of Childhood and Adult Obesity in the United States, 2011–2012." *Journal of the American Medical Association* 311(8): 806–814.

Pollack, Herbert. 1969. "Hunger USA 1968: A Critical Review." *American Journal of Clinical Nutrition* 22(4): 480–489.

Public Health Surveillance and Informatics Program Office. 2013. *About the Behavioral Risk Factor Surveillance System*. Centers for Disease Control and Prevention, Division of Behavioral Surveillance, http://www.cdc.gov/brfss/about/about_brfss.htm (accessed August 20, 2013).

Skinner, Asheley C., and Joseph A. Skelton. 2014. "Prevalence and Trends in Obesity and Severe Obesity Among Children in the United States, 1999–2012." *Journal of the American Medical Association Pediatrics*. http://dx.doi.org/10.1001/jamapediatrics.2014.21

Swan, Patricia B. 1983. "Food Consumption by Individuals in the United States: Two Major Surveys." *Annual Review of Nutrition* 3: 413–432.

U.S. Census Bureau. 2013. *Current Population Survey, 1960 to 2013*. Annual Social and Economic Supplements, https://www.census.gov/hhes/www/poverty/data/incpovhlth/2012/figure4.pdf (accessed August 20, 2014).

USDA (U.S. Department of Agriculture). 1980. *The Hassle-Free Guide to a Better Diet*. Science and Education Administration Leaflet No. 567. Washington, D.C.: U.S. Government Printing Office.

———. 1992. *The Food Guide Pyramid*. Human Nutrition Information Service, Home and Garden Bulletin 249. Washington, D.C.: U.S. Government Printing Office.

———. 2012. *Building a Healthy America: A Profile of the Supplemental Nutrition Assistance Program*. Food and Nutrition Service, Office of Research and Analysis, http://www.fns.usda.gov/sites/default/files/BuildingHealthyAmerica.pdf (accessed May 6, 2014).

———. 2013a. *A Short History of SNAP*. http://www.fns.usda.gov/snap/short-history-snap (accessed August 21, 2013).

———. 2013b. *Program Data: Child Nutrition Data, National Level Annual Summary Tables FY 1969–2012*. Food and Nutrition Service, http://www.fns.usda.gov/pd/cnpmain.htm (accessed August 21, 2013).

———. 2014. *Supplemental Nutrition Assistance Program Education Guidance*. Nutrition Education and Obesity Prevention Grant Program, http://snap.nal.usda.gov/snap/Guidance/FY2015snap-EdGuidance.pdf (accessed May 6, 2014).

USDHEW (U.S. Department of Health, Education, and Welfare). 1979. *Healthy People: The Surgeon General's Report on Health Promotion and Disease Prevention*. Office of the Assistant Secretary for Health and Surgeon General, Public Health Service Publication No. 79-55071. Washington, D.C.: U.S. Government Printing Office.

USDHHS (U.S. Department of Health and Human Services). 1959–1962. *U.S. National Health Examination Survey, Cycle I, 1959–1962*. Centers for Disease Control and Prevention. Hyattsville, Md.: National Center for Health Statistics.

———. 1971–1974. *National Health and Nutrition Examination Survey I.* Centers for Disease Control and Prevention. Hyattsville, Md.: National Center for Health Statistics.

———. 1976–1980. *National Health and Nutrition Examination Survey II.* Centers for Disease Control and Prevention. Hyattsville, Md.: National Center for Health Statistics.

———. 1980. *Nutrition and Your Health: Dietary Guidelines for Americans.* U.S. Department of Agriculture, Home and Garden Bulletin No. 232. Washington, D.C.: U.S. Government Printing Office.

———. 1985. *Nutrition and Your Health: Dietary Guidelines for Americans.* U.S. Department of Agriculture, Home and Garden Bulletin No. 232. Washington, D.C.: U.S. Government Printing Office.

———. 1988. *Surgeon General's Report on Nutrition and Health.* Public Health Service Publication No. 88-50210. Washington, D.C.: U.S. Government Printing Office.

———. 1988–1994. *National Health and Nutrition Examination Survey III.* Centers for Disease Control and Prevention. Hyattsville, Md.: National Center for Health Statistics.

———. 1990. *Nutrition and Your Health: Dietary Guidelines for Americans,* 3rd ed. U.S. Department of Agriculture, Home and Garden Bulletin No. 232. Washington, D.C.: U.S. Government Printing Office.

———. 1995. *Nutrition and Your Health: Dietary Guidelines for Americans,* 4th ed. U.S. Department of Agriculture, Home and Garden Bulletin No. 232. Washington, D.C.: U.S. Government Printing Office.

———. 2000. *Dietary Guidelines for Americans,* 5th ed. U.S. Department of Agriculture, Home and Garden Bulletin No. 232. Washington, D.C.: U.S. Government Printing Office.

———. 2001. *Surgeon General's Call to Action to Prevent and Decrease Overweight and Obesity.* Rockville, Md.: Public Health Service, Office of the Surgeon General.

———. 2005. *Dietary Guidelines for Americans,* 6th ed. U.S. Department of Agriculture, Home and Garden Bulletin No. 232. Washington, D.C.: U.S. Government Printing Office.

———. 2010a. *Dietary Guidelines for Americans 2010,* 7th ed. U.S. Department of Agriculture, Home and Garden Bulletin No. 232. Washington, D.C.: U.S. Government Printing Office.

———. 2010b. *The Surgeon General's Vision for a Healthy and Fit Nation.* Rockville, Md.: Public Health Service, Office of the Surgeon General.

U.S. Senate Select Committee on Nutrition and Human Needs. 1977. *Dietary Goals for the United States,* 2nd ed. Washington, D.C.: U.S. Government Printing Office.

7. How Home Economists Taught American Women to Dress, 1910–1950

LINDA PRZYBYSZEWSKI

In 1927, the U.S. Department of Agriculture (USDA) issued a new scorecard. The USDA had already issued a great many scorecards to ensure fair judging of the entries at hundreds of county and state fairs across the country. This one distributed its points among a variety of categories:

Becomingness of color	5 points
Modesty	5 points
Value in relation to cost	5 points
Occasion	10 points
Posture and carriage (if worn by contestant)	5 points
Effect of underwear	5 points

Although other scorecards were used to judge livestock and vegetables, this one was designed to judge the work produced in the clothing clubs organized for women and girls by the USDA. With it, the women working in the Bureau of Home Economics hoped to "establish standards for economical, becoming, and healthful apparel" (O'Brien, Campbell, and Davis 1927, inside cover). This scorecard was issued because of squabbles among judges and clothing club leaders as to whether an entry of racy colorful underwear should be marked down in favor of underwear in demure white.

Were these criteria echoes of Renaissance Europe's sumptuary laws? Such laws were passed by rulers in order to control consumption, and were intended to distinguish at a glance between a duke and an uppity merchant and between a respectable matron and a prostitute. Why should any government care about design in dress or elsewhere? Jules Lubbock in *Tyranny of Taste: The Politics of Architecture and Design in Britain, 1770–1960* (1995) asked, why should the government care about the design of a teacup? Answer: because people in power for hundreds of years believed that design had moral and so-cial effects, not merely economic ones. These beliefs existed into the twen-tieth century: the British government relocated thousands of former slum-dwellers and then coaxed them to choose modern furniture designs for their new homes, and it mandated rationing for some fabrics during World War II (Lubbock 1995).

Why did the U.S. federal government care about clothing design? More specifically, why did the women who ran the Bureau of Home Economics care? What did they and their counterparts in school and college classrooms teach about taste in creating and wearing apparel? This chapter tries to an-swer these questions by reviewing dress pamphlets and textbooks from the 1910s through the 1940s.

Past Perspectives on the Meaning of Apparel

Scholars, for example Wygant (1993) and Frank (2000), who write on the his-tory of fashion and the decorative arts, neglected the role of home econo-mists. Instead, they and others explored the relationship between haute cou-ture and the fine arts (Martin 1987, 1998; Troy 2003) and architecture (Wigley 1995). Even books about sewing often omitted aesthetic elements (Burman 1999; Gordon 2009). Historically, work in the Foods and Nutrition Division of the Bureau of Home Economics received more attention than work in the Textiles and Clothing Division, and historians of home economics too have given little consideration to clothing (Elias 2008; Stage and Vincenti 1997), yet dress, and the associated principles and skills, were prominent features of home economics.

The Bureau of Home Economics was created in the USDA in 1923 (Betters 1930). Louise Stanley, who held a PhD in biochemistry from Yale University and was in charge of home economics at the University of Missouri, was ap-pointed to head the bureau (Goldstein 2012). To lead the Textiles and Clothing Division, she hired Ruth O'Brien, who was reputed to rise up in wrath at the suggestion that "girl chemists" like herself should learn how to type instead of aiming for jobs in laboratories (M'Laughlin 1939). Clothing was one of the most popular of the Cooperative Extension clubs for girls run by the USDA. In 1932, over 324,000 girls joined clothing clubs (USDA 1933, 48). Cooperative Extension agents from thirty-nine states had published more than 250 publi-cations for clothing clubs by that year (Webb 1932). During the early 1940s the weekly radio broadcast *Farm and Home Hour* featured tips on sewing clothes (BHE 1942).

Home economics programs also grew in the schools during the first half of the twentieth century. By 1939, more than 90 percent of all but the smallest towns in the United States offered home economics courses, and most girls were required to take those courses (Halvenston and Bubolz 1999). Dress textbooks written by home economics educators for junior high, high school, and college courses were available from the major publishing houses—early on J. B. Lippincott and Charles Scribner's Sons, then Funk and Wagnalls, Macmillan, D. C. Heath, Houghton Mifflin, and McGraw-Hill—and they were published in multiple editions from the 1930s through the 1960s. Among the most prolific authors was Mildred Graves Ryan, the former head of the Department of Home Economics at a high school in Albany, New York. She wrote textbooks for a range of ages, including *Your Clothes and Personality* with editions in 1937, 1939, 1942, and 1949; *Junior Fashions* in 1944 and 1948; and *Clothes for You*, which she co-authored in 1947 and 1954. She also wrote books for adult women, including *Sew Smartly*, published in 1956, and *Dress Smartly* in 1956 and 1967.

Such publications allow us to examine the contents and purposes of an important effort to shape mass consumption, an effort that involved literally millions of girls and women in clothing clubs and classrooms across the country. Surveying the historiography of consumption, Meg Jacobs (2011) called for an investigation into how the state—which would include home economists employed in government agencies—entered into the history of consumption. The first scholars of consumption focused on the growth of the advertising industry and were highly critical of it (Ewen 1976; Fox and Lears 1983). Historians identified a significant shift from production toward consumption around 1900, and expressed fear that Americans had come to neglect political or religious engagement for the seductions of mass consumption (Leach 1993; Cohen 2003). Fashion was specifically criticized because women in particular were depicted as wasting time consuming when they might have been improving their political status (Ewen 1976; Rapp and Ross 1986).

Complicating this account are historians of colonial America who report that increased consumption first occurred in the late eighteenth century, thus implying that no pure pre-consumption world existed before 1900 (Breen 2005; Martin 1993). Other accounts indicated that fashion could challenge the status quo, such as the story of the Daughters of Liberty who made homespun clothing in order to signal their independence from Britain (Norton 1980; Roberts 1993; Stewart 2008), and the American suffragists on parade who wore white dresses to symbolize the need to clean up politics with women's "purer" votes. Young working-class women used clothing—whether ladylike or tough—to express their self-respect and solidarity in labor struggles (Clemente 2006; Enstad 1999). Newly employed women's wages used to buy new clothes, and consumption by women migrants to the city, gave women both pleasure and an exhilarating feeling of independence (Cahn 2007, 136–137;

Hackney 1999; Leach 1984). Consumer choice and abundance have become central concepts in historians' accounts of consumption (Lears 1994; Steigerwald 2006).

Americans took their excursions into the marketplace as political opportunities. Housewives protested against the high cost of living, while clubwomen used their power as shoppers to demand higher wages for women in factories (Jacobs 2005). Clearly, mass consumption was more than a frivolous waste of time, and an analysis of home economists' advice about dress can reveal the goals and assumptions of one nationwide effort to shape American women's taste in clothing.

The dress advice offered by home economists in the early twentieth century also allows a challenge to Warren Susman's characterization of American culture as shifting around 1900 from an emphasis on character to an obsession with personality. Character required *"citizenship, duty, democracy, work, building, golden deeds, outdoor life, conquest, honor, reputation, morals, manners, integrity,* and above all, *manhood"* (Susman 1984, 273–274, emphasis in original). That this definition of character did not apply to women did not worry Susman. Personality was linked to being *"fascinating, stunning, attractive, magnetic, glowing, masterful, creative, dominant, forceful"* (ibid., 277, emphasis in original). Some historians have noticed that Americans blurred the lines between the two concepts (Enstad 1999; Schorman 1996). Evidence from dress textbooks indicates that their authors saw character and personality as different yet equally valuable. Home economists at the Cleveland public schools declared, "we can at any age be improved in those personal traits that build up sterling character and make us congenial, interesting, and pleasing companions" (Van Duzer et al. 1936, 353). Grace Margaret Morton at the University of Nebraska thought that only someone who appreciated beauty *and* had high ideals of character could teach clothing design through fine art (Morton 1926). In her book on clothing, Lillian C. W. Baker (1931), who graduated from Kansas Agricultural College (now Kansas State University) and earned a master's degree at the University of Chicago, noted that Funk and Wagnalls' dictionary defined personality through character. For the home economists who wrote about dress, good taste meant something more than charm and looks. It reflected inner values.

What Is Good Taste in Dress?

Historians have not fully considered the question of what is good taste in dress, and a variety of judgments exist. Gordon (2009, 40–42) seemed to prefer the "flashy" dress of working-class women. Other scholars argued that middle-class observers condemned working-class style as in "bad taste," but they did so without analyzing what constituted "bad taste" or "good taste" (Connolly 1994; Joselit 2001; Schorman 2003). None of these authors analyzed the aesthetics in question in any detail.

Enstad saw "good taste" as social class oppression. Mid-nineteenth-century middle-class ladies' fashions—high heels, tight corsets and sleeves, voluminous skirts—prevented them from working, but they disingenuously insisted "(except in rare revealing moments) that 'tasteful' dress was available to all" (Enstad 1999, 27). By the early twentieth century, working-class women followed the latest trends, wearing the shocking new styles, while middle-class women demonstrated their good taste by wearing formerly shocking fashions that had become commonplace (Enstad 1999).

But home economists' understanding of good taste in dress was actually bent on undermining class oppression. Their rules on good taste relied on three intertwined beliefs: first, that the principles of art as they applied to dress were transcendent and unchanging; second, that it never cost more money to apply these principles to dress; and third, that appropriate dress meant a woman was clothed so that she could move efficiently and beautifully into any of the spheres opening to her in the twentieth century: home, business, or civic life. These interests—art, thrift, and practicality—were never entirely separate. Their message was artistic, democratic, and modern. The work of home economists gave an ambitious twist to the traditional work of dressmaking and dressing. Well-dressed modern women would not only be beautiful, they would be empowered to fulfill the many roles then opening to them, including those in business and civil affairs (for further discussion, see Przybyszewski 2014).

Art and Everyday Life

Art became identified with spiritual concerns and thus with women during the nineteenth century. Although women artists remained largely unappreciated, art appreciation became part of women's sphere. Home economists took several ideas from the arts and crafts movement and turned them to their own use. As a home economist at Cornell University put it in 1915, women should appreciate the relationship between orderliness in the home and tranquility of the soul (Young 1915). Good design was declared good for the soul, not just the eyes (Goldstein and Goldstein 1925).

By the early twentieth century, educators championed the movement to make art a part of everyday life, so that everyone could enjoy its elevating benefits. "Beautiful clothes should be part of contemporary art," declared Helen Goodrich Buttrick (1925, 7), who taught at Michigan Agricultural College (now Michigan State University), "not beautiful clothes for a few, but

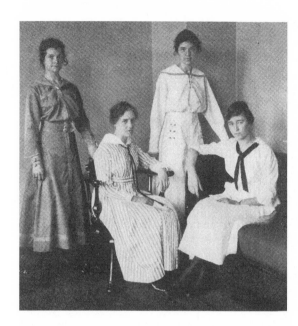

PHOTO 7.1. "Simple cotton dresses." Dresses made and modeled by home economics students at Iowa State College. Source: *Planning the Costume* 1916. Photograph courtesy Linda Przybyszewski, personal collection.

beautiful clothes for everybody, and at a cost that all can afford." The founder of the Parsons School of Design declared that all people possessed "the innate, inborn feeling for beauty, consistency and truth" just as they hungered for food and drink (Parsons 1912, 271).

So strong was women's hunger for beauty that when the USDA asked farm women what it might do for them in 1914, a woman from Tennessee wrote that a girl would not be so eager to leave the farm if she could "really see that there is an art in the farm life, and that she can dress as prettily and have her home as neatly furnished as the city girl can" (USDA 1915, 53). A woman from Idaho thought that a pamphlet on "the art and appropriateness of dress" would be much appreciated (ibid., 56). The desire to create beauty in the home, yard, and surroundings also was apparent in the responses from the USDA. Cooperative Extension home economics agents, such as Leona Hope at the University of Illinois, were eager to satisfy these requests. She set the pattern by writing *Fashion: Its Use and Abuse* in 1919 and followed up with a pamphlet on artistic dress (Hope 1919a, 1919b).

At institutions of higher education, faculty in departments of clothing and textiles encouraged students to value art in everyday life. Harriet Goldstein (1919, 300) of the University of Minnesota explained to students that "the art of a fine painting . . . is just the same expression that [a woman] finds . . . in a beautiful dress." All they had to do was learn the five art principles that European artists had used for centuries. Home economists also drew on the writings of two influential American art teachers. The first was Arthur Wesley Dow, who made Columbia University's Teachers College the most important art education program in the country through his book *Composition* (1899). The second was Denman Waldo Ross, who taught at Harvard and published *A Theory of Pure Design: Harmony, Balance, Rhythm* in 1907. According to Professors Harriet Goldstein and Vetta Goldstein (1925), the five art principles were proportion, balance, rhythm, emphasis, and harmony, which included shape, size (which really meant proportion all over again), color, texture, and idea. The Goldstein sisters illustrated their books with fashions from the past in order to emphasize that neither time nor place nor personal taste can alter the principles that govern beauty in dress.

However, White home economists failed to acknowledge the diversity in American society when they wrote of beauty in dress. Their art principles were taken almost entirely from the European tradition with a dash of influence from Japanese prints, and they ignored the continent of Africa. They gave advice on complexions no darker than those of the Latina movie stars of the 1920s and 1930s. But African American home economists worked to fill the void. "The peoples of dark skin have been forgotten," wrote Ella Mae Washington in her book *Color in Dress: For Dark-Skinned Peoples* (1949, 11). And yet personal appearance was essential to their success: "They must look the part if they are to reach the height to which the race is aspiring" (ibid.). Charleszine Wood Spears earned a master's degree in home economics, but never saw her own coloring in the textbooks she was assigned. So, after teaching in the Kansas City public schools, she decided to write a textbook that covered "the darker races" (Spears, 1937, 8). The civil rights movement and Black Is Beautiful awareness made the failings of White home economists apparent; subsequently, they made efforts to include African American models in their textbooks. Spears's book was so valuable that it continued to a fifth edition in 1974.

Emphasizing the importance of art in everyday life, Buttrick (1925, 162) asserted: "Garments that cover the body in a durable and physically adequate manner but ignore the element of attractiveness fail to fulfill the whole purpose of clothing and tend to starve the love of beauty with which most human beings are endowed." Think of the body as a canvas, the fabric as the oil paints, and the woman's personality as the idea to be given visible form, urged home economics faculty members at Kansas State College (Latzke and Quinlan 1935). They observed that clothing was the one remaining opportunity for creativity in the machine age and was still available to women. Claiming that men's clothing had become deadly dull (ibid., 2), the home economists put both design and creation firmly in the hands of women by teaching the art of dress and the craft of sewing.

Until the 1910s women's ready-to-wear clothing was generally considered the last resort of the poor. As ready-to-wear improved, it became clear that more women would be buying rather than making their clothes or hiring a dressmaker. Choosing from the myriad offerings of America's great department stores was an opportunity for artistry. The Goldstein sisters declared that the principles of art still held. "The clerk who chooses the right hat and dress for a customer has done a piece of work that calls for much the same kind of knowledge as the man who designs and paints a picture" (Goldstein and Goldstein 1925, 4). The same was true for a woman shopping on her own; thus every woman could be an artist.

The intellectual contribution of the home economists who focused on dress was their application of the principles of fine and decorative arts to dress. Furthermore, they believed that nature, art, and science agreed when it came to beauty in dress. They claimed that a modern American woman would gain psychologically from understanding the principles of design. If a woman "can learn to see the relation between orderliness of arrangement and tranquility of the soul, between confusion and nervousness, between harmony of color and harmony of mind, between honesty of form and directness of thought,—then she will have realized the essential meaning of art in daily life," wrote Young (1915, 150) for the Cornell reading courses for women in New York state. Morton (1943, 17) argued similarly thirty years later that a neat appearance reflected a mind that is "clear and organized," while a sloppy appearance indicated a mind that is "unorganized or ill-disciplined."

Dressing with a Purpose

The first generation of home economists came of age during the period of industrialization when the ideas of Frederick Winslow Taylor were taking the country by storm. Taylor, an engineer turned industrial manager, wrote *The Principles of Scientific Management* (1911). Efficiency became a watchword among Americans, especially home economists who were eager to prove that they used the most up-to-date ideas. They applied the concepts of efficiency along with psychology and art to their study of dress. For example, two home economists wrote, "The sense of being appropriately clothed for the occasion or occupation reacts on the mental attitude to give poise and dignity to the wearer, and a sense of efficiency" (McGowan and Waite 1919, 228).

One of the home economists' first efforts to influence style, infused with the element of efficiency, featured children's clothing. Freeing children from petticoats and corsets in the name of self-help and hygiene made sense. The home economists wanted clothing that encouraged self-reliance, a solid virtue of character. Hooks, snaps, bows, and elastic were all discarded in favor of loops, tabs, and buttons on the front of garments. They recommended looser clothing in order to prevent poor circulation, bad digestion, shallow breathing, round shoulders, weak muscles, lame feet, bad nerves, and the "displacement of certain organs" (Leiby 1925, 4; McGowan and Waite 1919, 250). Residents of orphanages around Washington, D.C., near where the Bureau of Home Economics was located, tested self-help bibs, sunsuits and sundresses (to encourage absorption of vitamin D), rainsuits, and rompers, all in the name of science (Betters 1930).

"The clothes of the young child help make the man" (and, presumably, the woman), declared one USDA publication (Davis 1927, 1). Aesthetics were not ignored. Helen Atwater (1929, 36) explained, "A child's clothing can be used to start his appreciation of color and design and thus lay the foundations for good taste and enjoyment, not only in matters of clothing but in other fields of art as well." O'Brien (1930, 285) was happy to report "a noticeable effect on children's clothing throughout the country" after the bureau sent out traveling exhibits. In 1939, the Singer Sewing Machine Company's *Style Digest* featured the offerings of six major pattern lines (Vogue, Butterick, Du Barry, Simplicity, McCall, and Hollywood) under the headline "The Modern Child Goes to a Party in 'Self-Help' Clothes" (1939, 7–8).

Just as they offered children's clothing with a definite purpose, so home economists of the early twentieth century defined the purpose of women's clothing: to be taken seriously as wage earners. Some home economics educators saw the previous decades as a turning point in women's opportunities. Where once women had dressed in order to catch a husband and then dressed to show off his wealth, now they enjoyed "a new freedom" that allowed them to work and travel for themselves, and "to resort less and less in dress to what was designated as 'woman's wiles'" (Baxter and Latzke 1938, 26). Some women had always worked for wages, but women were being hired increasingly as secretaries, typists, and sales clerks. In 1920, about 37 percent of young women between the ages of sixteen and twenty-four were employed outside the home (Kleinberg 2010).

Just as the scorecards had instructed girls and women at county fairs, home economists taught women how to dress in their textbooks. Buttrick (1925, 4) observed, "the number of women who are earning a living in occupations outside the home is constantly growing," and these "working women must appear at their best at all times." What was their best? An ideal job candidate mirrored business itself when she looked precise, focused, practical, and rational. "The idea which distinguishes business from other activities— the idea of accuracy and correctness"—is what should be found in business dress (Story 1930, xxi). Aesthetics also justified clothing that allowed women to move in the workplace. Clothing so tight that a woman could not move freely violated the harmony of shape. Tight clothing was declared nothing short of a disability (Hope 1919b). The twin barbarities of the period were corsets and high, pointy shoes (Roberts 1977). The 1920s introduced a looser silhouette, but shoes continued to be a problem. Buttrick (1925, 124) argued that such shoes handicapped women: "Fashion has caused women to compress their feet into shoes having soles . . . narrower than the foot. . . . Not only this, but the foot is tilted forward and the whole ankle and instep thrown into an abnormal position by a high narrow heel, and the toes are compressed into a point." Armed with X-rays, home economists explained that women were rendering themselves inefficient.

Illustrations of appropriate and inappropriate dress on the job were included in home economists' dress textbooks. In *Art in Home and Clothing* (1936), Trilling and Williams illustrated the clothes of two job candidates. One of the women will not get the job. Her dress is so narrow that it restricts her movement, hence the slit which makes walking possible, but also draws undue attention to her legs. Her sleeves are childishly puffy and restrictively tight. Her hat is frivolously flowered and will not shield her eyes from the sun during her morning commute. Her cheeks are over-rouged, a dozen bangles will clang constantly, and she has a superfluous necklace as well. The other woman wears a more modest, precise, quiet ensemble that does not constrict either her gait or the movement of her arms. It is more physically revealing than a man's suit, yet it is its equivalent down to the scarf/tie at the throat. Her hat shields her eyes from the sun. Dressed appropriately, she gets the job. At a time when most young women did not expect to work for wages after marriage, it is startling how much emphasis was put into early dress textbooks in order to teach them how to dress for paid work.

But the home economists did not ignore clothing for the woman at home. They called homemaking "the *greatest* of the professions—greatest in number and greatest in its effect on the individual and on society" (American School of Home Economics 1911, 3). The term "housedress" may conjure up shabby images, but its reality was far from it. Pickens (1939, 45) defined the housedress as a "dress suitable for morning wear at home. Usually of gaily printed, washable cotton fabric. Often perky in silhouette, smartly made and trimmed." Indeed, housedress patterns in the 1930s were detailed with bows, collars, eyelet trim, and shaped skirts. Housedresses followed fashion's hemline dictates up and down over the decades, but they always had short sleeves to make cooking and cleaning easier.

As income-earning women themselves, the writers and teachers about dress lauded the business potential of their talented students. One story (Laselle and Wiley 1913, 50) told of a student who appeared at school "in a gingham dress so beautifully cut and made" that her teacher asked her where the dress had come from. Surprisingly, the girl herself had designed and made it. The teacher arranged for the student to take a specialized course in dressmaking at a technical high school to prepare her for a career in design. "Teaching Your Daughter to Sew" was a featured chapter in a book by Constance Talbot (1943), who had worked for both Butterick and Simplicity pattern companies, and it included sections called "Developing Talents" and "Career Women."

Over and over, the home economists wrote that a woman could dress beautifully and appropriately without spending a fortune. Cooperative Extension home economists working in the rural South emphasized self-sufficiency, primarily through food production, preservation, and marketing, but they also taught women to renovate clothes and to use a variety of materials, such as the cloth used for feed and flour sacks. Home demonstration clubs held contests specifically focused on dresses made from these sacks. A 1933 report from Louisiana told about a girl who had quit school because of embarrassment over her poor clothing. After she and her mother attended a sack dress contest, the mother related that her daughter "ain't a bit ashamed to wear sack dresses now" and that they had made four (qtd. in Rieff 2006, 133). At the other extreme, the author of *The Girl Today, the Woman Tomorrow* invented the fictional Marjorie to symbolize all the middle school girls who had yet to learn the wisdom of home economics. She wrote: "It is strange, but true, unfortunately, that Marjorie with several complete costumes provided by indulgent parents is constantly bewailing her lack of the proper thing to wear" (Hunter 1932, 63). A junior high textbook from 1948 explained, "*Anyone can have an attractive wardrobe who takes time to plan it wisely and to make purchases carefully*" (Todd 1948, 131, emphasis in original). Even First Lady Eleanor Roosevelt, a close friend of Martha Van Rensselaer, the head of home economics at Cornell University, set forth the same ideals: "I have seen women who spend very small amounts on their clothes but who plan them carefully, frequently look better-dressed than women who waste a great deal of money and buy foolishly and without good taste" (Roosevelt 1933, 46).

Democracy in Dress

The essentially democratic character of thrift and appropriate dressing was taught explicitly to home economics students. "Every girl, especially of high school age, has seen unhappiness inflicted on the plainly dressed student by the supercilious attitude toward her of some better dressed classmate," explained a textbook from 1919 (McGowan and Waite 1919, 229). This was not right. "The girl of true American spirit will use her example and influence against such snobbishness" (ibid., 229–230). Home economists, including Mary Lockwood Matthews, the founding dean of Purdue University's School of Home Economics, supported a trend in the 1920s for schools to prescribe matching simple white graduation dresses. In *Elementary Home Economics* she wrote, "A girl never looks appropriately dressed when she wears clothing that may make her companions feel uncomfortable because it is more expensive than that which they are wearing" (Matthews 1928, 433). One home economics book included in the appendix proof that the girls of North Central High School in Spokane, Washington, had that true American spirit. Their school dress code banned "satin slippers, high heels, silk and velvet afternoon or party dresses" in 1925 (Gibson 1927, 307).

According to the home economists, dress could lead any girl or woman to success in life. "Beautiful and becoming clothing that contributes to one's attractiveness gives poise and assurance and thus contributes to success," concluded Buttrick (1925, 162) after noting the natural desire for beauty, which clothing can satisfy. Home economists saw young women as citizens in the making. The scope of ambitions that the educators envisioned for their well-dressed audience in the modern age was expansive. "Since the code of life of the modern girl includes an ideal of health and strength and an ideal of activity and leadership," explained Buttrick (ibid., 107), "her clothing must contribute to these ideals by giving her freedom of action and the chance to develop all the grace and strength of her body." In their college textbook, Mildred Graves Ryan and Velma Phillips, the dean of the College of Home Economics at the State College of Washington, made clear their ambitions for their young woman reader: "It is hoped that through its study she will gain that inner confidence which will allow her to think about something besides herself—to see herself in relation to the family, the community, and the world" (Ryan and Phillips 1954, v). This ambitious message never disappeared. By dressing well, a woman can gain "a basic sense of security and self-respect," and thus she is released "from the tensions caused by concern about her appearance" and is free "to give her full attention to more vital matters, for herself and for the welfare of others" (McJimsey 1963, 4–5).

Home economics programs on dress were not actual sumptuary laws, but for their era they were nearly the equivalent: a formidable government-sponsored program aimed at teaching American women how to dress. (Incidentally, Hunt [1996] argued that dress codes at work constitute the persistence of sumptuary laws; however, he gave no attention to the work of home economists.) The teachings of home economists differed from traditional sumptuary laws in a number of ways. They were peculiarly American in that they were democratic. They were democratic because they were designed to diminish the distinctions in dress that reflected distinctions in wealth and because they were designed to bring beauty into the lives of the many. They drew on the nineteenth-century designation of morality and art as part of women's sphere, combined it with a concern with efficiency, and sent their students off to serve in the home, the workplace, and the civic arena. As one of the first home economics land-grant college educators put it: "It is a trite saying, nevertheless true, that all art is not in a frame" (Hope 1919a, 3).

REFERENCES

American School of Home Economics. 1911. *The Profession of Home Making: A Condensed Home-Study Course on Domestic Science: The Practical Application of the Most Recent Advances in the Arts and Sciences to the Home Industries.* Chicago: American School of Home Economics.

Atwater, Helen W. 1929. *Home Economics: The Art and Science of Home Making.* Chicago: American Library Association.

Baker, Lillian C. W. 1931. *Clothing Selection and Purchase.* New York: Macmillan.

Baxter, Laura, and Alpha Latzke. 1938. *Modern Clothing.* Philadelphia: Lippincott.

Betters, Paul V. 1930. *The Bureau of Home Economics: Its History, Activities, and Organization.* Washington, D.C.: Brookings Institution.

BHE (Bureau of Home Economics). 1942. *Bureau of Home Economics in Wartime.* Washington, D.C.: U.S. Department of Agriculture, BHE.

Breen, T. H. 2005. *The Marketplace of Revolution: How Consumer Politics Shaped American Independence.* New York: Oxford University Press.

Burman, Barbara, ed. 1999. *The Culture of Sewing: Gender, Consumption and Home Dressmaking.* Oxford: Berg.

Buttrick, Helen G. 1925. *Principles of Clothing Selection.* New York: Macmillan.

Cahn, Susan K. 2007. *Sexual Reckonings: Southern Girls in a Troubling Age.* Cambridge, Mass.: Harvard University Press.

Clemente, Deirdre. 2006. "Striking Ensembles: The Importance of Clothing on the Picket Line." *Labor Studies Journal* 30(Winter): 1–15.

Cohen, Lizabeth. 2003. *A Consumers' Republic: The Politics of Mass Consumption in Postwar America.* New York: Vintage.

Connolly, Marguerite A. 1994. "The Transformation of Home Sewing and the Sewing Machine in America, 1850–1929." PhD diss., University of Delaware.

Davis, Mary Aleen. 1927. *Children's Rompers.* Leaflet 11. Washington, D.C.: U.S. Department of Agriculture, BHE.

Dow, Arthur Wesley. 1899. *Composition: A Series of Exercises Selected from a New System of Art Education.* New York: Baker.

Elias, Megan J. 2008. *Stir It Up: Home Economics in American Culture.* Philadelphia: University of Pennsylvania Press.

Enstad, Nan. 1999. *Ladies of Labor, Girls of Adventure: Working Women, Popular Culture, and Labor Politics at the Turn of the Twentieth Century.* New York: Columbia University Press.

Ewen, Stuart. 1976. *Captains of Consciousness: Advertising and the Social Roots of the Consumer Culture.* New York: McGraw-Hill.

Fox, Richard Wightman, and T. J. Jackson Lears, eds. 1983. *The Culture of Consumption: Critical Essays in American History 1880–1980.* New York: Pantheon.

Frank, Isabelle. 2000. *Theory of Decorative Art: An Anthology of European and American Writings, 1750–1940*. New Haven, Conn.: Yale University Press.

Gibson, Jessie E. 1927. *On Being a Girl*. New York: Macmillan.

Goldstein, Carolyn M. 2012. *Creating Consumers: Home Economists in Twentieth-Century America*. Chapel Hill: University of North Carolina Press.

Goldstein, Harriet. 1919. "Related Art for Home Economics Courses in Smith-Hughes Schools." *Journal of Home Economics* 11: 300–306.

Goldstein, Harriet, and Vetta Goldstein. 1925. *Art in Everyday Life*. New York: Macmillan.

Gordon, Sarah A. 2009. *"Make It Yourself": Home Sewing, Gender, and Culture, 1890–1930*. New York: Columbia University Press.

Hackney, Fiona. 1999. "Making Modern Women, Stitch by Stitch: Dressmaking and Women's Magazines in Britain 1919–1930." In *The Culture of Sewing: Gender, Consumption and Home Dressmaking*, edited by Barbara Burman, 73–95. Oxford: Berg.

Halvenston, Sally I., and Margaret M. Bubolz. 1999. "Home Economics and Home Sewing in the United States, 1870–1940." In *The Culture of Sewing: Gender, Consumption and Home Dressmaking*, edited by Barbara Burman, 303–325. Oxford: Berg.

Hope, Leona. 1919a. *Artistic Dress*. Extension Circular No. 34. Urbana, Ill.: Extension Service in Agriculture and Home Economics.

———. 1919b. *Fashion: Its Use and Abuse*. Extension Circular No. 33. Urbana, Ill.: Extension Service in Agriculture and Home Economics.

Hunt, Alan. 1996. *Governance of the Consuming Passions: A History of Sumptuary Law*. New York: St. Martin's.

Hunter, Lucretia P. 1932. *The Girl Today, the Woman Tomorrow*. Boston: Allyn and Bacon.

Jacobs, Meg. 2005. *Pocketbook Politics: Economic Citizenship in Twentieth Century America*. Princeton, N.J.: Princeton University Press.

———. 2011. "State of the Field: The Politics of Consumption." *Reviews in American History* 39: 561–573.

Joselit, Jenna W. 2001. *A Perfect Fit: Clothes, Character, and the Promise of America*. New York: Metropolitan.

Kleinberg, S. J. 2010. "Women's Employment in the Public and Private Spheres, 1880–1920." In *Becoming Visible: Women's Presence in Late Nineteenth-Century America*, edited by Janet Floyd et al., 81–103. Amsterdam: Rodopi.

Laselle, Mary A., and Katherine E. Wiley. 1913. *Vocations for Girls*. Boston: Houghton Mifflin.

Latzke, Alpha, and Beth Quinlan. 1935. *Clothing: An Introductory College Course*. Chicago: Lippincott.

Leach, William R. 1984. "Transformations in a Culture of Consumption: Women and Department Stores, 1890–1925." *Journal of American History* 71: 319–342.

———. 1993. *Land of Desire: Merchants, Power and the Rise of a New American Culture*. New York: Pantheon.

Lears, T. J. Jackson. 1994. *Fables of Abundance: A Cultural History of Advertising in America*. New York: Basic.

Leiby, Cora Irene. 1925. *Clothes for Little Folks*. Ames: Iowa State College of Agriculture and Mechanic Arts.

Lubbock, Jules. 1995. *Tyranny of Taste: The Politics of Architecture and Design in Britain, 1770–1960*. New Haven, Conn.: Yale University Press.

Martin, Ann Smart. 1993. "Makers, Buyers and Consumerism as a Material Culture Framework." *Winterthur Portfolio* 28: 141–157.

Martin, Richard. 1987. *Fashion and Surrealism: Wearable Art*. New York: Rizzoli.

———. 1998. *Cubism and Fashion*. New York: Metropolitan Museum of Art.

Matthews, Mary Lockwood. 1928. *Elementary Home Economics*. Boston: Little, Brown.

McGowan, Ellen B., and Charlotte A. Waite. 1919. *Textiles and Clothing*. New York: Macmillan.

McJimsey, Harriet T. 1963. *Art in Clothing Selection*. New York: Harper and Row.

M'Laughlin, Kathleen. 1939. "Sidelines Stressed for Girl Chemists." *New York Times*, April 16, 25.

"The Modern Child Goes to a Party in 'Self-Help' Clothes." 1939. *Singer Style Digest* (Fall–Winter): 7–8.

Morton, Grace Margaret. 1926. "Related Art in Clothing Selection." *Journal of Home Economics* 18: 25–28.

———. 1943. *The Arts of Costume and Personal Appearance*. New York: Wiley.

Norton, Mary Beth. 1980. *Liberty's Daughters: The Revolutionary Experience of American Women, 1750–1800*. Boston: Little, Brown.

O'Brien, Ruth. 1930. "The Program of Textile Research in the Bureau of Home Economics." *Journal of Home Economics* 22: 281–287.

O'Brien, Ruth, Maude Campbell, and Mary Aleen Davis. 1927. *Score Cards for Judging Clothing Selection and Construction*. Miscellaneous Circular No. 90. Washington, D.C.: U.S. Department of Agriculture.

Parsons, Frank A. 1912. "A Rational Application of Art to Daily Life." *Journal of the American Association of University Women* 5: 266–272.

Pickens, Mary Brooks. 1939. *The Language of Fashion*. New York: Funk and Wagnalls.

Planning the Costume. 1916. Home Economics Bulletin No. 9. Ames: Iowa State College of Agriculture and Mechanic Arts.

Przybyszewski, Linda. 2014. *The Lost Art of Dress: The Women Who Once Made America Stylish*. New York: Basic.

Rapp, Rayna, and Ellen Ross. 1986. "The 1920s: Feminism, Consumerism, and Political Backlash in the United States." In *Women in Culture and Politics: A Century of Change*, edited by Judith Friendlander et al., 52–61. Bloomington: Indiana University Press.

Rieff, Lynne. 2006. "Revitalizing Southern Homes: Rural Women, the Professionalization of Home Demonstration Work, and the Limits of Reform, 1917–1945." In *Work, Family, and Faith: Rural Southern Women in the Twentieth Century*, edited by Melissa Walker and Rebecca Sharpless, 135–165. Columbia: University of Missouri Press.

Roberts, Helene E. 1977. "The Exquisite Slave: The Role of Clothes in the Making of the Victorian Woman." *Signs* 2: 554–569.

Roberts, Mary Louise. 1993. "Samson and Delilah Revisited: The Politics of Women's Fashion in 1920s France." *American Historical Review* 98: 657–684.

Roosevelt, Eleanor. 1933. *It's Up to the Women.* New York: Stokes.

Ross, Denman Waldo. 1907. *A Theory of Pure Design: Harmony, Balance, Rhythm.* New York: Houghton Mifflin.

Ryan, Mildred Graves, and Velma Phillips. 1954. *Clothes for You,* 2nd ed. New York: Appleton-Century-Crofts.

Schorman, Rob. 1996. "The Truth About Good Goods: Clothing, Advertising, and the Representation of Cultural Values at the End of the Nineteenth Century." *American Studies* 37: 23–49.

———. 2003. *Selling Style: Clothing and Social Change at the Turn of the Century.* Philadelphia: University of Pennsylvania Press.

Spears, Charleszine Wood. 1937. *How to Wear Colors: With Emphasis on Dark Skins.* Minneapolis, Minn.: Burgess.

Stage, Sarah, and Virginia B. Vincenti, eds. 1997. *Rethinking Home Economics: Women and the History of a Profession.* Ithaca, N.Y.: Cornell University Press.

Steigerwald, David. 2006. "All Hail the Republic of Choice: Consumer History as Contemporary Thought." *Journal of American History* 93: 385–403.

Stewart, Mary Lynn. 2008. *Making Modern Frenchwomen: Marketing Haute Couture, 1919–1939.* Baltimore, Md.: Johns Hopkins University Press.

Story, Margaret. 1930. *Individuality and Clothes: The Blue Book of Personal Attire.* New York: Funk and Wagnalls.

Susman, Warren I. 1984. *Culture as History: The Transformation of American Society in the Twentieth Century.* New York: Pantheon.

Talbot, Constance. 1943. *The Complete Book of Sewing.* New York: Book Presentations.

Taylor, Frederick W. 1911. *The Principles of Scientific Management.* New York: Harper.

Todd, Elizabeth. 1948. *Clothes for Girls.* Boston: Heath.

Trilling, Mabel B., and Florence Williams. 1936. *Art in Home and Clothing.* Philadelphia: Lippincott.

Troy, Nancy J. 2003. *Couture Culture: A Study of Modern Art and Fashion.* Cambridge, Mass.: MIT Press.

USDA (U.S. Department of Agriculture). 1915. *Domestic Needs of Farm Women.* Report 104. Washington, D.C.: U.S. Government Printing Office.

———. 1933. *Report of Extension Work in Agriculture and Home Economics in the United States.* Washington: D.C.: USDA.

Van Duzer, Adelaide Laura, Benjamin R. Andrews, Ethelyn Bobenmyer, and Edna M. Andrix. 1936. *Everyday Living for Girls.* Chicago: Lippincott.

Washington, Ella Mae. 1949. *Color in Dress: For Dark-Skinned Peoples.* Langston, Okla.: Ella Mae Washington.

Webb, Edith J. 1932. *Boys' and Girls' 4-H Club Work in the United States: A Selected List of References.* Washington, D.C.: U.S. Department of Agriculture, Office of Cooperative Extension Work.

Wigley, Mark. 1995. *White Walls, Designer Dresses: The Fashioning of Modern Architecture*. Cambridge, Mass.: MIT Press.

Wygant, Foster. 1993. *School Art in American Culture, 1820–1970*. Cincinnati, Ohio: Interwood.

Young, Helen B. 1915. *The Arrangements of Household Furnishings*. Farmhouse Series No. 7. Ithaca, N.Y.: New York State College of Agriculture at Cornell University.

8. New Patterns for Women's Clothing

Consumption versus Sustainability

MARGARETE ORDON

Most consumers in the United States are awash in a sea of clothes. Fabrics and garments pack container ships, moving from producing country to consuming country on their cross-ocean voyages. Clothes overflow from bedroom closets, while cast-offs pile up in corners before being sent off to a local charity. Massive bales of discarded garments are resold to international secondhand clothing markets or recycled into scrap.

Embroiled in a culture of consumerism, we face a global glut of clothing that perpetuates unfulfilled needs and hinders the well-being of both clothing producers and consumers. Although clothes are cheap and plentiful in the United States, the structure of production, sale, consumption, and disposal has many environmental, economic, and social costs. Clothing production and consumption demands intensive inputs of raw materials, energy, water, toxic chemicals, and human labor while simultaneously generating dangerous outputs of chemical-saturated water effluent, air emissions, and solid waste.

This chapter analyzes issues in clothing consumption (e.g., acquisition, use, maintenance, and disposal) as they relate to environmental and social sustainability. In particular, my thesis is that multisensory interactions with clothing, particularly as they manifest in perceptions of and attitudes toward quality, are pivotal factors in women's clothing practices and are potential sites of intervention for sustainable initiatives. In-depth interviews with nineteen women about their clothing choices and care practices provide substance for the discussion.[1] The interviews were conducted in 2010–2012, a period of increased scholarly and public attention to global environmental issues and sustainability. This chapter illustrates that home economics theory, research, and education can be applied to build consumer and textile knowledge and skills, cultivate creative and conscientious consumption, and situate those practices in environmental and social systems.

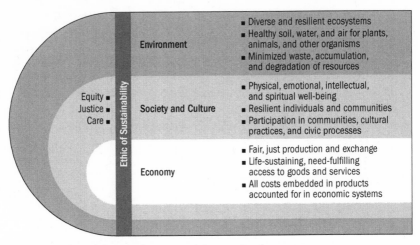

FIGURE 8.1. Conditions for Systems Supporting Sustainability.[2]

Defining Sustainability

Sustainability has become a buzzword in contemporary news, popular culture, and consumer marketing; however, scholars from a variety of disciplines have focused on issues of sustainability for years. The World Conservation Union (aka the International Union for Conservation of Nature), the United Nations Environment Programme, and the World Wide Fund for Nature (IUCN/UNEP/WWF 1991, 10) have adopted the following definition: Sustainability is "improving the quality of human life while living within the carrying capacity of supporting ecosystems." In order to understand the complexity of the concept, a broad, holistic definition of sustainability is needed—one that encompasses the complex, dynamic system of interlocking environmental, social, and economic dimensions (see also Jackson 2006; Max-Neef, Elizalde, and Hopenhayn 1991). Furthermore, sustainability includes an ethic that challenges—and corrects—interconnected injustices that have emerged from current systems of production and consumption (Dresner 2002; Held 2006). Such a model is presented in figure 8.1.

Environmental and Social Injustices
Along the Clothing Life Cycle

Clothing is enmeshed in complex systems of production and consumption, including dynamic networks of trade, consumer use, and disposal (see figure 8.2). In addition, social constructions of gender and cultural codes of meaning related to clothing consumption are parts of the system, though less tangi-

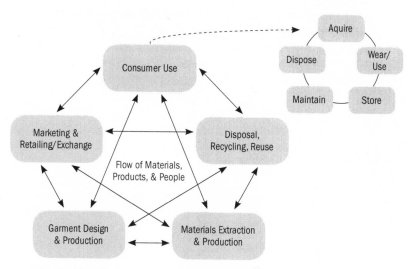

FIGURE 8.2. Clothing Life Cycle Components, Interconnections, Consumer Subcycle.[3]

bly. While commodity chains are often depicted as independent, linear movements of goods, they are, in fact, complex, fluid, multidirectional, and interconnected webs. Furthermore, each of the system's components is situated in historical and cultural contexts; has its own subcycles; and links to other cycles in different geographic places, product industries, trade systems, local economies, and individual lives (Fletcher 2008; Leonard 2010; McDonough and Braungart 2002). My analysis of women's clothing consumption and sustainaiblity focuses on the consumer experience in this life cycle system.

Producing fabrics on the vast scales to supply consumers with cheap, plentiful apparel has transformed global economies and ecosystems. Cotton agriculture is labor-, land-, and water-intensive and frequently relies on toxic pesticides. The drilling and processing of petroleum-based synthetic materials draw on finite reserves of fossil fuels. The dyeing and finishing to create ever-changing seasonal color palettes or easy-care fabrics introduce carcinogens and neurotoxins into workers' bodies, finished products, and waterways (Fletcher 2008; Leonard 2010).

The increasing quantity of offerings and the speed of change in the fashion system exacerbate a variety of challenges. The pressure on women consumers to keep up with fashion and maintain their social status has psychological, social, and economic consequences (Kasser 2003; Schor 1999). While improvements in technology have facilitated fast, cheap fashion, many environmental and social costs are not accounted for in the purchase price. For example, the cross-oceanic shipping of fabrics and finished products guzzles fossil fuels and pollutes waterways with ballast (Welters 2008). Despite idealistic company mission statements, economic, social, and political circumstances, as well as U.S. consumers' demand for cheap clothing, result in egregiously hazardous working conditions, low wages, elevated stress, and job insecurity for garment workers (Rosen 2002; Ross 1997). These challenges do not stop with production.

Despite a significant role in a garment's life cycle, laundering clothes and maintaining (or failing to maintain) clothing entails environmental costs that are often invisible, notwithstanding the publicized toxicity of the dry cleaning fluid perchloroethylene (Fletcher 2008). Laundering polyester and acrylic sheds microplastic debris that contaminates marine habitats (Browne 2011). Many factors contribute to these impacts: garment fiber, frequency of wear before washing, water temperatures, efficiency of washing or drying machines, type and quantity of detergents, the presence of bleaches, and ironing.

Vast quantities of textile scraps from production and cast-off garments end up in landfills, despite sustainable disposal options. (Natural fibers are biodegradable and synthetic fibers are recyclable; Allwood et al. 2006.) Many neighborhoods do not have textile recycling, few stores or companies offer take-back programs, and mixed fibers—ubiquitous in comfort stretch garments—do not easily compost. Donating and reselling clothes have ethical implications, such as raising money for a charity's particular agenda or affecting local industries in countries receiving used clothing for resale (Hansen 2000).

Understanding Unsustainable Clothing Consumption

Despite the well-documented litany of environmental and human rights abuses in the global apparel industry and U.S. consumption habits, this unsustainable pattern persists. For example, Rachel primarily bought lower-priced T-shirts, even though she regularly had problems with the fabric graying or being so thin that her bra was visible. She recently threw away a nicer, more expensive white shirt but felt remorse, as she explained, "I spilled something on it, first week I had it. . . . It kills me!" Louise felt compelled to buy certain clothes because of limited plus-size options, not because she particularly liked them, leaving her with a wardrobe of unsatisfying, unworn garments.

Navigating through the vast ocean of clothing choices can be a complicated process. Women balance fit, comfort, personal style, sensory preferences, fashion, social norms, convenience, cost, and available products, as well as their own skill sets, as they decide what garments to buy and how to wear them. Invisible, intangible production conditions and environmental costs fall to the bottom of the list of considerations, if women are conscious of them at all (Joergens 2006; Kim, Littrell, and Ogle 1999; Rudell 2006; Valor 2007). Additionally, even when consumers do express pro-environmental or other social values, researchers consistently identify gaps with actual behaviors (Carrigan and Atalla 2001; Kennedy et al. 2009).

Two theoretical approaches, when combined, help to explain the unsustainable behavior patterns. Stern and his colleagues (1999) in their value-belief-norm (VBN) model cited the influence of internal factors (values and beliefs) on activating an individual's pro-environmental norms and behaviors. Guagnano, Stern, and Dietz's (1995) attitudes-behavior-content (ABC) theory postulated that the gap between expressed attitude and behavior can be explained by positive or negative contextual variables (such as convenience, rewards, regulations, time pressures, or financial costs), which affect behavior regardless of one's attitude toward the behavior's environmental or social impacts. Combining the VBN and ABC models allows us to consider consumption as a system of interactions, so that we can assess the internal barriers and motivations and the external factors that influence clothing practices (McKenzie-Mohr and Smith 1999; Zepeda and Deal 2009).

Assessing Quality

As revealed through my interviews and observations, the aesthetic, affective, and subjective perceptions of quality dominated as barriers to sustainable consumption. Low-quality products challenge sustainability because they decrease how long garments last physically and stylistically, thus increasing total resources consumed and discarded. Furthermore, they decreased consumer satisfaction by perpetuating unfulfilling relationships with clothes. Participants' stories revealed that they (1) assessed quality through aesthetic or sensory criteria rather than technical criteria, (2) felt that current apparel options were not of sufficient quality to warrant large investments of time or money, and (3) evaluated themselves as limited in skills and resources to make those investments.

Participants evaluated apparel quality through a range of criteria, such as fabric characteristics, construction, fit, design, care needs, brand, and price. Women intuitively sensed quality based on multisensory aesthetic, affective experiences, and did not assess quality primarily by closely inspecting the garment's yarn, fabric structure, construction, or other technical criteria—let alone production practices or environmental impacts. The following comments were typical: "The quality of the fabric, you could *feel* it" (Melanie). "If it's a shirt that's all fakey fabric, and flimsy fabric, you know, it's not going to hang right or sit right on your body" (Camilla).

Interviewees framed sensory assessments through subjective understandings of tastes, social expectations, and use. For example, Rachel pulled several cashmere sweaters from her closet and contrasted their drastically different qualities despite the nominally identical fibers. The sweater from a high-end retailer purchased twenty years ago was faring pretty well, especially compared to the now pilled and stretched sweater purchased from a big-box chain only a few years ago. Although she still wore the former sweater to work, she had demoted the other to weekend, at-home wear. The real contrast materialized when Rachel selected a cashmere sweater that her mother wore sixty years ago. This piece was in pristine condition. No pills. Sturdy fabric. As Rachel exclaimed, "Look at how *gorgeous* it is!"

Overall, the women lacked both a language to describe sensory aesthetic pleasures and technical expertise about garment construction. Women's attention to how things feel, but their struggle to articulate it, is illustrated in their awkward responses. For example, "Like, it's, I mean like, it. Hmm. It doesn't feel good," attempted Camilla. Sandra said, "If something is coming from [a department store] or something like that, they usually have, you know, pretty good, uh, pretty good quality, . . . and then maybe, I mean, I'm not an expert on any of this." While part of the women's inability to articulate experiences may be due to their qualitative, subjective nature, the issue bears further examination. Knowledgeable consumers ideally would be able to link the primary affective, tactile experiences with specific information.

Women's stories revealed that relationships with their clothes were at the heart of their attitudes toward quality. While plenty of companies name their shirt "the perfect" or "the essential," this label was only earned through repeated wearing and laundering. A perfect shirt was one that lived with a woman. One of Megan's much-loved shirts, thinned through use, had provided a high-quality, needs-fulfilling experience (even though she had transferred it to a less formal use: sleepwear). Her description of finally throwing away the worn T-shirt conveyed a sense of loss. Stories of a well-worn garment revealed pleasurable and satisfying engagements that reflected high physical, sensual, and emotional qualities, as Chapman (2005) also reported.

When garments pilled, snagged, shrunk, stretched out, or stained easily, women were frustrated, and they explained how they not only reassessed these items as lower quality, but also questioned whether to continue to wear them, to donate them, or to throw them away. As seen in Rachel's stories, given the abundance of cheap cashmere sweaters or white T-shirts, it is easy enough for consumers to use lower-quality clothes until worn, torn, or stained. Instead of developing technical expertise to identify and maintain quality apparel, participants primarily focused their consumer energies on finding a good deal, even if that sometimes meant a lower-quality product or disappointing performance.

Clothing Maintenance

Connected to women's skeptical perceptions of the apparel industry's practices and products was a reluctance to invest time or money in maintaining products with mending or alterations. Repairs were relegated to primarily special or favorite items. Eunice paid for upkeep on her favorite leather accessories, but discarded clothes when her size changed. Torn or worn items regularly ended up in landfills, because they were not worth repairing or their owners lacked the appropriate skills. As Zoe reported, "If it was a tear in the actual fabric, then I would probably [pause], I probably don't have the skill to mend that." Unaware of or unwilling to invest in invisible or creative patching, several participants avoided mending projects because they believed it would lower the aesthetic quality of a garment. "I think there's like a casual jean where you could, like, mend them, and it would be part of the style of them. . . . But it wasn't my style," observed Eunice.

Participants' reluctance to engage in these practices may also have been an effort to resist a domestic identity, as Lanser (1993) found. Tina expressed it this way: "I don't really like doing that sort of thing, you know. It's a little more domestic stuff [laughs] than I'm interested in doing." Despite their contribution to caring practices and family life, domestic chores from shopping to laundering to mending continue to be feminized, marginalized, and devalued (Laermans and Meulders 1999; Oakley 1974; Strasser 1982). Moreover, this idealized and domesticated feminine private sphere perpetuates real and symbolic sites of oppression (Lanser 1993; Oakley 1974). Additionally, rational, efficient consumption and domestic practices, promoted in part by twentieth-century home economists and others, have increased women's emotional labor of managing work both inside and outside the home, a phenomenon that Hochschild (2001) termed the "third shift" (also see Goldstein 2012).

A Knowledge and Skills Gap

The interviews revealed a dichotomy of attitudes about sewing and fashion. As Hanson (1990) also observed, participants in my study mirrored cultural stereotypes trivializing and feminizing apparel consumption. Felicity and Niki described looking at fashion magazines or watching fashion television shows as their "guilty pleasures" or something a "serious mom oughta not be doing." Jessica associated needing mending skills with a future domestic life, not her current professional one. She said, "How much time and energy do I want to devote to something like that? I can pay somebody else to do that. But I think it might be one of those things, maybe like in a different stage in my life, where, like, maybe, if I had kids or something, I would want to learn how to do that." Contrastingly, some women enjoyed these skills because of the distinction and aesthetic pleasure they afforded. For example, Niki reported, "There's that special sort of pride of ownership that I *made* this. While I was at this party, where I was wearing it [a hand-knit sweater], people were like, 'That's lovely. Where'd you get it?' 'I made it.' So it's nice to make something and to feel good about wearing it."

The absence of language to talk about clothing creation and care might be a symptom of an overall lack of product knowledge and expertise—less often taught in homes or schools now—that was available to women of earlier generations. Norum (2013) found that having clothing maintenance skills, including sewing, was more prevalent among the older generations, the Baby Boomers and Generation X, compared to Generation Y (ages eighteen to thirty-eight). In the early twenty-first century, only a quarter of secondary school students took home economics courses. Additionally, these programs varied from general life skills to more vocationally oriented content, such as popular culinary arts courses, and did not necessarily cover apparel (Werhan and Way 2006). Goldstein (2012) has suggested that home economists emphasized women's roles as "domestic consumers" rather than "homemakers," emphasizing marketplace rather than maintenance skills.

Most women in my study had no formal consumer or apparel training. Felicity was one of several who struck out on her own to find sewing classes and knitting circles, primarily for the pleasurable, sensual process; the expressive, unique products; and the intimate friendships—and less because of concerns about environmental abuses or labor exploitation in the garment industry.

Patterns of Sustainable Clothing Practices

Individual consumers, educators, designers, and others in the apparel industry can harness existing behaviors to craft ecological and ethical practices. These behaviors reduce the consumption of energy, water, resources, materials, and unwanted, unsatisfying, poor-quality garments (see table 8.1). The specific clothing practices fall into four categories of behavior across the clothing life cycle stages.

Women in my study variously engaged in some of these practices. However, they sometimes perceived barriers of limited time, money, skills, and quality options, especially given their goals to have positive embodied, multisensory aesthetic experiences and to use clothing to symbolically communicate their tastes, identities, and social roles. Expanding individuals' consumer, textile, and apparel skills can help women identify, talk about, and maintain quality apparel in their wardrobes. Perhaps providing girls and young women (and boys and young men) with knowledge about textiles and the economy, as well

TABLE 8.1. Clothing Practices for Sustainable Consumption

Acquire	Wear and Use	Store and Maintain	Dispose
■ Purchase sustainably produced apparel	■ Wear clothes that can be adapted to different sizes	■ Wash less frequently	■ Wear until completely worn
■ Acquire fewer items	■ Repurpose clothes to different uses if quality changes	■ Spot clean	■ Reduce number of garments discarded
■ Invest in physically and stylistically long-lasting pieces		■ Use less water, soap, and other products	
	■ Wear clothes that fit personality, not latest trends	■ Avoid dry cleaning	■ Avoid putting clothes in trash
■ Share or swap clothes		■ Air dry	
■ Buy secondhand or vintage garments	■ Wear patched or mended clothes	■ Mend invisibly or visibly	■ Reuse textiles, materials, and components
■ Consider making garments or collaborating with designers and makers	■ Wear multiple times before cleaning	■ Alter or customize instead of discarding	■ Recycle or compost materials
	■ Wear what you own	■ Learn or improve sewing, mending, and alteration skills	■ Donate clothes if still wearable
		■ Use mending or alteration services	

Across Clothing Life Cycle Changes
■ Be mindful of consumption experiences, including multisensory aesthetic pleasures, connections to people and places, and impact on environment and others' well-being
■ Value and respect materials, resources, energy, and labor embedded in garments and care

as sewing and maintenance skills, would also foster understanding of the social and environmental impacts of consumer choices. Combining these ecological and ethical purchasing and care practices with emotionally durable, qualitative experiences could go far in transforming our clothing consumption's impact (Chapman 2005). Women's stories about mindfully, thoughtfully, and creatively learning textile skills and engaging with garments revealed how through these activities they also fostered positive multisensory aesthetic experiences, restyled garments to fit their bodies and personalities, mended favorite dresses to extend their life, cultivated social relationships, and participated in creative practices.

Felicity's story about why she attended sewing classes captures a resurgence of interest in domestic arts, which is often associated with a pursuit of self-sufficient, meaningful livelihoods and a rejection of consumer culture (Coyne and Knutzen 2010; Hayes 2010; Matchar 2013). In refashioning the clothing life cycle into a closed-loop system that builds on and extends these objectives, we can seek to design products that enable needs-fulfilling, high-quality consumption practices; produce them in ways that support the well-being of workers and environments; consume them in ways that extend their usable life; and transform used garments into restyled garments or reusable raw materials (Fletcher 2008; McDonough and Braungart 2002).

Repairing Relationships Between Consumption and Sustainability

Women's stories about quality direct our attention to aesthetic, affective, and subjective experiences as factors in sustainable practices. Home economics can bring these topics into sustainability initiatives and help to answer—in theory and practice—the following questions: What if we attended to the interlocking relations between ourselves, our clothing, other people, and the environment? What if we made consumption choices based not on lowest price points but on high-quality apparel that supports the well-being of our family as well as the environment and the other people on which that well-being depends? How can we teach skills and ways of thinking *about* and *for* sustainability, within and outside of formal education settings, in collaborative and participatory projects? (Stibbe 2009).

In some ways, the emphasis on individual consumption perpetuates the individualization and domestication of problems and solutions, shifting accountability away from industry (Maniates 2002). For example, focusing on learning and applying skills suggests that it is the consumer's responsibility to evaluate product quality, purchase organic and fairly traded T-shirts, spend time and money customizing jeans, and care for garments in individualized domestic contexts. Although home economics may appear to reinforce individualized solutions in domestic settings, the discipline gives us a framework through which to understand and move beyond historically and culturally gendered-female skills, and to personalize issues without individualizing their solutions. A life cycle, systems approach expands the conversation and solutions to ways the apparel industry, retailers, marketers, policy makers, and educators can create social and physical environments that foster individual, environmentally sustainable, conscious behaviors (Kolodinsky 2012).

Home economics' conventional association with skills education can help position individuals as global citizens able to cultivate respect for mutual interdependencies (Dewhurst and Pendergast 2011; Elias 2008; Pendergast 2003). Moreover, home economics research, education, and outreach initiatives can reinvigorate how we value labor—in the home and in the garment factory. Connecting otherwise unseen, unarticulated clothing practices with their broader political contexts; grounding them in everyday practices; and decoupling skills from gender, race, and class could help normalize them as "sometimes necessary, sometimes pleasurable, and sometimes onerous work worthy of respectable status and, when performed for wages, respectable reward" (Lanser 1993, 50).

Home economists have been historically involved in teaching consumer skills, cultivating aesthetic sensibilities, and exploring the interdependencies of environmental and social systems (Elias 2008; Goldstein 2012; Stage and Vincenti 1997). Nevertheless, in much sustainable consumption literature, home economics is absent from the discussion. Perhaps it is because gendered-female applied knowledge often has been marginalized (Pendergast 2003). Or perhaps it is because home economists have not gone far enough in examining the values, beliefs, and meanings that underlie unsustainable consumption behaviors (Dewhurst and Pendergast 2011; Hill and Solheim 1993). Sustainability researchers continue to put out the call to address the emotional and cultural dimensions of behavior in order to understand why people persist in making harmful choices (Gibson and Stanes 2011; Maniates 2002). By framing sustainable clothing systems within the aesthetic, affective, and subjective dimensions of assessing and maintaining apparel quality, this chapter reaffirms the continued role home economics can play, and the leadership role the discipline's theorists, researchers, and educators should assume in crafting a sustainable future.

ACKNOWLEDGMENTS

This work was supported in part by an Emerging Scholar Fellowship I received at the multidisciplinary conference "Home Economics: Classroom, Corporate, and Cultural Interpretations Revisited" (University of Georgia, 2012). Funds were also received from the Department of Design Studies and the School of Human Ecology, University of Wisconsin, Madison. I would like to thank the nineteen women who generously opened their homes and shared their stories with me. I thank the editors of this volume, Sharon Y. Nickols and Gwen Kay, for their suggestions for the chapter, and my academic advisor, Beverly Gordon, for her support throughout the research process. In addition, thanks to the senior and fellow emerging scholars at the 2012 conference for their comments and conversations about this work and the field of home economics.

NOTES

1. I collected these data between November 2010 and January 2012 through semi-structured interviews, ethnographic observations during home visits, and material culture object studies, combining fieldwork observations with in-depth interviews that followed a "levels of abstraction" model (moving from concrete examples to reflection) (Patton 2002). The participants were nineteen women (ages twenty-four to seventy; two Asian American and seventeen Euro American) from the greater Madison, Wisconsin, area. The interviews, two with each woman, were recorded and transcribed. Following a heuristic model of grounded theory (Charmaz 2006), I identified themes and coded the corresponding interview sections. Participants are referred to by pseudonyms.

2. I developed this model based on previous work by Dresner (2002), IUCN/UNEP/WWF (1991), Held (2006), Jackson (2006), Max-Neef, Elizalde, and Hopenhayn (1991), and others.

3. I developed this model based on previous work by Fletcher (2008), Leonard (2010), McDonough and Braungart (2002), and others.

REFERENCES

Allwood, Julian M., Søren Ellebæk Laursen, Cecilia Malvido de Rodríguez, and Nancy M. P. Bocken. 2006. *Well Dressed? The Present and Future Sustainability of Clothing and Textiles in the United Kingdom.* Cambridge: Institute for Manufacturing.

Browne, Anthony. 2011. "Accumulation of Microplastic on Shorelines World Wide: Sources and Sinks." *Environmental Science and Technology* 45(21): 9175–9179.

Carrigan, Marylyn, and Ahmad Atalla. 2001. "The Myth of the Ethical Consumer: Do Ethics Matter in Purchase Behavior?" *Journal of Consumer Marketing* 18(7): 560–577.

Chapman, Jonathan. 2005. *Emotionally Durable Design: Objects, Experiences, and Empathy.* London: Earthscan.

Charmaz, Kathy. 2006. *Constructing Grounded Theory: A Practical Guide Through Qualitative Analysis.* Los Angeles: Sage.

Coyne, Kelly, and Erik Knutzen. 2010. *Making It: Radical Home Ec for a Post-Consumer World.* New York: Rodale.

Dewhurst, Yvonne, and Donna Pendergast. 2011. "Teacher Perceptions of the Contribution of Home Economics to Sustainable Development Education: A Cross-Cultural View." *International Journal of Consumer Studies* 35(5): 569–577.

Dresner, Simon. 2002. *The Principles of Sustainability.* London: Earthscan.

Elias, Megan. 2008. *Stir It Up: Home Economics in American Culture.* Philadelphia: University of Pennsylvania Press.

Fletcher, Kate. 2008. *Sustainable Fashion and Textiles: Design Journeys.* London: Earthscan.

Gibson, Chris, and Elyse Stanes. 2011. "Is Green the New Black? Exploring Ethical Fashion Consumption." In *Ethical Consumption: A Critical Introduction*, edited by Tania Lewis and Emily Potter, 169–185. New York: Routledge.

Goldstein, Carolyn M. 2012. *Creating Consumers: Home Economists in Twentieth-Century America.* Chapel Hill: University of North Carolina Press.

Guagnano, Gregory A., Paul C. Stern, and Thomas Dietz. 1995. "Influences on Attitude-Behavior Relationships: A National Experiment with Curbside Recycling." *Environment and Behavior* 27(5): 699–718.

Hansen, Karen Tranberg. 2000. *Salaula: The World of Secondhand Clothing and Zambia.* Chicago: University of Chicago Press.

Hanson, Karen. 1990. "Dressing Down, Dressing Up: The Philosophic Fear of Fashion." *Hypatia* 5(2): 107–121.

Hayes, Shannon. 2010. *Radical Homemakers: Reclaiming Domesticity from a Consumer Culture.* Richmondville, N.Y.: Left to Write Press.

Held, Virginia. 2006. *The Ethics of Care: Personal, Political, and Global.* Oxford: Oxford University Press.

Hill, Paulette P., and Catherine Solheim. 1993. "Home Economists as

Environmentalists: Setting a Research Agenda." In *Cross Cultural Approaches to Home Management*, edited by Rosemarie von Schweitzer, 51–64. New York: Westview.

Hochschild, Arlie Russell. 2001. *The Time Bind: When Work Becomes Home and Home Becomes Work*. New York: Holt.

IUCN/UNEP/WWF. 1991. *Caring for the Earth: A Strategy for Sustainable Living*. Gland, Switzerland: IUCN.

Jackson, Tim. 2006. "Readings in Sustainable Consumption." In *The Earthscan Reader in Sustainable Consumption*, edited by Tim Jackson, 1–23. London: Earthscan.

Joergens, Catrin. 2006. "Ethical Fashion: Myth or Future Trend?" *Journal of Fashion Marketing and Management* 10(3): 360–371.

Kasser, Tim. 2003. *The High Price of Materialism*. Cambridge, Mass.: MIT Press.

Kennedy, E. H., T. M. Beckley, B. L. McFarlane, and S. Nadeau. 2009. "Why We Don't 'Walk the Talk': Understanding the Environmental Values/Behaviour Gap in Canada." *Human Ecology Review* 16(2): 151.

Kim, Soyoung, Mary A. Littrell, and Jennifer L. Paff Ogle. 1999. "The Relative Importance of Social Responsibility as a Predictor of Purchase Intentions for Clothing." *Journal of Fashion Marketing and Management* 3(3): 207–218.

Kolodinsky, Jane. 2012. "A Systems Approach to Food Future Proofs the Home Economics Profession." In *Creating Home Economics Futures: The Next 100 Years*, edited by Donna Pendergast, Sue L. T. McGregor, and Kaija Turkki, 157–169. Bowen Hills: Australia Academic Press.

Laermans, Rudi, and Carine Meulders. 1999. "The Domestication of Laundering." In *At Home: An Anthropology of Domestic Space*, edited by Irene Cieraad, 118–129. Syracuse, N.Y.: Syracuse University Press.

Lanser, Susan S. 1993. "Burning Dinners: Feminist Subversions of Domesticity." In *Feminist Messages: Coding in Women's Folk Culture*, edited by Joan Newlon Radner, 36–53. Urbana: University of Illinois Press.

Leonard, Annie. 2010. *The Story of Stuff: How Our Obsession with Stuff Is Trashing the Planet, Our Communities, and Our Health—and a Vision for Change*. New York: Free Press.

Maniates, Michael. 2002. "Individualization: Plant a Tree, Buy a Bike, Save the World?" In *Confronting Consumption*, edited by Thomas Princen, Michael Maniates, and Ken Conca, 43–66. Cambridge, Mass.: MIT Press.

Matchar, Emily. 2013. *Homeward Bound: Why Women Are Embracing the New Domesticity*. New York: Simon and Schuster.

Max-Neef, Manfred A., Antonio Elizalde, and Martín Hopenhayn. 1991. *Human Scale Development: Conception, Application and Further Reflections*. New York: Apex.

McDonough, William, and Michael Braungart. 2002. *Cradle to Cradle: Remaking the Way We Make Things*. New York: North Point.

McKenzie-Mohr, Doug, and William Smith. 1999. *Fostering Sustainable Behavior: An Introduction to Community-Based Social Marketing*. Gabriola Island, B.C.: New Society.

Norum, Pamela S. 2013. "Examination of Apparel Maintenance Skills and Practices: Implications for Sustainable Clothing Consumption." *Family and Consumer Sciences Research Journal* 42(2): 124–137.

Oakley, Ann. 1974. *The Sociology of Housework*. New York: Pantheon.

Patton, Michael Quinn. 2002. *Qualitative Research and Evaluation Methods*, 3rd ed. Thousand Oaks, Calif.: Sage.

Pendergast, Donna. 2003. "From the Margins: Globalization With(out) Home Economics." *International Journal of Consumer Studies* 27(4): 331–334.

Rosen, Ellen Israel. 2002. *Making Sweatshops: The Globalization of the U.S. Apparel Industry*. Berkeley: University of California Press.

Ross, Andrew, ed. 1997. *No Sweat: Fashion, Free Trade, and the Rights of Garment Workers*. New York: Verso.

Rudell, Frederica. 2006. "Shopping with a Social Conscience: Consumer Attitudes Toward Sweatshop Labor." *Clothing and Textiles Research Journal* 24(4): 282–296.

Schor, Juliet. 1999. *The Overspent American: Why We Want What We Don't Need*. New York: HarperPerennial.

Stage, Sarah, and Virginia B. Vincenti, eds. 1997. *Rethinking Home Economics: Women and the History of a Profession*. Ithaca, N.Y.: Cornell University Press.

Stern, Paul C., Thomas Dietz, Troy Abel, Gregory A. Guangnano, and Linda Kalof. 1999. "A Value-Belief-Norm Theory of Support for Social Movements: The Case of Environmentalism." *Human Ecology Review* 6(2): 81–97.

Stibbe, Arran. 2009. *The Handbook of Sustainability Literacy: Skills for a Changing World*. Totnes, England: Green Books.

Strasser, Susan. 1982. *Never Done: A History of American Housework*. New York: Pantheon.

Valor, Carmen. 2007. "The Influence of Information About Labour Abuses on Consumer Choice of Clothes: A Grounded Theory Approach." *Journal of Marketing Management* 23(7–8): 675–695.

Welters, Linda. 2008. "The Fashion of Sustainability." In *Sustainable Fashion: Why Now? A Conversation About Issues, Practices, and Possibilities*, edited by Janet Hethorn and Connie Ulasewicz, 7–29. New York: Fairchild.

Werhan, Carol, and Wendy L. Way. 2006. "Family and Consumer Sciences Programs in Secondary Schools: Results of a National Survey." *Journal of Family and Consumer Sciences* 98(1): 19–25.

Zepeda, Lydia, and David Deal. 2009. "Organic and Local Food Consumer Behavior: Alphabet Theory." *International Journal of Consumer Studies* 33(6): 697–705.

III. Race and Gender in Home Economics Careers

The chapters in this part explore the intersections of institutional settings, employment, race, and gender as experienced by home economists, as well as the potential of home economics to influence the expansion of career opportunities for girls and women. While there has been extensive study of gender segregation in the workforce, of the influence of race in academic and employment settings, and of the efficacy of policies to address these issues, most research was at the macroeconomic or societal level, and none of it included home economics. The following three chapters attend to aspects of these intersections, seeking to understand critical points where gender and race impact home economics as a field of study and home economists themselves.

In chapter 9, "'It Was a Special Time': African American Deans of Family and Consumer Sciences in Predominantly White, Comprehensive Universities," Penny A. Ralston chronicles the experiences and insights of three African American women who were home economics academic deans between 1987 and 2004. This was a barrier-breaking period in the late twentieth century. Throughout its history, the mission of home economics has been inclusive and universal; however, the contributions of people from diverse backgrounds have received limited attention. This chapter, which uses oral histories, adds to the story of the evolution of home economics from a history of discrimination to a field that values diversity in top leadership positions.

Chapter 10, "'Cookin' with Gas': Home Economists in the Atlanta Natural Gas Industry, 1950–1995" by Sharon Y. Nickols, is based on interviews with home economists employed by the Atlanta Gas Light Company during the last half of the twentieth century. These home economists were liaisons between the company and consumers; they pioneered televised cooking programs, held leadership roles, and represented the company in the community. The specialization of their work virtually guaranteed that it would be gender-segregated. Demand for home economics graduates in the natural gas industry was strong through the 1980s; however, changes in the economy and deregulation of the natural gas industry led to the elimination of these jobs.

In chapter 11, "Science Matters: Home Economics and STEM Fields of Study," Peggy S. Meszaros traces the life of Ellen H. Richards from her education as a chemist through her career as a researcher, educator, author, and organizer in the home economics movement. Overcoming many obstacles facing women during the mid-nineteenth century, Richards is still a role model for today's girls and women facing cultural and social constraints. Meszaros describes the Appalachian Information Technology Extension Services (AITES) program that she designed to foster cultural change and to address the science, technology, engineering, and mathematics (STEM) talent crisis on a regional basis. While the content of AITES is new, the delivery system is based on the classic model of Cooperative Extension (described in chapter 2), which provides information and leadership for transformative community change.

9. "It Was a Special Time"

African American Deans of Home Economics in Predominantly White, Comprehensive Universities, 1987–2004

PENNY A. RALSTON

Historically and currently, home economics is a field of study concerned with the quality of life of individuals, families, and communities. Although the mission of the field is inclusive and universal, the actual involvement of people from diverse backgrounds has been uneven with regard to professionals and those whom they serve. Home economics has been disparaged for its lack of inclusion of people of color and of males (Vincenti 1997). In particular, the field has been criticized historically for discriminatory practices in professional organizations and for the training-oriented curricula offered at Black colleges and universities (Ralston 1978). Yet, strides have been made over the years to rectify these problems, including the development of African American leaders who have served in key positions in higher education institutions and in professional societies, such as the presidencies of the American Association of Family and Consumer Sciences, the Council of Administrators of Family and Consumer Sciences, and the Board on Human Sciences. How the field evolved from discrimination to vaulting African Americans to positions of power and prestige is a fascinating story.

One untold aspect is how African Americans secured top leadership positions as deans in home economics units in predominantly White institutions. African American deans of home economics in predominantly Black institutions—such as Flemmie Kittrell at Howard University—were well known for their leadership during the formative years of the field (Ralston 1994). Yet there were no African Americans in leadership roles in major land-grant and comprehensive research institutions until the late 1980s. Between 1987 and 2004 four African Americans served as deans of home economics units in comprehensive universities. Three are highlighted in this chapter: Esther Fahm, Julia Miller, and Retia Walker. The fourth dean is Penny Ralston, the author of this chapter. Due to the historical, cultural, and gender contexts of this period, serving in these key positions placed African American deans in the spotlight. The purpose of this chapter is to examine the leadership opportunities and challenges, governance and management strategies, and professional achievements of these deans during their tenures as administrators.

Esther Fahm served as dean of the School of Home Economics at the University of Wisconsin, Stout (UW-Stout) from 1990 to 1996. Julia Miller was dean of the College of Human Ecology at Michigan State University (MSU) from 1987 to 2004. Retia Walker held the dean's position at the College of Human Environmental Sciences at the University of Kentucky (UK) from 1994 to 2002. Interviews with the three deans provided insights regarding the similarities and uniqueness of each woman's experience. A review of documents, as well as interviews with selected faculty, staff, and former students at each institution provided perspectives regarding the institutional contexts and the perceptions of stakeholders.[1]

Higher Education Context

The recruitment and selection of African American deans in home economics in the 1980s and 1990s reflected the broader social forces of the civil rights and women's movements in the 1960s and 1970s. Universities, like other societal institutions, developed nondiscrimination policies and practices to break down race and gender barriers (Bowen and Bok 1998). In reality, universities remained places dominated by White men (May, Moorhouse, and Bossard 2010). In response, higher education institutions began developing special programs to encourage diversity not only in the faculty ranks but also in administrative positions. This occurred at the three institutions where the deans of home economics became employed: UW-Stout had an emphasis on diversity at the system level (E. Fahm, pers. comm.); MSU had a series of platforms, or cross-disciplinary priority areas, and diversity was one of these platforms (J. Miller, pers. comm.); and UK had diversity as a priority, perhaps to rectify its historical slowness in improving race and gender equity (R. Walker, pers. comm.; see also Todd 2002 on UK's Commission on the Status of Women). Because diversity was a priority in these three universities, leaders employed aggressive techniques to ensure a diverse pool in their deanship searches.

A "dean" can be defined as a person with significant authority over an academic unit or a specific area of concern in an educational institution. In comprehensive universities, deans have significant power to shape the direction of their respective disciplines and are expected to assertively advocate for their units by employing effective strategies to compete for university resources. Deans must be respected scholars and provide leadership for academic programs. At the same time, deans must relate to students and work effectively with external groups, including alumni, donors, and industry leaders. The search for a new dean for an academic unit is a rigorous process in which candidates are vetted thoroughly by a variety of stakeholders.

For the three deans who are the focus of this chapter, the search process was typically exhaustive. Getting the candidates into the pool was the first challenge. The initial recruitment contacts were met with skepticism by all three women. They were well aware of the normative strategy used by search committees: ensuring that the pool was diverse but not being truly serious about diversity in the hiring process (Aguirre 2001). Retia Walker was contacted twice by members of the search committee for the deanship at UK, but she told them she was not interested (R. Walker, pers. comm.). Julia Miller was nominated for the position, but was conducting research in Kenya when the first contact was made. The search committee attempted to track her down while she was out of the country (J. Miller, pers. comm.). In contrast, Esther Fahm was looking to relocate in Wisconsin to be closer to her husband, who had accepted a position at UW-Plattsville. Although she saw the announcement for the position at UW-Stout, she initially did not think about applying for it (E. Fahm, pers. comm.).

What happened next in all three cases was a sincere effort on the part of the universities to encourage these women to submit applications. Miller was intrigued that someone from MSU wanted to find out where she was in Africa. She then learned that MSU had a diversity platform spearheaded by the provost (J. Miller, pers. comm.). Walker was personally recruited by the UK chancellor, a scholar of African American literature. He shared with her that he had contacted the American Home Economics Association (AHEA) and asked Gladys Gary Vaughn, a well-known African American scholar and AHEA administrator, for the names of possible candidates. This convinced Walker to apply because, as she recalled, "The AHEA contact showed his seriousness" (R. Walker, pers. comm.). In Fahm's case, the advertisement for the deanship at UW-Stout was brought to her attention by her husband's department chair at UW-Plattsville, who informed her that the Wisconsin university system had diversity as a priority. Miller, who by then was in the deanship at MSU, encouraged Fahm to apply (E. Fahm, pers. comm.).

The relationships between Fahm, Miller, and Walker had been established as a result of all three serving as chairs of home economics units at historically Black universities. Fahm was the chair at Alcorn State University (1982–1990), Miller at Virginia State University (1974–1986), and Walker at the University of Maryland, Eastern Shore (1983–1994). All three were active in the 1890 Administrators of Home Economics organization and had collaborated on the 1890 regional research project, "Quality of Well-Being of the Rural South-

PHOTO 9.1. Julia R. Miller. Photograph by Okemos
Studio of Photography.

ern Elderly—Food, Clothing and Shelter," funded by the U.S. Department of
Agriculture.

Miller was the first of these African American women to be recruited as
dean, joining MSU in 1987. She relied on the support of family to help make the
decision to take the position (J. Miller, pers. comm.). Both Fahm and Walker
looked to Miller for advice and support during the search process. Fahm trav-
eled to East Lansing to visit Miller, who gave her guidance on preparing the
application and later provided coaching regarding how to handle the interview process (E. Fahm, pers. comm.). Walker sought advice from Miller and
from Ralston, who was serving as dean at Florida State University, especially
after the offer was made and the negotiations began (R. Walker, pers. comm.).

All three of these women made the cut after an initial screening of appli-
cants, were successfully interviewed, and perceived a welcoming environment during this process. What followed was a quick progression where offers were made, negotiations handled, and details of appointments finalized.
They reported that their offers were substantial. For example, all received full
professor status and competitive salaries. Two negotiated funds for facility
renovations. A third was able to negotiate two faculty lines and assurance of
support for a doctoral program that had been put on hold, along with other
programs, at the system level.

Although the recruitment process went smoothly, some of the challenges
these deans would face during their tenures as administrators were revealed.
Fahm had discussed with the provost resource allocations and the direction
he saw for academic units at the university; however, the provost left for an-

PHOTO 9.2. Retia Scott Walker. Photograph by Tim Collins of ProImaging for the University of Kentucky, School of Human Environmental Sciences.

other position before she arrived (E. Fahm, pers. comm.). She also learned during the interview process that there were some historical internal issues in the unit. In reflection, she observed, "Wish I had asked more questions [to] understand the issues" (E. Fahm, pers. comm.). Similarly, Walker learned soon after arriving at UK that the chancellor was taking a position at another university; she was "disappointed he was not there during [my] first year of adjustment" (R. Walker, pers. comm.).

In contrast, MSU's provost, whom Miller felt was quite dynamic, stayed in the position for seven years. Miller said that under his leadership, "it was a special time" at MSU. Yet internal issues dogged the home economics unit, and she recalled that she had been cautioned by a few people to think carefully about whether to take the position (J. Miller, pers. comm.). In all three cases, however, these deans put their challenges in the context of typical issues in higher education and saw the opportunity to lead their respective units as an important next step for the profession and their careers.

Leadership: Opportunities and Challenges

Leading as a dean is a complex process of assessing needs internally and externally, determining goals and priorities, developing strategies and tactics, and taking action. Deans learn early on that as this process unfolds, there are opportunities that should be seized as needs are assessed. Yet, even with opportunities, the process must be handled with the thorough support of and aligned action from others. Department heads, faculty, staff, students, and alumni must, in essence, be on the same page. In reality, this process is fraught with the competing interests of stakeholders, thus contributing to the challenges of leading as a dean.

For these three deans, the opportunities were similar. The development of funding, curricula, and programs were the key areas where all reported being successful in advancing their units. Fundraising was a university priority at all the institutions, and securing nonstate sources of support for their units was essential for viability. Fahm discussed how the funding formula at her institution was based mostly on teaching productivity, which resulted in year-to-year fluctuations in allocations. Securing private funds allowed her to provide enhancements for students and faculty, including student development experiences, scholarships, and faculty development activities. She was particularly proud of being able to establish a minority scholarship fund and to garner $1 million for an endowed chair (E. Fahm, pers. comm.). Similarly, at UK, fundraising was tied to the university's quest to become a top tier research university. Walker's fundraising efforts resulted in more than $2 million for fellowships, scholarships, and four endowed professorships, each matched with state funds (R. Walker, pers. comm.).

Miller also focused on private giving and as part of the Campaign for MSU (2003) set a multimillion-dollar goal for the college. She raised $8 million toward the $12 million goal. In addition, she prioritized increasing research funding. MSU tied external funding, especially federal funding, to keeping its Association of American Universities status. Miller was concerned with the ebb and flow of research dollars in her unit and wanted to see more stability. She instituted a faculty partners program where selected faculty received intense training on obtaining federal funding. The $50,000 she secured as "seed funds" resulted in a return of $1.4 million in federal contracts and grants after the first year of the program (J. Miller, pers. comm.).

With regard to curriculum/program development, all three deans were able to sustain most of their academic programs and develop new initiatives. Fahm, working with faculty, developed a new program in service management, a four-year degree curriculum to provide leadership in the service industry. The only other program of its kind at the time was at Harvard University (E. Fahm, pers. comm.). Walker secured approval for a PhD program in family studies, a master's degree program in hospitality and dietetics administration, and a 2+2 program in early childhood education in conjunction with a community college in Lexington (R. Walker, pers. comm.). Miller expanded the Institute for Children, Youth and Families by hiring a nationally acclaimed scholar. She also was instrumental in MSU joining the Great Plains Interactive Distance Education Alliance for an online master's program in youth develop-

PHOTO 9.3. Esther Fahm with students, 1993. Photograph courtesy University of Wisconsin, Stout Archives.

ment, and she established the university's first online program, which offered a certificate in facilities management and could be accessed internationally (J. Miller, pers. comm.).

Two of the deans, Miller and Fahm, expanded international programs for their units. Miller, who already had significant experience in international work in countries in Africa, shifted her focus to Asia upon her arrival at MSU due to the university's established master's program in community service at the Kadena Air Base in Okinawa, Japan (J. Miller, pers. comm.). She grew this program by establishing a study-abroad program wherein students from Okinawa studied at MSU. In addition, Miller hired an associate dean who provided an international thrust for the college. Fahm (pers. comm.) continued an existing exchange program with a higher education institution in Monterrey, Mexico, and explored relationships with universities in Cuba.

The recruitment of faculty and students that resulted in greater diversity was an important achievement for Miller and Walker. When she arrived at MSU, Miller and two Asian Americans were the only faculty of color in the college (J. Miller, pers. comm.). Among the faculty she hired during her tenure, five were from diverse backgrounds. She secured a grant from the provost to work with historically Black colleges and universities on student recruitment. Miller summed up these efforts by saying that she always asked herself while serving as dean, "What is it that I could do for my people?"

In the same vein, the diversification of faculty and staff, especially the recruitment of African Americans, was a priority for Walker (pers. comm.). When she arrived at UK, there were four faculty and one staff member of African descent in her unit. When she left the deanship, there were six faculty and three staff members of African descent (*Research and Faculty Expertise* n.d.). Fahm (pers. comm.) was able to sustain an exchange program with Tuskegee University, a historically Black institution.

Other singular achievements were Fahm's collaboration with other UW-Stout deans on the university's initiative to evaluate the scholarship of teaching. Walker established the Hall of Fame to recognize alumni, launched Human Environmental Sciences Week to promote the unit through lectures and other activities, and instituted a faculty and staff recognition program. All three deans also were instrumental in continuing specialized accreditations for academic programs, furthering student development through enhancing student governance, and developing undergraduate research programs.

The challenges faced by the three deans were similar, including internal relations in the academic unit, financial support for the unit, and reorganization in the university. Internal relationships, especially among faculty, are not an unusual challenge for academic deans and have been described by Aguirre (2001): "the academic workplace is characterized by group struggles over the definition of knowledge and about what it means to be a knowledgeable person. To survive in the academic workplace, faculty members must align themselves with and participate in institutional networks that define one's position in a knowledge hierarchy."

For home economics units, which have been predominantly female, the pressures to remain viable are well documented (Bailey et al. 1993; Haley, Peggram, and Ley 1993; Nerad 1999; Rossiter 1997). As described by Miller, "There was often the [internal] fear of 'takeover.'" The internal struggles in home economics units could manifest as competing disciplines and individuals fighting for respect in the broader university, competing against each other for scarce resources within the academic unit, and combating the fear that the university would not find them worthy to remain as a unit or, worse yet, exist at all. Managing these internal struggles in the context of broader university priorities became one of the key challenges for all three deans, although they each viewed these issues differently.

Fahm perceived the internal relationship issues in the context of the leadership styles of previous administrations. Her goal was to restore trust. Miller viewed the internal relationships in her unit as human resource issues where networks of faculty operated without communicating with her and in some instances appeared to purposefully undermine her. Walker perceived the internal relationships at UK from the standpoint of racism since the university, and more broadly the state of Kentucky, was still attempting to improve race relations. Having been raised in the segregated South, Walker felt she was able to "read" people and their actions. Sharing how she perceives racism, she stated, "I notice how people act and react to experiences. I'm sensitive to this" (R. Walker, pers. comm.). She viewed various incidents and actions as subtle rather than overt racism.

As a second challenge, the financial pressures on the home economics units of the three deans were significant. Fahm shared that the funding formula at UW-Stout, which she viewed as "inflexible," led to financial instability in her unit. For example, a faculty position was lost after the first year of her deanship. She then worked strategically to improve funding by establishing service courses and initiating external fundraising. Walker discussed the disproportionately limited resource allocations to her unit, which she viewed as historical and political. She stated, "The issue was not about [our college's] productivity in enrollment, retention, and fundraising. I spent so much time trying to demonstrate productivity" (R. Walker, pers. comm.). Yet the traditional allocation of resources to the College of Human Environmental Sciences prevailed. This is a typical struggle for home economics units, especially those in land-grant universities where agriculture, engineering, and other male-dominated programs have historically been the power base on campuses (Vincenti 1997). For Miller, the financial issues were generally related to maintaining stable external grant funding.

The third and biggest challenge for all three deans was reorganization in their universities, which in the end resulted in major changes in how the home economics programs were configured in the institutions. In general, reorganization in higher education is a result of external pressures to meet efficiency expectations, often driven by the economic climate in a given geographical area with action taken at the central administrative level (Gumport 2000; Olson 2010). Yet, in home economics, the faculty and administrators often perceived reorganization as a threat to the viability of the field (Firebaugh et al. 2010; Haley, Peggram, and Ley 1993). In other words, it was believed that units would be separated in order to break up or dismantle home economics as a unified discipline on campus.

Home economics units were vulnerable to reorganization for a variety of reasons. During the 1980s and 1990s, home economics was increasingly becoming a field of specialities. Qualified faculty for research positions were often hired with degrees in these specialities, and they sometimes lacked a philosophical viewpoint consistent with home economics. Professional accreditations further created autonomy in specialized programs, and units were not always successful in incorporating the focus of these programs into a coherent conceptual framework. Moreover, communicating this "new" home economics to faculty, students, and external decision makers could be challenging. Thus, a lack of conceptual clarity and clear communication about the interdependence of various areas of study within home economics made units vulnerable (Vincenti 1997). And to be fair, given the specialization of programs, some reorganization might on the surface have made sense conceptually (e.g., marriage and family therapy could be joined with social work, or human nutrition with animal nutrition). Yet the underpinnings of home economics—its focus on individuals, families, and communities in the context of well-being or the quality of life—was clearly understood and promoted by higher education organizations in the field (Simerly et al. 2000). Further, how the reorganizations affected the African American deans featured in this chapter demonstrates the political nature of these actions.

Each reorganization began as a directive from the university's key leader. At UW-Stout, the reorganization was a top-down mandate from the chancellor (E. Fahm, pers. comm.). Prior to the restructuring, there were four academic schools; his mandate was to reorganize into three colleges. Fahm reported that the chancellor engaged the faculty senate to develop a university model for the reorganization. At MSU, a new president, who had worked in central administration and was hired after an internal search, announced the reorganization (J. Miller, pers. comm.). However, Miller felt that the announcement seemed to be a "smoke screen" for eliminating the home economics unit. She stated, "I have been told [by] people who retired that the culture [of MSU] is that once administration makes a decision about eliminating programs, they use reorganization as the process" (J. Miller, pers. comm.). Walker perceived the reorganization at her university as retribution on the part of the new provost (the former graduate school dean), related to her advocacy for the PhD program in family studies and the strong fight she waged to keep the budget allocated for nutrition after three faculty were transferred out of the college (R. Walker, pers. comm.).

How the reorganization played out in the academic units and with external stakeholders was different at each university. Fahm noted that at UW-Stout, the faculty senate developed models wherein the home economics unit either was split up, with programs going to different units, or was combined with the School of Education. She held several meetings with faculty where the senate representatives from her unit communicated what was going on. She and the faculty developed a strategy to involve alumni in writing letters to the chancellor. On campus, there was the perception that nothing would happen to the home economics unit because of the chancellor's support. Indeed, when

Fahm met with the chancellor, he indicated his support, dissuaded her from involving alumni, and emphatically stated, "Trust me" (E. Fahm, pers. comm.). However, because of the unpopularity of the reorganization, the chancellor came under his own pressures, ultimately receiving no-confidence votes from both faculty and academic staff. Weakened, he supported the merger of the Schools of Home Economics and Education, with retail management being moved to the Department of Management. Fahm indicated regret for not involving alumni and other stakeholders. But involving external groups might not have been feasible, she observed in retrospect, because the chancellor was able to push the reorganization through quickly.

For Miller (pers. comm.), the challenges began when faculty networks were formed that operated outside her purview. Miller was influenced by Bolman and Deal's (1991) organizational leadership framework, which included structural, human resources, political, and symbolic components. In retrospect, she acknowledged that a great deal of her time was by necessity spent on relationship building, representing the human resources frame. The new provost did not discourage direct contact from faculty, as had been the practice of the previous administration. Miller viewed this change as an attempt to gather information that could be used against the college in the reorganization process. Although the college showed evidence of productivity and had sound academic programs, some of the networks of faculty were not supportive of Miller's leadership. In the end, most of the programs were dispersed to other colleges on campus, and the programs in merchandising, apparel design, and textiles were eventually eliminated. Miller summed up the reorganization by stating, "Our college was the only one they got rid of. . . . One of the things I say to any unit, once faculty start going to central administration and forming alliances, there are problems" (pers. comm.).

At UK, the reorganization of the college became a power struggle between the provost, representing the university, and the home economics stakeholders (R. Walker, pers. comm.). Walker recalled that relations between her and the provost, the former dean of the graduate school, had started off rocky as she moved the family studies PhD proposal through the approval process with support of the chancellor. At the time, the graduate dean did not favor the PhD program in family studies, which he believed would compete with his home discipline of psychology. As provost, he initiated the reorganization of the university, stating that he wanted to examine academic programs by asking the question, "Which programs should continue?" Walker stated, "Everyone could see his plan. He even told others, [the home economics unit] was the low-hanging fruit." After announcing the reorganization, the provost began quiet negotiations with select faculty in home economics to provide incentives for them to leave the unit. Most of these contacts followed previous discussions with other deans. In particular, he proposed that the master's program in nutritional sciences be linked to the medical school and administered in the graduate school. According to Walker, he enticed three nutrition faculty members to leave the unit by establishing new lines for them elsewhere. He also proposed relocating other programs (food science to agriculture, interior design to architecture, marriage and family therapy to social work, and early childhood to education). Walker felt that his actions were motivated by their earlier disagreements. Given this context, she was determined to "fight him all the way" (R. Walker, pers. comm.). She rallied the alumni and the faculty through a series of meetings, but they picked their battles. When the interior design faculty expressed interest in moving to architecture, other faculty in the unit agreed that they should go, and then worked on keeping the rest of the programs together.

In the end, it was the alumni who helped to preserve the unit as a school affiliated with home economics within the College of Agriculture, as opposed to merging the departments into other colleges. Two home economics alumni on the UK board of trustees made it clear that they would not vote for eliminating the College of Human Environmental Sciences and sending programs to other academic units, but they would support school status (R. Walker, pers. comm.). They had graduated in home economics when it was formerly a part of agriculture and believed that administering the school there would be a good fit. Thus the board of trustees supported school status to keep an intact home economics unit. In the end, only the program in interior design, early childhood education (including the Early Childhood Center), and three of the four faculty members in nutrition left the unit (R. Walker, pers. comm.).

Leadership Processes

Given these opportunities and challenges, how did the deans perceive their own leadership styles? Specifically, what strategies did they use to take advantage of opportunities and handle the array of challenges? All three deans viewed their leadership styles as collaborative, an important observation since, in all three cases, they had been recruited to academic units that had internal relationship problems. Fahm (pers. comm.) stated that she worked hard to be perceived as "open," working "bottom-up" to gather ideas, but not hesitant to propose her own ideas for consideration. She would state a vision and goals so that faculty could see where she wanted to take the unit, but at the same time she fostered open discussion and collaboration to get their buy-in. She worked hard to establish trust.

Walker (pers. comm.) described her approach as "shared governance," working collaboratively with faculty and staff to establish annual goals in the home economics unit. She established committees or task forces to study particular areas that needed attention. She involved department chairs in decision making and believed it was important to have people involved in all aspects of decisions.

Miller (pers. comm.) discussed how MSU had a collaborative culture where joint appointments and multidisciplinary research were encouraged. Thus, she established a structure to ensure collaborative decision making. The administrative council, composed of department chairs and associate deans, was already established when she arrived, and she used this group as the central decision-making body. In addition, a staff council was formed to provide input into decision making. When asked, "What is your vision?," Miller always responded, "We have to have a collaborative vision" (J. Miller, pers. comm.). Thus, all three deans viewed their leadership as working with various constituencies to move the home economics unit forward.

Leaving a Legacy and Moving On

The legacy of leadership for these three deans is perhaps another chapter to be written. Although their academic units were reconfigured, the programs they initiated (i.e., service management at UW-Stout; the *Institute for Children, Youth and Families* and the Great Plains online master's degree in youth development at MSU; and the PhD program in family studies and the 2+2 early childhood education program at UK) live on. Earnings from the endowed funds secured by these deans still provide substantial support for students and faculty at their institutions. Although the academic programs no longer are unified as a home economics unit at UW-Stout and MSU, most of the areas of study still exist and have healthy enrollments. Clearly, these three African American deans left a legacy of achievement as administrators in three predominantly White comprehensive universities.

The three deans have moved on in their professional lives. In many ways, they used their experiences as deans as springboards to wider activities. Fahm went on to serve as an associate vice chancellor at UW-Stout for two years and, after leaving that position, worked at the UW system level, helping to align high school competencies with requirements for Wisconsin universities. She now works with the Higher Learning Commission and has chaired several site visits for the higher education regional accrediting body. She has written a manuscript for a textbook on nutrition for young children to be used in two-year higher education programs, and she conducted work on child nutrition and older adult programs in South Africa during a sabbatical.

Miller now has a faculty position, served as the principal investigator of a collaborative research-outreach project on homelessness with the city of Lansing, consulted with the Ministry of Women and Children's Affairs in Ghana, and co-edited the book *African American Women: Contributions to the Human Sciences* (Miller, Mitstifer, and Vaughn 2009). She continues other research and outreach initiatives, teaches online courses, and serves on several local and regional community boards. She served as president of the National Coalition for Black Development in Family and Consumer Sciences, an organization that she helped to establish in 1984.

After her deanship, Walker was appointed to be the vice president for academic outreach and public service, a new position at UK. After retiring in 2005, she worked to implement a Housing and Urban Development (HUD) grant she had garnered while at UK and served as an external evaluator on a $20 million HUD-funded housing redevelopment project in Lexington (Walker 2006). Walker accepted a temporary position as executive assistant to the interim president and was then promoted to interim provost and vice president for academic affairs at the University of Maryland, Eastern Shore, going "back home" to the institution where she had served as the department chair of human ecology (R. Walker, pers. comm.). Clearly, in each instance, these women of high achievement have continued to thrive in their post-deanship years.

Continuing Issues and Future Promises

For the field of home economics to have four African American women serving as deans in predominantly White comprehensive universities for two decades was a landmark achievement. This is especially extraordinary considering the field's challenges to be a diverse discipline. The history of home economics is filled with examples where it was not an open, welcoming field to people of color. Given this history, the strides to become more of a model in terms of diversity and cultural competency are to be commended. At the three institutions discussed in this chapter, there were serious and effective strategies employed to recruit people of color for the deanships. Interestingly, in all three cases the African American women who assumed these positions were administrators at historically Black universities. This argues for the recognition of the talent in these universities, and the need to increase efforts in mentoring for administrative roles.

The achievements and challenges of the three African American deans discussed in this chapter bring up the question, where are we now in mentoring for administrative roles in our profession? Knowing that the talent pool for administration comes from tenured faculty, the first question to ask is, what is the status of African American faculty in home economics and related fields? Broadly speaking, progress in the hiring of African American and other faculty of color has stalled, at best, in all disciplines in higher education. Nationwide, in 2007 African Americans were 5.2 percent of full-time faculty members at colleges and universities ("Black Faculty in Higher Education" 2007). However, few of the top-ranked private and state colleges and universities reached this national average at the time. Data from 2011 show that only three state or land-grant universities with home economics units exceeded an average of 5 percent African American full-time faculty ("Race, Ethnicity and Gender" 2013). Interestingly, the University of Kentucky, which ranked the best among state institutions in 2007, had regressed to only 3.8 percent in 2011, suggesting that the efforts started when Retia Walker was hired have not continued.

On a more promising note, the number of doctoral degrees granted to African Americans has grown. In 1999–2000, 2,762 African American men and 4,316 African American women were granted doctoral degrees in all disciplines. By 2009–2010, doctoral degrees grew by 31.1 percent to 3,622 for African American men and by 57.4 percent to 6,795 for African American women (National Center on Educational Statistics 2012). While this progress is certainly exciting, the path to academic positions following the doctoral degree is less clear given recent employment trends (Patton 2012) and the lack of African American hires in state flagship universities, where major home economics programs are housed. Clearly, the most pressing issue is to get African Americans into the pipeline for tenure track positions so that sufficient candidates for administrative positions can be mentored and nurtured for these roles.

The status of African Americans in higher education today demonstrates the importance of what Esther Fahm, Julia Miller, and Retia Walker were able to achieve in their time. Their impressive achievements in curricula, programs, and fund development have been sustained. Yet how they addressed the challenges is equally impressive. They coped with changing university agendas and issues within their home economics units. They had to sort out the effects of race, gender, and the academic bias against home economics (Stage 1997) in addressing these challenges—clearly, a complex and confusing process. However, through it all, these deans stepped forward to accept administrative positions with courage, despite knowing some of the barriers they would encounter. They understood that certain challenges they faced were typical for academic administrators, and took advantage of opportunities to advance their units, home economics as a field of study, and their own careers. Finally, they found the silver linings during their tenure, leveraged lessons learned for new opportunities, and moved on with gusto and grace to continue to achieve professionally—epitomizing the strength of African Americans as a people. It was a special time, and these African American women took full advantage of it.

ACKNOWLEDGMENTS

I express my appreciation to the three African American deans who are the focus of this chapter for giving freely of their time in interviews and providing access to background documents. Thanks also to others who were interviewed and provided materials.

NOTE

1. This study is based on in-depth interviews, a frequently used method employed by qualitative researchers. In-depth interviews are appropriate when the researcher has a particular topic on which he or she wants to focus, and it assumes that individuals have unique and important knowledge about the social world (Hesse-Biber and Leavy 2011). In-depth interviews are useful for accessing "subjugated knowledge," the "hidden experiences and knowledge" often excluded from mainstream research methods due to the marginalization of women, people of color, and other groups (ibid., 98).

I conducted personal interviews, following an outline of predetermined topics, with the deans as follows: Esther Fahm, December 8, 2011, and January 19, 2012; Julia Miller, January 10 and February 2, 2012; Retia Walker, December 5, 2011, and January 27, 2012. The interviews were tape recorded; extensive notes were also taken. The deans were asked to identify stakeholders (faculty, staff, former students) who could be contacted to provide additional institutional context and information about their tenure as deans. Interviews were then conducted with seven of those ten individuals. Each dean provided a copy of her curriculum vitae and other documents that helped verify the information provided in the interviews. Notes and recordings from the interviews were transcribed and reviewed to identify key patterns and themes. The stakeholder interviews and documents provided supplementary data to substantiate the themes. Fahm, Miller, and Walker reviewed various drafts and the final manuscript to assure accuracy and to confirm the overall integrity of the chapter.

REFERENCES

Aguirre, Adalberto. 2001. "Women and Minority Faculty in the Academic Workplace: Recruitment, Retention, and Academic Culture." *Eric Digest*, www.ericdigests. org/2001-3/women.htm (accessed August 11, 2013).

Bailey, Lena, Francille Firebaugh, Elizabeth G. Haley, and Sharon Y. Nickols. 1993. "Human Ecology in Higher Education: Surviving Beyond 2000." *Journal of Home Economics* 85(4): 3–10.

"Black Faculty in Higher Education: Still Only a Drop in the Bucket." 2007. *Journal of Blacks in Higher Education*, http://www.jbhe.com/features/55_blackfaculty.html (accessed August 11, 2013).

Bolman, Lee G., and Terrence E. Deal. 1991. *Reframing Organizations: Artistry, Choice and Leadership*. San Francisco, Calif.: Jossey-Bass.

Bowen, William G., and Derek Bok. 1998. *The Shape of the River: Long-Term Consequences of Considering Race in College and University Admissions*. Princeton, N.J.: Princeton University Press.

"Campaign for MSU Kicks Off: College of Human Ecology Set $12 Million Goal." 2003. *Ecologue* (newsletter of the College of Human Ecology, Michigan State University), 10–11. In author's possession.

Firebaugh, Francille M., Sharon Y. Nickols, Jorge H. Atiles, and Kaija Turkki. 2010. "Sustaining FCS in Higher Education: A 2010 Perspective." *Journal of Family and Consumer Sciences* 102(4): 17–23.

Gumport, Patricia J. 2000. "Academic Restructuring: Organizational Change and Institutional Imperatives." *Higher Education* 39(1): 67–91.

Haley, Elizabeth G., Rosemary S. Peggram, and Connie J. Ley. 1993. "Enhancing Program Viability." *Journal of Home Economics* 85(4): 11–17.

Hesse-Biber, Sharlene, and Patricia Leavy. 2011. *The Practice of Qualitative Research*, 2nd ed. Thousand Oaks, Calif.: Sage.

May, Ann Mari, Elizabeth A. Moorhouse, and Jennifer A. Bossard. 2010. "Representation of Women Faculty at Public Research Universities: Do Unions Matter?" *Industrial and Labor Relations Review* 63(4): 699–718.

Miller, Julia, Dorothy I. Mitstifer, and Gladys Gary Vaughn, eds. 2009. *African American Women: Contributions to the Human Sciences*. East Lansing, Mich.: Kappa Omicron Nu.

National Center on Educational Statistics. 2012. "Doctor's Degrees Conferred by Degree-Granting Institutions, by Race/Ethnicity and Sex of Students: Selected Years, 1976–77 Through 2009–10." http://nces.ed.gov/fastfacts/display.asp?id=72 (accessed August 11, 2013).

Nerad, Maresi. 1999. *The Academic Kitchen: A Social History of Gender Stratification at the University of California, Berkeley*. Albany: State University of New York Press.

Olson, Gary A. 2010. "Why Universities Reorganize." *Chronicle of Higher Education*, http://chronicle.com/article/Why-Universities-Reorganize/123903 (accessed August 11, 2013).

Patton, Stacey. 2012. "Doctoral Degrees Rose in 2011, but Career Options Weren't So Rosy." *Chronicle of Higher Education*, http://chronicle.com/article/Doctoral-Degrees-Rose-in-2011/136133 (accessed August 11, 2013).

"Race, Ethnicity and Gender of Full-Time Faculty at More than 4,3000 Institutions." 2013. *Chronicle of Higher Education*, http://chronicle.com.proxy.lib.fsu.edu/article/Race-EthnicityGender-of/142607 (accessed June 1, 2014).

Ralston, Penny A. 1978. "Black Participation in Home Economics: A Partial Account." *Journal of Home Economics* 70(15): 34–37.

———. 1994. "Flemmie P. Kittrell: Her Views and Practices Regarding Home Economics in Higher Education." *Journal of Home Economics* 86(1): 16–24, 41.

Research and Faculty Expertise. N.d. College of Human Environmental Sciences, University of Kentucky. Personal collection of R. Walker.

Rossiter, Margaret W. 1997. "The Men Move In: Home Economics, 1950–1970." In *Rethinking Home Economics: Women and the History of a Profession*, edited by Sarah Stage and Virginia B. Vincenti, 96–117. Ithaca, N.Y.: Cornell University Press.

Simerly, Coby B., Penny A. Ralston, Lynda Harriman, and Barbara Taylor. 2000. "The

Scottsdale Initiative: Positioning the Profession for the 21st Century." *Journal of Family and Consumer Sciences* 92(1): 75–80.

Stage, Sarah. 1997. "Home Economics: What's in a Name?" In *Rethinking Home Economics: Women and the History of a Profession*, edited by Sarah Stage and Virginia B. Vincenti, 1–13. Ithaca, N.Y.: Cornell University Press.

Todd, Lee. 2002. "Women Have Made Real Progress at U.K." *Lexington Herald Leader*, December 16.

Vincenti, Virginia B. 1997. "Home Economics Moves into the Twenty-First Century." In *Rethinking Home Economics: Women and the History of a Profession*, edited by Sarah Stage and Virginia B. Vincenti, 301–320. Ithaca, N.Y.: Cornell University Press.

Walker, Retia Scott. 2006. "Building Community Leadership: From the 'Grassroots Up' and 'Inside Out.'" Paper presented at the Community Outreach Partnership Centers Conference, Baltimore, Md., March 30.

10. "Cookin' with Gas"

Home Economists in the
Atlanta Natural Gas Industry, 1950–1995

SHARON Y. NICKOLS

From the early days of the natural gas industry, cooking schools were a mainstay in the promotion of natural gas appliances and natural gas as a source of energy in the home. These programs continued to be popular in Atlanta, Georgia, in the 1980s. One such event sponsored by the Atlanta Gas Light Company featured a local celebrity chef assisted by two gas company home economists, one of whom was Katrina Graham. Gumbo was the chef's first dish. When the flour and oil mixture for the roux separated, there was a moment of panic, but Graham and her colleague quickly switched to the next recipe. While the chef continued onstage, the home economists worked backstage to prepare another roux. When they presented the fresh roux to the chef, he expressed surprise and appreciation for the perfectly prepared roux. To which Graham responded, "Well, we're cookin' with gas!" (K. Graham, pers. comm.). "Cooking with gas" had become an everyday idiom, meaning performing to perfection. Its origins are British, related to the superior performance of natural gas for cooking (Wentworth and Flexner 1967).

As liaisons between the company and the consumer during the twentieth century, home economists employed in the utility industries—electricity and natural gas—responded to multiple expectations. The goal of their employers was to expand the market for their products. Customers depended on home economists to be a source of information and solutions to problems. Home economists juggled many tasks as they educated consumers, marketed products, projected a positive image of the company in the community, and served as "agents of modernity" (Kline 1997) by carrying out a "mediating role" between industry and consumers (Goldstein 2012).

This chapter, which is based on personal interviews, examines the work of home economists employed by the Atlanta Gas Light Company (AGL) from the middle to the end of the twentieth century. I focus attention on their work experiences and positions in the corporation's organizational structure.[1] The home economists contributed to the expansion of AGL, served as the primary link between the company and residential consumers, and provided a presence for the company in a variety of community settings. They experienced great satisfaction in their work. Yet their jobs were abruptly terminated in 1995 in anticipation of deregulation of the natural gas industry in Georgia. Despite their sudden displacement, the home economists continued to take pride in their past contributions, and many maintained the social and professional networks that had been a significant part of their professional identities.

A dichotomy has existed in the popular image of the home economist in business: it is either a glamorous position with lots of company perks, or the job of a manipulator who convinces unwitting consumers to purchase certain products. Neither of these stereotypes is accurate. This chapter allows a group of home economists in business (the "gas ladies" of AGL) to speak for themselves and through their voices to provide a clearer understanding of their work. From a broader economic perspective, their experiences provide a case study of the gender segregation in the workforce that existed for most of the twentieth century.[2] The chapter captures many attributes of home economists: service to others, high standards of professionalism, in-group camaraderie, resilience, and the absence of institutional clout.

History of the Atlanta Gas Light Company

By the mid-twentieth century, the Atlanta Gas Light Company had a prominent place in Atlanta with satellite offices and services in many other Georgia cities. However, the origins of the company were hardly auspicious. The gas works that produced gas from coal was built in the 1850s (Tate 1985). A few businesses and homes soon adopted indoor gas lighting. Following the Civil War, the gas plant was rebuilt and gas service gradually was restored during the 1870s. Gas water heaters, small space heaters, and cook stoves were developed in the 1880s (Cowan 1983; Herbert 1992; Lief 1961). Cooking with gas was encouraged in advertisements in the Atlanta newspapers in the 1890s (AGL Collection n.d.).

AGL pioneered in consumer relations by employing Mrs. Henrietta Dull in 1910 to give demonstrations on the use of the gas cook stove (Georgia Women of Achievement 2013). Although she did not have a degree in home economics, Dull wrote a food column for the *Atlanta Journal*, compiled a popular cookbook, and conducted cooking schools throughout the South, while also working for the gas company as a "demonstrator." Similar positions already were prevalent in the British gas companies in the 1890s (Clendinning 2004). The British "lady demonstrators," who were trained in home economics, held an elite professional status among their home economics peers as they promoted the use of natural gas in the home at trade exhibitions and worked in marketing natural gas.

Gas ranges were selling especially well across the United States by the mid-1920s, in part because new enameled ranges and cabinet-style enclosures had replaced the exposed burners and high black metal ovens of the original models (Herbert 1992; Lief 1961). In Atlanta, sales of gas appliances in the early 1900s probably also were fueled by the decision among AGL's management to espouse a philosophy of customer service. In the 1920s, AGL established a Home Service Department in which only women with degrees in home economics were employed (Tate 1985). The department was expanded in anticipation of growth in the industry; however, cuts in staff during the 1930s Depression left only one home economist in AGL's employ. As economic conditions improved, positions were reinstated and the department's scope and size increased.

When AGL celebrated its hundredth anniversary in 1956, it was the second oldest corporation in the state of Georgia, and natural gas service had been extended to forty cities, including Macon, Rome, and Savannah (Tate 1985). As part of the anniversary celebrations, Home Service Department home economists prepared recipes from a century-old cookbook on the weekly *Blue Flame* television show that had premiered in 1951 (on black-and-white TV). Additional home economists were employed in the 1960s and 1970s; by the 1980s there were thirty-two home economists employed by AGL across the state of Georgia. The unit was renamed Consumer Information and Education (CI&E) in 1984.

Home Economists in Business

Employment opportunities for graduates of home economics colleges became available in the food and home products industries in the 1920s and 1930s. Companies such as Corning Glass Works, the Kellogg Company, and General Mills employed home economists, some with advanced degrees, to develop new products and equipment, as well as educational materials and media programs (Blaszczyk 1997; Copeland 1996; Goldstein 1997, 2012; Rossiter 1982). Utility companies hired women with degrees in home economics to build consumer interest, educate them about their new appliances, and promote the sales of kitchen ranges and other appliances. These second-generation home economists, who were essentially excluded from male-dominated occupations in the sciences and business, followed the example of their college teachers into feminized niches as authorities on things connected with hearth and home (Blaszczyk 1997; Goldstein 1997, 2012; Rossiter 1982).

Corporate home economists began developing a cohesive group identity in 1920 when, with the leadership of Mary Keown of the American Washing Machine Manufacturers Association, a separate section of the American Home Economics Association was initiated (Goldstein 1997, 2012). The Home Economics in Business (HEIB) section was formally recognized in 1923. "Within six years this group grew to 217 women engaged . . . with commodities ranging from aluminum to yeast" (MacLeod 1938, 3). The Home Service Committee was formed within the American Gas Association in the early 1920s. At its 1930 meeting in Chicago, Ruth Soule, the committee's chair, reported that various subcommittees kept members informed about developments in gas appliances, promoted the "Blue Star Home" (one fully equipped with gas), maintained contacts with colleges and universities to promote courses about gas appliances, and published articles in trade journals and women's magazines (Soule 1930).

College bulletins and books advised home economics students about career opportunities, including working for public utilities. The home economics program at Iowa State College (now Iowa State University) was in the forefront of developing college curricula focused on household equipment based on the premise that "women could and should acquire a practical yet scientifically based understanding of household technologies" (Bix 2002, 730). Although young women were warned in one career compendium that they should expect to "accept smaller jobs at less pay, work harder, and wait longer for advancement" during the Great Depression, it was also assumed that their opportunities in home economics positions would be less affected than other jobs "since no men are equipped to handle the work" (MacLeod 1938, 15). Some utility companies reduced staff size or temporarily discontinued their home service departments during World War II, but most refocused their work on educating the public about the care and conservation of equipment and economical food preparation after the war (Goldstein 2012). During the war, AGL offered Atlanta homemakers the loan of pressure canners so they could preserve garden produce to help maintain food security ("Your Gas Co." 1945).

After World War II the expansion of U.S. industries to meet consumers' demand for household appliances and convenience products opened additional opportunities in business for home economics graduates (Rossiter 1995). As household income rose and the 1950s culture of domesticity encouraged women to focus on home and family, manufacturers introduced new products for the civilian market and increased their educational and promotional efforts. As a consequence, "the demand for business home economists exceeded supply in the immediate postwar period" (Goldstein 2012, 258). A 1955 report on the kinds of positions held by 63,927 employed home economists identified 3,400 in positions in business, comparable to the 3,442 identified as faculty, administrators, and researchers connected with colleges and universities (Hemphill 1955).

By the 1970s the majority of U.S. homes had an array of household appliances. As home equipment ownership became even more commonplace in the following decades, manufacturers began to assume that specialized education about these products was no longer needed (Emmel et al. 2010). Furthermore, "the energy crisis had severe consequences for home economics work in utility companies" (Goldstein 2012, 280). Economic factors, including stockholders' demands for profit and the challenge of demonstrating positive benefits to the company's bottom line from the expenditures on consumer services departments, contributed to the elimination of positions in many companies in the 1980s (Rebecca Lovingood, pers. comm.).

AGL Home Economists on the Job

The job description of the AGL home economists in the second half of the twentieth century was remarkably similar to the expectations in previous decades: teach the public about the features of natural gas appliances, provide customer service in using gas appliances, and be ambassadors for AGL in the community. The original job title was "home economist," but late in the 1970s it was changed to "consumer information and education specialist." AGL's headquarters and its largest market were in the metropolitan Atlanta area, and thus the largest concentration of home economists was in metro Atlanta with one or two home economists employed at each of the regional offices.

Producing programs tailored to specific audiences, including students in home economics classes, adults in civic organizations, women's clubs, and cooking school events were primary assignments. Pearl Solomon (pers. comm.) in Macon recalled her experience with the schools: "I would go to the home economics classroom and do a range demonstration. I liked to call them that instead of a food demonstration [to emphasize the appliance, instead of cake or brownies]. In the Living Skills class, I would do a presentation on the gas dryer."

Carol Cofer, who was employed at the Athens office, reported that she mainly worked with the University of Georgia's College of Home Economics and the schools in Clarke and nearby counties. "They had equipment on loan from the company and I would do demonstrations and teach them how to use the equipment," she explained (pers. comm.). The appliance consignment system provided home economics departments in schools and colleges with gas ranges and, sometimes, dryers. The schools purchased one range and the company loaned two or more. Once the relationship was established, the loans continued over several years with new ranges provided every three years.

In the 1980s the AGL home economists began making presentations in science classes, where their lessons included the source of natural gas, the structure of the natural gas industry, and safety. For example, the city of Savannah, where Jackie Ogden was located, used natural gas–powered vehicles, which were good illustrations in her presentations to classes at the middle and high schools and the area technical college during the 1980s and 1990s (J. Ogden, pers. comm.). The historically strong emphasis on sciences in the college home economics curriculum created a solid foundation for the home economists' science presentations.

Cooking schools continued to draw large audiences from the 1950s into the 1980s, providing AGL home economists with the opportunity to showcase the company's products and their own expertise. The schools were designed to demonstrate all aspects of the gas range, from the top burners to the oven and broiler. In Atlanta the most prominent cooking schools were held during the Atlanta Dogwood Festival in a large auditorium in AGL's building at Peachtree Center. Cooking demonstrations were presented at big trade shows, and smaller sessions were provided for charitable organizations. Zena Brown (pers. comm.) declared that she did so many cooking schools during her thirty years with AGL, "I couldn't count them all. Instead of calling me 'the gas lady,' one church group nicknamed me their 'cooking school woman.'"

The home economists described their role as being a liaison between consumers and the company; they were employed by AGL because they were skilled in public relations. Janet Joseph (pers. comm.) described the home economists' job as "selling ease": "It was our job to show the consumer just how easy it was to use the gas appliances so that they would want to have them in their homes. We were there to influence future customers . . . in the schools and in the community." Many of the home economists described themselves as "the face of the company" in the community, saying it was a role they thoroughly enjoyed.

Next to the symbol of the blue flame (the insignia of AGL), "the Calendar" was reportedly the most recognizable icon of the company. Annual production of the Calendar was a major undertaking for the home economists. Recipes were invited from customers and then tested in the AGL kitchens. Outstanding recipes were selected for each month. Newly employed home economists learned the science and art of recipe testing from the experts. Graham (pers. comm.) explained, "Zena Brown, Gladys Powell, and Mildred Almdale were the ones that had the most experience with recipe testing. We all learned a lot from them . . . to write recipes correctly, very specific . . . how to set it up. Zena always had a wealth of information in putting together a recipe." Brown, who was in charge of the Calendar's production for many years, admitted to one mistake in a printed recipe, for which she continued to be teased a long time afterward. "I worked with the printer and we laid out each page and proofed it. One time, I had 'add eggs, one at a time' in the instructions, but there were no eggs in the list of ingredients," she said with a chuckle (Z. Brown, pers. comm.).

Going to a consumer's home to provide individual instruction or to investigate problems was a regular experience for the home economists. When a customer purchased a gas appliance from AGL, a home economist followed up to make sure it was operating properly and demonstrated how to use and clean it. Home economists also worked in tandem with men from the service department when a customer complained that her gas range was not working. As Solomon (pers. comm.) described, "If a customer called in and complained that they couldn't get the range to bake right, I would go out and usually our service man would meet me at the house. I would bake biscuits, because if a range will bake biscuits, it's pretty much working okay. I would do biscuits, the service man would have the thermocouple connected to the range, and we would check the range out thoroughly." Most of the instructional visits were to women, but men sometimes requested a home visit, as Diane Pulley (pers. comm.) recalled: "When gas grills became popular in the 1980s, men were very interested in learning how to use their new gas grill."

As ambassadors of the company in the community, the home economists were encouraged by AGL management to be actively engaged in civic organizations. LeeAnn Wynns (pers. comm.) formed "tons of partnerships within the community and really put a face to the organization" by collaborating with the Cobb County Chamber of Commerce, the Georgia Youth Science Center, and other organizations in her district. Solomon (pers. comm.) described the purpose of her activities with the Macon Home Builder's Association, the Macon Arts Alliance, and the United Way campaign, among others: "They [AGL administrators] wanted the home economists to show that AGL was not a company that was just taking from the community, but that we were giving back." Giving back to the community meant not just an investment of time, but sometimes also providing facilities. Because the Cooperative Extension offices in southeastern Georgia did not have kitchens suitable for demonstrations, AGL opened its demonstration kitchen in Savannah for extension's home food preservation lessons on proper use of the pressure canner and for 4-H youth programs (J. Ogden, pers. comm.).

While the home economists were very positive in describing their community involvement, they also conveyed the weight of responsibility they felt to represent AGL effectively. As Janet Joseph (pers. comm.) summarized, "We were the face of the company; therefore, it was emphasized to us the importance of conveying a positive image. Atlanta Gas Light was a public utility, consequently, it was imperative that the public perceived value from the company in terms of its service to the community."

Job Satisfaction and Challenges

The AGL home economists participating in this study unanimously expressed satisfaction with their jobs and their immediate work environment. The most frequent response to questions about their experience working at AGL was "I loved my job." Many aspects contributed to their job satisfaction: relationships with people (including customers and co-workers), autonomy and flexibility in completing their work, employee benefits, and prestige in the field of home economics. Cofer (pers. comm.) observed, "Home economists in my generation were very versatile and we were trained to do a lot of different things. We worked well with people. We were kind of the problem solvers [with customers] for the company. I felt very respected."

Joseph (pers. comm.) offered another perspective: "People outside the company may have thought we just cooked various recipes. We did prepare food, but there was a lot more to the job than that. I definitely think we were recognized as professionals." However, AGL's internal culture also exploited their culinary and organizational skills. Management called on the home economics staff to plan for and to prepare food and beverages for company employee retirements, receptions, and office parties. This was bothersome for some, but Joseph rationalized, "I don't think it was out of disrespect. We had the skills and access to the test kitchens, so it kind of made sense." When Mary Davis (pers. comm.), the manager of CI&E in the Atlanta division, documented to upper management that it would be less expensive to hire a caterer rather than use CI&E specialists' time to organize and prepare for these events, AGL began using caterers.

The flexibility to manage their work appeared throughout the interviews as an advantage of working for AGL. Most of the home economists controlled their own schedules, such as when to do programs in the schools or for community groups, and which community meetings to attend. With autonomy came accountability: monthly reports were required, listing how many programs, types of audience, and potential customers reached. Pulley (pers. comm.) put this in perspective, "There was a lot of accountability, but being able to be creative and almost control your own destiny was an entrepreneurial-type feeling. It was a great job."

Other home economists assigned to specific projects had more structured schedules. For example, two of the home economists on the *Blue Flame* television show, Zena Brown and Marian McCullers, had a schedule of each day's

PHOTO 10.1. Frances Tegeder (*left*) and Marian McCullers were among the home economists who appeared on a televised cooking show for the Atlanta Gas Light Company in the early 1950s. Atlanta Gas Light Collection, VIS 185, Kenan Research Center at the Atlanta History Center, Atlanta, Georgia.

activities to prepare for the weekly program. Brown recalled, "We would buy the food on Monday and write key sentences for the director and the cameraman, so he would know when I said a certain thing he should move the camera. We practiced in the AGL kitchen on Tuesday and Wednesday with food. The food we cooked on Wednesday was shown as the finished product at the end of Thursday's show. Otherwise, we did the show ad lib, but we knew what we were doing!" The TV show was produced for ten years in the 1950s and 1960s, originally with a weekly budget of $10.

Along with other responsibilities, Solomon became a local television personality in the late 1960s. She recalled, "I contacted a local television station about doing a cooking show and they surprised me when they said yes. There were few African Americans on television anywhere at the time, and this was Macon, Georgia" (P. Solomon, pers. comm.). Solomon invited the viewing audience to send recipes, which she tested: "The gas company built a portable demonstration kitchen for my program. I got [a local grocery store] to give the person whose recipe I demonstrated a $50 gift certificate."

Among their benefits, the home economists valued the use of a car (with the blue flame logo on the side) for company business, an expense account to pay for the products used in demonstrations, health insurance, and being vested in the company's retirement plan after five years of employment. Six weeks of maternity leave were available. AGL encouraged the home economists to join professional organizations, paid some of their dues, and helped support their attendance at professional conferences. AGL home economists were members of the Georgia and American Home Economics Association, and active in local and national HEIB and American Gas Association activities. Several, including McCullers and Davis, held state and national positions in these associations.

Enjoying a congenial work environment was a consistent theme as the home economists reflected on their work with AGL. Wynns worked in a suburban Atlanta office with five other home economists. She recalled, "My fellow home economists were my good friends. . . . we were very close. We had a lot of fun and still keep in touch" (L. Wynns, pers. comm.). An element of prestige was associated with being an AGL home economist, especially when compared to the confined routine and lower salary of teaching. The prestige came, in part, from the AGL home economists themselves, who perceived that as a group they were highly professional women. However, several home economists expressed frustration about their compensation. They were aware that their pay was not comparable to the salaries paid to men in similar public relations and managerial positions. Brown (pers. comm.) recalled that when she was designated as the supervisor of home services in the Atlanta division in 1972, she received the new title, but no pay raise.

While the home economists were overwhelmingly positive about their AGL employment experiences, they were acutely aware of the lack of channels for them to advance in the corporate structure. After fourteen years as a kitchen designer for AGL, Davis approached her home service director to inquire about a different assignment, emphasizing that she had completed a master's degree. She recalled, "I was promoted to supervisor of home service in Atlanta, responsible for supervising ten home economists, hiring, the unit budget, and the test kitchen where work for the Calendar was done. When the department name was changed to Consumer Information and Education [in 1984], my job title changed to manager" (M. Davis, pers. comm.). But despite her managerial experience, master's degree, and twenty-seven years of experience at the company, there was no avenue for advancement into corporate administration. Davis recollected, "It had a demoralizing effect . . . being a home economist with a graduate degree and seeing engineers without graduate degrees being promoted. Some male managers' attitudes toward the home economists and women in general were negative, but they tried not to show it, and we tried to ignore it."

Cofer, who also had a master's degree, was employed from 1978 to 1995, and she corroborated Davis's observation: "Well, it was a man's world. Men without college degrees got promoted" (C. Cofer, pers. comm.). Another AGL veteran with a master's degree, Joseph, elaborated, "Almost all of the upper management was male. We had home economics graduates as the supervisors of our positions, but all of the home economists were female. That made networking and moving [up] within the company hard."

A great deal of pride and optimism among AGL home economists accompanied Marian McCullers's appointment as corporate vice president for Consumer Information and Education in 1986. McCullers had begun working for AGL in 1946. During her forty-one-year career, she held supervisory positions in the Home Service Department and was widely respected. But like other home economists who had long careers before being appointed to high-level administrative roles in business, McCullers had little opportunity to effect change in the corporate culture before her retirement (see Goldstein 2012, 266–267).

Gender in the Workplace

Studies of gender and paid work, especially those published in the 1980s and 1990s, shed light on the experiences of the AGL home economists. The structure and dynamics of the workplace have formal and informal organizational components (Taylor 1988). The formal organization is composed of the hierarchy of authority, the specialization of work, values, and explicitly stated policies. The informal organization develops among employees through tradition, attitudes, friendships, and selective application of the formal rules. In the workplace of the mid- to late twentieth century, the formal structure favored men, whose occupational job ladders linked one level of responsibility to higher levels (Reskin and Padavic 1994; Taylor 1988).

The gender typing of positions in an industry is a manifestation of specialization. Historically in the United States the more specific the occupational categories, the more gender segregation (Fox and Hesse-Biber 1984; Spitze 1988). Reskin (1984) observed that despite changes in occupational structure and the shifting gender composition of the labor force, occupational segregation levels were extraordinarily stable throughout most of the twentieth century. Two consequences of specialization have been the gender gap in pay (Bielby and Baron 1984) and women's restricted opportunities for corporate advancement (Fox and Hesse-Biber 1984). These factors manifested in the occupational experiences of the AGL home economists. While this helps explain the disparities in pay and opportunities for advancement, what accounts for the AGL home economists' high level of job satisfaction?

In both the formal and informal components of the workplace, some de-

gree of social control is present, but within such parameters there is varia-
tion in the degree of autonomy (Stewart and Cantor 1982). Job satisfaction
is closely tied to employees' perceptions about the level of control they have
over their work. Given that the home economists had the training and skills
needed to perform the work of CI&E, which occupied a distinct niche in AGL,
they had a relatively high degree of autonomy. Independence in managing
their work and the collegial network of friendships among the home economists strongly influenced their positive job satisfaction.

The experiences of the AGL home economists were consistent with research by Michael and Hunt (1987), who found that home economists perceived very limited opportunities for advancement to managerial positions
in the appliance and related product industries in the mid-1980s. Regarding
mentoring in the utility and home appliance industries, Michael (1988) reported that home economists believed that they were not chosen for mentor-
ship programs because they were women in a male-dominated industry, and
furthermore, being women in a traditionally female field was a hindrance.

Gender was not the only factor that shaped the AGL work environment.
Patterns of occupational opportunity by race and gender were evident in the
group photographs of employees in the internal company newsletters of the
mid-twentieth century (AGL Collection n.d.). Manual laborers (blue-collar
employees) were all Black men, whereas managers were all White men. Cleri-
cal personnel (few in number) were White women. The exception was in the
home economics unit, where African American and Euro American professionals had worked together since the 1940s, yet there were some historical
disparities even there. Davis (pers. comm.) recounted the career of Gladys
Powell: "She was the first African American home economist hired by a utility
company in the nation. She was hired in 1940 and first worked in the Atlanta
housing projects, where many African Americans lived, to show residents
how to use the gas ranges. As a professional woman she was smart and intelligent, but while other home economists got a company car to make their calls,
Gladys got on a streetcar and made the home visits. As times and attitudes
changed, she was assigned a company car and eventually became assistant
director for [AGL home service] statewide programs." Powell was employed
at AGL for nearly forty years and retired in 1977. Powell's supervisory appointment may have helped pave the way for African American men, who were appointed to positions in the corporate structure in later years.

Solomon, the only African American woman in a professional position
in the Macon AGL division from 1968 to 1995, recalled a racially tainted encounter with a customer while making a home visit. Solomon (pers. comm.)
explained, "If there were ever issues, I had bosses that knew how to resolve them. The lady needed a home economist to help her with her range.

I knocked at the front door." When the woman opened the door, she used a racial epithet and told Solomon that people like her did not enter the front door of her house. Solomon recalled that she excused herself, went back to the company car, returned to the office, and reported the incident to the manager, a White man. Solomon remembered, "He called her [the customer] and said, 'Well, ma'am, if she [Solomon] can't come to the front door, she can't come at all.' The AGL management stood behind you. That was the end of that.' He was not going to send anybody else. I had a wonderful job and I loved it."

External Change and Internal Adjustments

Many changes from mid-century through the 1990s directly or indirectly had an effect on the work of the AGL home economists. The labor force participation rate of women in most age groups nearly doubled, with over 75 percent of women aged twenty-five to fifty-four employed outside the home by the 1990s (Fullerton 1999). With fewer women at home, home visits were less feasible. Customers' employment schedules precluded going to exhibitions and cooking schools during the day, and attendance fell. Schools changed the areas of emphasis in the curriculum. Home economics courses, including many of the food classes, were no longer taught. AGL dropped the equipment consignment program in the 1990s. The 1970s energy crisis decreed a greater emphasis on energy conservation. Household appliances powered by electricity rather than natural gas increasingly dominated the market. In 1984, for example, 61 percent of the ranges produced were electric compared to 39 percent gas, and electric dryers (81 percent) far exceeded gas dryers (19 percent) (Appliance Statistics 1984).

Davis (pers. comm.) summarized the budgetary challenges for CI&E: "By the 1990s it seemed like every year we had to justify the existence of our department. Money was a concern. We couldn't look at our budget and say how much money we brought in. So we constantly had to justify it [CI&E] in other ways. We were diversifying and going in a lot of different directions." Similar challenges had been experienced in the 1970s by home economists in many types of business (Goldstein 2012), and college and university programs that educated professionals on home equipment declined as consumer education services offered by many manufacturers and marketers of appliances were curtailed in the 1980s and 1990s (Emmel and Lovingood 2003).

Despite inklings that changes were taking place in AGL and despite some public discussion about natural gas deregulation, most AGL home economists were caught unaware when the company began downsizing and CI&E was eliminated in 1995. In 1997 the Georgia General Assembly passed Senate Bill 215, thus becoming the first state in the United States to deregulate the natural gas industry (Grenier 1997). Natural gas services were "unbundled" so that the sale of the gas itself, distribution services, and marketing to consumers were conducted by separate entities. Theoretically, deregulation was intended to increase competition and reduce costs. In fact, the initial result was mass confusion on the part of consumers (Hardin 2002).

In retrospect, Cofer observed, "I felt like the company was making a mistake, moving away from being customer-oriented by doing away with us [CI&E]." After twenty-seven years of employment with AGL, Solomon reflected, "I never felt like it was time for me to leave. I was downsized. . . . we were the last utility company to eliminate home economics. The company had a different direction they were going. Consumers said they wanted deregulation; this was part of deregulation. I'm not sure the universe has been helped by deregulation."

Downsizing also eliminated positions in many other units of AGL. Following the purge, AGL offered employees the opportunity to reapply for the remaining jobs, but only a few home economists were rehired into different positions. Some were place-bound and could not relocate, while others took early retirement at a substantially reduced benefit level. Solomon and Ogden parlayed their long experience working with the public into positions with Cooperative Extension. Other AGL home economists took positions in community service agencies, education, and commercial enterprises. Fifteen years after the end of their employment with AGL, when they participated in this study, the home economists displayed resilience in having moved on with their professional careers and personal lives. They express pride in their work with AGL, and most maintain contact with their colleagues and attend an annual HEIB gathering where they reminisce about cookin' with gas.

ACKNOWLEDGMENTS

I express my deep gratitude to the home economists who participated in this study. While it was not possible to include the reflections of each person, every interview contributed to the synthesis of experiences and insights. Thanks to the graduate students without whose engagement the project would not have been completed, and to Carolyn M. Goldstein, Megan J. Elias, and Gwen Kay, who reviewed earlier drafts of this chapter. The research was supported by funds from the Janette M. Barber Distinguished Professorship, College of Family and Consumer Sciences, University of Georgia.

NOTES

1. Personal interviews were conducted with fourteen home economists employed by the Atlanta Gas Light Company between 1950 and 2000 and who were residing in Georgia at the time of the interviews. The study was informed by phenomenology, an empirical research approach in which participants are encouraged to reflect ret-

rospectively on lived experiences, and the researcher interprets the essence of their experiences to derive general meanings and structure (see deMarrais 2004). The method for obtaining participants followed the "network selection" strategy, in which one person who fits the selection criteria is contacted and that individual refers the researcher to others who also fit the criteria. Semi-structured interviews were conducted from November 2009 through February 2010 by me and by graduate students, who were trained in a research seminar. The interviews were tape recorded and transcribed. I and a trained graduate student then read the transcripts and identified and labeled themes. I selected representative narratives to illustrate patterns in interviewees' experiences and observations or to highlight unique experiences. The narrative includes observations from the oldest interviewee, who earned her bachelor's degree in 1938 and worked at AGL from 1955 to 1985, and the youngest, who received her bachelor's degree in 1984 and immediately began employment with AGL. Years of employment with AGL ranged from nine to thirty. Three interviewees were African American and eleven were Euro American. All of the home economists had bachelor's degrees; five also held master's degrees.

2. This examination of the employment experiences of AGL home economists was informed by scholarship on gender issues in the workplace in the 1970s–1990s. See Blaxall and Reagan 1976; Fox and Hesse-Biber 1984; Reskin 1984; Reskin and Hartmann 1986; Reskin and Padavic 1994; Stromberg and Harkess 1988.

REFERENCES

AGL (Atlanta Gas Light Company) Collection. N.d. Atlanta History Center, Atlanta, Ga.
"Appliance Statistics." 1984. *Appliance* (June): 22.
Bielby, William T., and James N. Baron 1984. "A Woman's Place Is With Other Women: Sex Segregation Within Organizations." In *Sex Segregation in the Workplace: Trends, Explanations, Remedies*, edited by Barbara Reskin, 27–55. Washington, D.C.: National Academies Press.
Bix, Amy Sue. 2002. "Equipped for Life: Gendered Technical Training and Consumerism in Home Economics, 1920–1980." *Technology and Culture* 43(4): 728–754.
Blaszczyk, Regina Lee. 1997. "Where Mrs. Homemaker Is Never Forgotten: Lucy Maltby and Home Economics at Corning Glass Works, 1929–1965." In *Rethinking Home Economics: Women and the History of a Profession*, edited by Sarah Stage and Virginia B. Vincenti, 163–180. Ithaca, N.Y.: Cornell University Press.
Blaxall, Martha, and Barbara Reagan, eds. 1976. *Women and the Workplace: The Implications of Occupational Segregation*. Chicago: University of Chicago Press.
Clendinning, Anne. 2004. *Demons of Domesticity: Women and the English Gas Industry, 1889–1939*. Hampshire, England: Ashgate.
Copeland, Marcia. 1996. "The Home Economists Behind Betty Crocker." *Kappa Omicron Nu Forum* 9(2): 66–77.
Cowan, Ruth Schwartz. 1983. *More Work for Mother: The Ironies of Household Technology from the Open Hearth to the Microwave*. New York: Basic.
deMarrais, Kathleen. 2004. "Qualitative Interview Studies: Learning Through

Experience." In *Foundations for Research: Methods of Inquiry in Education and the Social Sciences*, edited by Kathleen deMarrais and Stephen D. Lapan, 51–68. Mahwah, N.J.: Erlbaum.

Emmel, JoAnn M., and Rebecca P. Lovingood. 2003. "Home Equipment Education: A Dinosaur or a Phoenix?" *Journal of Family and Consumer Sciences* 95(3): 46–51.

Emmel, JoAnn M., Rebecca P. Lovingood, Carol M. Michael, and Joseph L. Wysocki. 2010. "Association of Home Equipment Educators—The Changing Face of Home Equipment Education." *Family and Consumer Sciences Research Journal* 38(3): 333–344.

Fox, Mary Frank, and Sharlene Hesse-Biber. 1984. *Women at Work*. Mountain View, Calif.: Mayfield.

Fullerton, Howard N. 1999. "Labor Force Participation: 75 Years of Change, 1950–98 and 1998–2005." *Monthly Labor Review* (December): 3–12.

Georgia Women of Achievement. 2013. www.georgiawomen.org/2013/03/dull-henrietta-stanley-s-r (accessed July 25, 2013).

Goldstein, Carolyn M. 1997. "Part of the Package: Home Economists in the Consumer Products Industries, 1920–1940." In *Rethinking Home Economics: Women and the History of a Profession*, edited by Sarah Stage and Virginia B. Vincenti, 271–296. Ithaca, N.Y.: Cornell University Press.

———. 2012. *Creating Consumers: Home Economists in Twentieth-Century America*. Chapel Hill: University of North Carolina Press.

Grenier, Edward J. 1997. "Georgia's Move to Gas Deregulation." *Natural Gas* (November): 27–29.

Hardin, Marie. 2002. "Turning Up the Heat." *Georgia Trend* 17(5): 75–80.

Hemphill, Josephine. 1955. "Home Economics Unlimited." *Journal of Home Economics* 47(9): 653–660.

Herbert, John H. 1992. *Clean Cheap Heat: The Development of Residential Markets for Natural Gas in the United States*. New York: Praeger.

Kline, Ronald R. 1997. "Agents of Modernity: Home Economists and Rural Electrification, 1925–1950." In *Rethinking Home Economics: Women and the History of a Profession*, edited by Sarah Stage and Virginia B. Vincenti, 237–252. Ithaca, N.Y.: Cornell University Press.

Lief, Alfred. 1961. *Metering for America: 125 Years of the Gas Industry and American Meter Company*. New York: Appleton-Century-Crofts.

MacLeod, Annie Louise, ed. 1938. *Business Opportunities for the Home Economist: Jobs in Consumer Service*. New York: McGraw-Hill.

Michael, Carol M. 1988. "Support Relationships in the Career Development of Home Economists in the Home Equipment and Related Product Industries." *Home Economics Research Journal* 16(3): 163–172.

Michael, Carol M., and Fern E. Hunt. 1987. "Opportunities for Advancement of Home Economists in the Home Equipment and Related-Product Industries." *Home Economics Research Journal* 16(1): 36–45.

Reskin, Barbara, ed. 1984. *Sex Segregation in the Workplace: Trends, Explanations, Remedies*. Washington, D.C.: National Academies Press.

Reskin, Barbara, and Heidi I. Hartmann, eds. 1986. *Women's Work, Men's Work: Sex Segregation on the Job*. Washington, D.C.: National Academies Press.

Reskin, Barbara, and Irene Padavic. 1994. *Women and Men at Work*. Thousand Oaks, Calif.: Pine Forge Press.

Rossiter, Margaret W. 1982. *Women Scientists in America: Struggles and Strategies to 1940*. Baltimore, Md.: Johns Hopkins University Press.

———. 1995. *Women Scientists in America: Before Affirmative Action, 1940–1972*. Baltimore, Md.: Johns Hopkins University Press.

Soule, Ruth. 1930. "Activities of American Gas Association's Home Service Committee." In *Proceedings of the First National Home Service Conference*, 44. New York: Charles Francis Press.

Spitze, Glenna. 1988. "The Data on Women's Labor Force Participation." In *Women Working: Theories and Facts in Perspective*, 2nd ed., edited by Ann Hilton Stromberg and Shirley Harkess, 42–60. Mountain View, Calif.: Mayfield.

Stewart, Phyllis L., and Muriel G. Cantor, eds. 1982. *Varieties of Work*. Beverly Hills, Calif.: Sage.

Stromberg, Ann Helton, and Shirley Harkess, eds. 1988. *Women Working: Theories and Facts in Perspective*, 2nd ed. Mountain View, Calif.: Mayfield.

Tate, James H. 1985. *Keeper of the Flame: The Story of the Atlanta Gas Light Company, 1856 to 1985*. Atlanta, Ga.: Atlanta Gas Light Company.

Taylor, Patricia A. 1988. "Women in Organizations: Structural Factors in Women's Work Patterns." In *Women Working: Theories and Facts in Perspective*, 2nd ed., edited by Ann Helton Stromberg and Shirley Harkess, 167–181. Mountain View, Calif.: Mayfield.

Wentworth, Harold, and Stuart Berg Flexner. 1967. *Dictionary of American Slang*. New York: Crowell.

"Your Gas Co. Will Lend You a Pressure Canner." 1945. *Atlanta Constitution*, July 4, 7.

11. Science Matters

Home Economics and STEM Felds of Study

PEGGY S. MESZAROS

The United States is experiencing a talent crisis in science, technology, engineering, and math (STEM), fields that affect our economic productivity, competitiveness, quality of life, and security (Committee on Science, Engineering, and Public Policy 2006). The country is not producing the needed workforce in numbers of people, skills, or diversity to continue the U.S. position as a global leader in innovation and technology. The talent crisis is especially evident when we consider women, who could fill the gap. While women are seeking college degrees in greater numbers than men, their share of college degrees in 2006 was 20.5 percent in computer science, 19.5 percent in engineering, and 20.7 percent in physics (NSB 2008, table C-5). Women now comprise 43.5 percent of workers with a college degree, but they are only 26 percent of the people in science and engineering occupations with a degree (ibid., table H-5).

The United States has been unsuccessful in tapping underutilized and more diverse populations due to inadequate educational preparation, gender stereotypes, inaccurate images of science professions, work and family pressures, and few incentives to change educational practices (Sevo 2009). These factors have been part of the U.S. culture for decades and have served to disadvantage women and minorities seeking access to the growing fields of science and technology. It is notable that these same gaps in the female science talent pipeline existed over a hundred years ago, when a chemist and the founder of home economics, Ellen Henrietta Swallow Richards, overcame these obstacles and created a path for women interested in science. She then went further, establishing a profession built on strong science foundations and dedicated to connecting science to improving the lives of individuals and families.

This chapter reviews the challenges facing women pursuing careers in science that have persisted for over a century, the emergence of home economics and the changing presence of science in its curriculum, and a role for current home economics professionals in advancing women in the STEM professions. The life and work of the recognized founder of home economics illustrate the obstacles that faced women in science in the late 1800s and provide inspiration for addressing contemporary challenges.

A Scientist and a Leader

Environmentalist Robert Clarke (1973) called Ellen Richards the "First Lady of Science and Technology." Her passion to extend the science professions to women and to use science to improve the quality of home life is legendary (Clarke 1973; Hunt 1980; Miles 2009a, 2009b; Stage 1997a). Richards was born in 1842, the only child of Peter and Fanny Taylor Swallow. Her parents were both educated and stressed education for their daughter, whom they home-schooled for the first seventeen years of her life. She then enrolled in Westford Academy where her classical education included French and German and her genius for mathematics emerged. Working in her father's general store after school allowed her the opportunity to observe the customers and the limited knowledge they had of the food they consumed. It was during this time in Westport, Massachusetts, that Ellen began to exhibit interest in living things beyond her observations of people (Clarke 1973). She collected plants and flowers and was concerned about air and water—early stirrings of what was to come in her scientific life. Richards faced work and family challenges throughout her formative years. In need of funds for tuition, she had to be frugal, and she worked at tutoring, cleaning, and caring for her sick mother. Her urge to learn was tremendous, but there were no colleges for women in New England then, and a woman's place was steadfastly thought to be in the home.

Educational opportunities for women in the 1860s–1870s were extremely limited with the prevailing attitude and belief being that women had smaller brains and weaker minds than men (Cremin 1980). There was also the fear that education might make a girl unfit for marriage and her subservient role as a wife. In fact, early academies and seminaries for women were targeted at preparing them to be good mothers and to be able to help their sons learn. While between 1850 and the 1870s there were a variety of models for collegiate education, such as private women's colleges, religiously oriented coeducational colleges, private coordinate women's colleges, secular coeducational institutions, and public single-sex vocational institutions, in 1870 only 0.7 percent of the female population went to college (Solomon 1985). Science education for women during this time period was extremely rare. As more educated women joined scientific organizations, men began to feel they were intruding on their domains, resulting in a series of incidents in the 1880s and 1890s that caused an almost total ouster of women from positions in science other than in subordinate roles (Rossiter 1982).

Fortuitously, in 1861 Matthew Vassar opened a college for women where Richards enrolled in 1868 at the age of twenty-six as a third-year student. Two Vassar College professors provided positive images of a scientist and influenced Richards's growing interest in astronomy and chemistry. Professor Maria Mitchell, a rare female faculty member for the time, deepened Richards's knowledge of astronomy, but it was Professor Charles S. Farrar whose strong influence persuaded her to pursue chemistry because of its potential to help in the solution of practical problems. Richards graduated from Vassar with a bachelor of science degree in 1870, but this was only the beginning of her journey to becoming a scientist. Experiences of gender stereotyping, which still sound familiar today, dogged Richards as she sought to advance her formal education.

The U.S. Civil War ended in 1865. Social conditions improved somewhat for women and African Americans, but science and technology continued to be dominated by Euro American men. Nevertheless, Richards was determined to follow her passion for chemistry. In 1871, she applied to the Massachusetts Institute of Technology (MIT), which had been established in 1861, and was accepted as a "special student," considered by many as an experiment to see if females really could learn science. Richards was fully conscious of her status as the only woman at MIT, and she was determined not to call undue attention to herself. She dressed very plainly, pulled her hair straight back, and walked quickly and quietly through the halls. She did simple tasks for the male professors, such as mending suspenders, but she did not think this was being subservient. Rather, these tasks expressed her altruism and caring for people in her life and, apparently, built trust among the professors, who gradually opened opportunities for her in their laboratories. It was also during this time that her walks around the city exposed her to filth, disease, and suffering, which deepened her resolve to find scientific solutions for the ills of ordinary people.

Richards completed the requirements for the bachelor of science degree in chemistry at MIT in 1873; she had been the first woman in the United States accepted to any school of science and technology, and now she was the first woman to earn a bachelor of science degree in chemistry. In the same year, Vassar conferred on her a master of arts in chemistry. She continued her studies at MIT for two more years, but was not awarded a doctorate, perhaps because MIT did not want its first PhD in chemistry to be awarded to a woman.

Much later, Smith College awarded Richards the honorary degree of doctor of science in 1910.

In 1875 Ellen Swallow married Robert Hallowell Richards, the chair of MIT's Mining Engineering Department. They settled in a house in the Boston suburb of Jamaica Plain, which became a laboratory for their theories in household efficiency. Determined to change educational practices for women, Richards volunteered her services and donated $1,000 annually to further women's science education at MIT. With support from the Women's Education Association of Boston, she established the "women's laboratory" in 1876. In 1879 she was given the title of assistant instructor, without pay. She taught courses in chemical analysis, industrial chemistry, mineralogy, and applied biology. Determined to further expand educational opportunities for women, in 1882 Richards and Marion Talbot were leaders in forming the Association of Collegiate Alumnae, later renamed the American Association of University Women. The special laboratory for women was closed in 1883 as MIT began awarding undergraduate degrees to women on a regular basis.

MIT appointed Richards as an instructor in sanitary chemistry in 1884. At the request of the Massachusetts State Board of Health, she and her assistants performed a survey of the quality of the inland bodies of water of Massachusetts, many of which were polluted with industrial waste and sewage. The scale of this survey was unprecedented and led to the first state water-quality standards in the nation as well as the first modern municipal sewage treatment plant in Massachusetts. She served as a chemist with the Manufacturers Mutual Fire Insurance Company from 1884 to 1894.

While at the women's laboratory, Richards had decided to apply scientific principles to domestic topics, including nutrition, pure foods, physical fitness, sanitation, proper clothing, and efficient practices that would allow women time for pursuits other than cooking and cleaning. She and Talbot published *Home Sanitation: A Manual for Housekeepers* (Richards and Talbot 1882). In her lifetime Richards published seventeen books on sanitation and home economics, including the first health food cookbook published in the United States. She organized public demonstrations of good nutrition and sanitation as she developed the New England Kitchen in 1890 and the Rumford Kitchen in 1893. A feature of the World's Columbian Exposition in Chicago, the Rumford Kitchen provided inexpensive but nutritious meals and informed people about nutrition and food preparation. Ten thousand people were served during the two months that it was open. Richards lobbied tirelessly for providing nutritious school lunches and courses in domestic science in Boston's public schools. The time was ripe for this new application of science to the practical problems of daily life.

Home Economics Foundation in Science

Home economics as a field of study and scientific investigation emerged in the United States at the end of the nineteenth century just as a greater focus on scientific explanations arose in the culture, industrialization transformed the economy, and immigration and urbanization altered population patterns. These dramatic changes contributed to a period of social activism and political reform from the 1890s to the 1920s known as the Progressive Era (Buenker, Burnham, and Crunden 1986; Diner 1998). Science and progressivism hoped to achieve efficiency by identifying old ways that needed modernizing, and they emphasized scientific, medical, and engineering solutions (Stage 1997b). This was the perfect environment for the emergence of Richards's vision of scientific applications to improve home and family life. By 1888 there were already efforts under way to introduce domestic science into the New York City public schools; earlier, in 1871–1874, there had been similar work at the college level at what are now known as Kansas State University, the University of Illinois, and Iowa State University (Bevier 1924). At that time, however, there was little coherence in the curricula being taught at each level of education. Action was needed to bring structure and order. It was time for Richards to use her organizational skills. The Lake Placid Conferences provided the venue.

At the turn of the twentieth century a group of professionals from diverse fields met together at the Lake Placid Club in New York State to discuss the welfare of the family. Ten Lake Placid Conferences were held from 1899 to 1908, bringing coherence to the efforts springing up in this new field, which had little unified direction. Curriculum matters were considered at each of the conferences. The second conference in 1900 described the necessity of making clear connections between study topics and their scientific underpinnings in the proposed curriculum to be taught in high schools (Lake Placid Conference 1901). The fourth Lake Placid Conference (1902, 70–71) developed a definition of the new field:

> Home economics in its most comprehensive sense is the study of the laws, conditions, principles and ideals which are concerned on the one hand with man's immediate physical environment and on the other hand with his nature as a social being, and is the study specially of the relation between those two factors. . . . In forming a complete definition, however, it may be possible to consider home economics as a philosophical subject, i.e., a study of relation, while the subjects on which it depends, i.e., economics, sociology, chemistry, hygiene and others, are empirical in their nature and concerned with events and phenomena.

As the annual Lake Placid Conferences ended in 1908, the American Home Economics Association (AHEA), today called the American Association of Family and Consumer Sciences (AAFCS), was chartered in Washington, D.C. Richards served as the first president and remained active until her death in 1911.

At AHEA's second annual meeting the Committee on Nomenclature was appointed for the purpose of encouraging unity and standards among home economics educators. The committee prepared the *Syllabus of Home Economics: An Outline of Subject Matter*, a forty-nine-page comprehensive statement of topics to be covered, although it allowed flexibility to adapt to the circumstances of various institutions (AHEA 1913). In any case, the foundation in science was clear.

Throughout the twentieth century the home economics curricula for secondary school and college courses were revisited periodically. Trilling and her colleagues (1920) critiqued the relatively new home economics programs in U.S. public schools as showing little evidence of a sequentially arranged curriculum. She asserted that standardized tests and scales were particularly needed to make home economics scientific. In contrast, McGrath (1968) retrospectively observed that in the 1920s home economics in higher education drew heavily on the physical and biological sciences in preparing secondary school teachers. (A complete and compelling overview of the McGrath report, as well as other developments in home economics, is found in the chapter "Protecting Home Economics: The Women's Field" in Rossiter 1995.)

In June 1927 the AHEA's Committee on the Revision of the Syllabus expanded the 1913 syllabus from its original divisions—food, clothing, shelter, and management—by adding institutional management, family relationships, and family economics. The AHEA appointed another committee in 1944 to study the standards for membership in the association and another committee to study the core curriculum (Branegan 1946). In 1949, after five years of work by the Committee on Criteria for Evaluating College Programs of Home Economics, there was no specific mention of science in *Home Economics in Higher Education: Criteria for Evaluating Undergraduate Programs* (Spafford 1949, nicknamed "the Bluebook"). During the ensuing years the AHEA dealt with accreditation issues and, later, certification issues.

At mid-century, secondary school educators examined the new curriculum guidelines. Directed by Beulah Coon of the Home Economics Division of the U.S. Office of Education, this study found a lack of balance in the curriculum, which primarily emphasized food preparation and clothing construction (Coon 1961). Subsequently, several home economics organizations sponsored a national conference at French Lick, Indiana, to address concerns among college and university faculties about the problems of articulation and differentiation in home economics subject matter at the secondary, college, and adult education levels (Vincenti 1997). From this and workshops conducted between 1961 and 1964, basic concepts and generalizations in five subject areas of home economics at the high school level were developed (AHEA 1967). Secondary educators later revised this curriculum guide and published *Home Economics Concepts: A Base for Curriculum Development* (AHEA 1989), which included an emphasis on "critical science" throughout.

In the 1989 yearbook of AHEA's Teacher Education Section, *Alternative Modes of Inquiry in Home Economics Research* (Hultgren and Coomer 1989), some authors reviewed the historic prevalence of empirical and analytic science in home economics while others argued for more interpretative modes of inquiry. Critical science was embraced by educators "to help their students develop more complex ways of reasoning and to provide a forum for social dialogue" (Coomer 1989, 197). As an advocate of critical science, Vincenti (1990, 189) urged home economics educators to develop curricula around the needs of society, teaching students to solve "perennial, practical problems by the inclusion of cognitive and affective processes . . . analysis of life situations . . . generation and criticism of alternative actions, and the making of value judgments," rather than training them solely for narrow, predesignated careers. In this paradigm, science was in the curriculum but took a different form from the empirical science approach in earlier syllabi.

As the end of the twentieth century approached, home economics leaders took stock of the substantial changes that had occurred in U.S. society and in the field itself, all of which had impacts on the curriculum. A conference, "Positioning the Profession for the 21st Century," was held in Scottsdale, Arizona, in 1993 to address multiple issues ("Conceptual Framework" 1994; Simerly et al. 2000; also see Kay, this volume). A significant outcome of the meeting was that AHEA changed the name of the association to the American Association of Family and Consumer Sciences (AAFCS). It is noteworthy that the new name included the word "sciences."

Anticipating the turn of the twenty-first century, and in keeping with the passage of the national Goals 2000: Educate America Act in 1994, administrators responsible for home economics in state departments of education in partnership with the Vocational Technical Education Consortium of States developed a comprehensive plan for public school programs: *National Standards for Family and Consumer Sciences Education* (1998). This plan sought to "prepare students for family life, work life, and careers in Family and Consumer Sciences by providing opportunities to develop [necessary] knowledge, skills, attitudes, and behaviors" (ibid., 1). *National Standards* encompassed academic and occupational content for family and consumer sciences, based on the "practical problems" approach (ibid., 16). Words such as "facts," "examine," "interpret," "technical action," and "reflection" echoed science concepts although the word "science" was not specifically used.

One director of family and consumer sciences education reported that she and her colleagues continue to use the National Standards as the basis for competency development in coordination with state-specific standards of learning (pers. comm., 2012). An emphasis on science is a thread that runs through the various career clusters with the aim of teaching the competencies needed in today's culture. Funding for these school programs varies as federal and state funding for education fluctuates.

In higher education, units that seek accreditation by the American Association of Family and Consumer Sciences must meet criteria related to the "discovery, integration, and application of knowledge," documenting that faculty members demonstrate scholarly or creative activity, advance knowledge through a variety of activities, and engage students in scientific experiences as appropriate (Council for Accreditation 2010). A wide variety of methods of inquiry are evident in the institutions of higher education and journals of the profession.

New Solutions for an Old Problem

Ellen Swallow Richards's life provides a useful backdrop against which to review the development of home economics curricula. As a highly gendered field, home economics provided a foundation for women to enter areas of applied science (Rossiter 1982), and women scientists dominated science and technology in home economics until the mid-twentieth century (Rossiter 1995, 1997). Sevo's (2009) examination of the talent crisis in science and engineering asks the question, in over a century has there been real progress for women interested in a broader spectrum of science careers? The answer is that there has been hardly any; the same challenges that plagued women in Richards's generation are still present. Gender stereotyping; inadequate educational preparation; narrow and inaccurate images of science, engineering, and technology professions; and weak legal and moral pressures to change educational practices continue and are related to the talent crisis in science.

While college education today is more available to women, who now outnumber men in undergraduate programs, the percentage of women earning degrees in STEM is still small. Women are entering engineering, some science fields, and mathematics as academic majors; however, the information technology (IT) career field today presents more barriers for women than even engineering or mathematics. Only one in four people in the IT workforce is female (ITAA 2007; U.S. Department of Labor 2012; Vegso 2005).

Researchers have struggled to understand why proactive efforts to recruit women to computer-based science fields often are not successful. Even when they have both the skills and interest in computers, females of all ages consistently express less confidence in their technological abilities (Gurer and

Camp 1998; Sax and Harper 2005). Many fail to make a connection between their skills and interests and a career choice (Meszaros, Lee, and Laughlin 2007; O'Brien and Fassinger 1993).

This problem has begun to be addressed in the twenty-first century. My research team at Virginia Tech, through a National Science Foundation–funded project, identified subtle and implicit biases in Appalachian culture, such as gender stereotyping, as significant factors deterring young women from viewing IT as a viable career choice (Meszaros, Lee, and Laughlin 2007; Creamer, Lee, and Meszaros 2007). These views, often held by school counselors, teachers, and parents, along with stereotypical ideas about the nature of all STEM careers, especially IT, communicate negative values and beliefs that are embedded in the local environment surrounding young girls and influencing their career decisions (Committee on Maximizing the Potential of Women 2007). Lack of encouragement from influential adults, preconceived notions, sexist attitudes, and stereotypes regarding IT are some of the most difficult barriers for girls to overcome. These findings echo Sevo's review noted earlier. They also echo the situation for females during Richards's time.

There are definite parallels between Ellen Richards in the 1870s and the girls in Appalachia in 2013. The Appalachian region of the eastern United States is home to over 20 million people and covers parts of thirteen states; it has a rugged topography and a distinct culture (Hurst 1992). The cultural values of strong family and community ties are shaped in part by geographic isolation from mainstream culture. Living far from cities and neighbors, often with poor or no roads, the inhabitants of Appalachia have been dependent on family and kin for their survival. Appalachian culture is predominantly patriarchal in its socialization process; traditional gender roles are valued and supported (Engelhardt 2005; Fiene 2002; Walker 2000). The basic elements of Appalachian culture, such as strong family, kinship, church, and community ties; high value on independence and an oral tradition; distrust of outsiders; and a preference for family responsibilities when they conflict with other values, such as education, mirror many of the values that shaped Richards as a young girl growing up in Massachusetts. Resources to bring about change in Appalachia in the twenty-first century continue to be scarce.

Enter family and consumer sciences professionals from five Appalachian states with a holistic view of problem solving. In October 2008 the National Science Foundation funded an Appalachian Information Technology Extension Services (AITES) grant for five years at $2.5 million. AITES spans five Appalachian states—Virginia, Kentucky, Tennessee, North Carolina, and West Virginia—focusing on two counties in each state. The overarching goal of AITES is to develop community capacity through a sustainable program of change, concentrating on educating the teachers, school counselors, and parents who are the supporters of middle and high school girls in these communities. Our research found that there is nothing "wrong" with the girls that would inhibit their interest in science; rather, it is the environment around them that is discouraging: the parents, teachers, school personnel, and community members with their traditional values and lack of support for females in nontraditional roles.

Appalachian residents have a higher poverty rate and a higher percentage of working poor than the rest of the nation. Fifty-seven percent of adults in central Appalachia did not graduate from high school compared to less than 20 percent in the general U.S. population (Hurst 1992). Almost 30 percent of Appalachian adults are considered functionally illiterate. Educational differences between men and women are greater in Appalachia than in the rest of the nation, resulting in other gender inequalities (Shaw, DeYoung, and Rademacher 2004). While county- and gender-specific data are not available, the college completion rate for both men and women in the ten Appalachian counties served by AITES ranges from 9.4 percent in Russell County to 28.7 percent in Forsyth County, the most metropolitan among the ten. Women in these Appalachian counties have traditionally been confined to the domestic sphere where resources and employment opportunities are limited. Just as in Richards's day, traditional views are held of what is appropriate for women, and parents generally do not value educating daughters for employment, which is likely to be outside the area.

Upon hearing about the AITES project, a local legislator predicted that parents would never support educating their daughters so that they would leave home. Fortunately, there are IT jobs right in the local communities since the old industries of coal mining and manufacturing are dying out and the new industry is technology-driven. There are not enough workers, female or male, to fill the job openings. These jobs promise higher salaries and hope for the future as the United States struggles to keep up with the world. The goal of AITES is to educate the surrounding environment through building partnerships between parents, schools, local IT industries, family and consumer sciences educators, 4-H Cooperative Extension agents, community economic development professionals, and other community stakeholders. The premise is that as the community increases its awareness of how to overcome gender stereotyping, broadens its knowledge of the breadth of IT opportunities locally, and expands strategies for supporting girls' involvement in IT, more girls will receive encouragement to explore all STEM careers, especially IT. Family and consumer sciences and 4-H professionals are ideally positioned to carry out this project given their commitment to improving both families and communities. They are trusted in their communities and familiar with setting goals, delivering programs, and measuring outcomes.

The AITES project builds community capacity to encourage more females to pursue a career in IT through forming community cohort teams (CCTs) of middle and high school teachers and counselors and Cooperative Extension agents in the two counties in each AITES state. The engagement design consists of yearly train-the-trainer workshops, where examples of gender stereotypes are identified and strategies to overcome them are discussed. Women working in IT in the local communities are profiled and strategies for supporting middle and high school girls' career decision making are formulated. The CCTs then carry out community workshops using this new information to train their peers, parents, and community leaders. These trained individuals then further extend the network of informed community leaders to influence others in their work, school, and community environments and ultimately to encourage the girls to seek IT career paths.

While the AITES project does not solve all the problems of interesting more women in science and technology, it is an example of outreach and engagement patterned after the holistic approach used by early pioneers in home economics. Family and consumer sciences professionals are leaders in each of the five states: they chair the state partners boards and use their organizational skills to bring other community stakeholders to the table. The state partners boards are composed of IT industry owners, school principals and superintendents, parent-teacher associations, mayors, chambers of commerce, local civic groups, and others. The Appalachian Information Technology Extension Services National Pioneer Partners Board is made up of industry representatives from Apple, Microsoft, and Cisco; local IT CEOs; Department of Education representatives from the various states; national media reporters; and Cooperative Extension personnel. These boards give guidance to the project annually, review evaluation results, and provide ideas for developing curricula and sustainability.

In the fifth year of operation of the CCTs, pre- and post-test AITES data reveal that they are having an impact by increasing awareness of gender stereotyping, of the broad range of IT jobs available in their communities, and of strategies to support girls' interest in IT and all STEM fields. An evidence-based best practices guide featured case studies of the participants in the project. When asked what changes they had noticed in their own growth through the project, one community cohort team member said, "I was not aware of my own prejudices about nontraditional jobs [for women] until this project. I can be a better counselor now that I recognize how I have changed" (Meszaros, Mutcheson, and Kimbrell 2013). A state partners board member and owner of an IT company remarked that the project had opened his eyes to the severe shortage of women IT workers educated in the United States. His company employed several females in IT, but when he checked he found they were all from Asia (pers. comm., 2012).

Efforts to sustain the AITES program's progress include the development of a mobile platform with content linking girls' interests to IT jobs in their communities. This resource will be accessible throughout the Appalachian region by the AITES teams and IT industry owners to continue the education and work with middle and high school girls. Boys and youth with disabilities will be added to the target audience of girls in the sustainability phase of the project.

On the national level, a number of laws forbid discrimination that impedes the participation of women in science and engineering. Most prominent is the Civil Rights Act of 1964, which outlaws employment discrimination on the basis of race, color, religion, sex, or national origin. Title IX of the Education Amendments of 1972 and the Perkins Act of 1978 also outlaw discrimination on the basis of sex in any educational program receiving federal funding. The American Association of University Women (AAUW), the organization that home economists Richards and Talbot were instrumental in founding, has reported on the problems facing women seeking STEM careers and has proposed recommendations to rectify the situation (Hill, Corbett, and St. Rose 2010). The AAUW offers scholarships to women, and its research findings advance women in STEM areas.

At least one federal agency has taken action to overcome some of the family issues preventing women from advancing in science careers. The Equal Opportunities for Women and Minorities in Science and Technology Act of 1981 mandates that the National Science Foundation (NSF) report statistics on underrepresented groups and initiate a suite of programs to increase diversity in the science and engineering workforce. The NSF's Career-Life Balance Initiative is one such program, designed to address the proportion of women attaining full professorship positions at U.S. colleges and universities by creating specific initiatives for both women and men to balance the conflicting demands of life, such as the birth or adoption of a child, raising children, or providing elderly dependent care. These actions are aimed at helping to enlarge and preserve the nation's domestic STEM talent pool with a coherent and consistent set of family-friendly policies and practices. These and other initiatives are promising, yet they are small programs dependent on local action and enforcement for success.

Science Still Matters

Has the home economics profession kept true to the strong science underpinning of its curriculum, which was so prominent in its formative years? A review of the events in curriculum development provides an ongoing picture of a profession constantly searching for its scientific moorings and willing to expand its understanding of science. A renewed focus on research, indicated by

the establishment of the Center for Research within the AAFCS, can do much to
stimulate awareness of the profession's grounding in science. Richards and her
collaborators set the profession on the right track. Now it is the task of today's
educators to move forward not just in the classroom, but also in the neighborhoods, businesses, and organizations of the community in order to foster the
development of women's potential to engage with matters of science.

REFERENCES

AHEA (American Home Economics Association). 1913. *Syllabus of Home Economics.*
Baltimore, Md.: AHEA.
——. 1967. *Concepts and Generalizations: Their Place in High School Home Economics
Curriculum Development.* Washington, D.C.: AHEA.
——. 1989. *Home Economics Concepts: A Base for Curriculum Development.*
Alexandria, Va.: AHEA.
Bevier, Isabel. 1924. *Home Economics in Education.* Philadelphia: Lippincott.
Branegan, Gladys. 1946. "Study of College Undergraduate Home Economics Programs
of Sixty Representative Schools or Departments: Report and Proposal from
the Committee on Standards for Membership." Unpublished report. American
Association of Family and Consumer Sciences Archives, Kroch Library. Cornell
University, Ithaca, N.Y.
Buenker, John D., John C. Burnham, and Robert M. Crunden. 1986. *Progressivism.*
Cambridge, Mass.: Schenkman.
Clarke, Robert. 1973. *Ellen Swallow: The Woman Who Founded Ecology.* Chicago: Follett.
Committee on Maximizing the Potential of Women in Academic Science and
Engineering. 2007. "Beyond Bias and Barriers: Fulfilling the Potential of Women
in Academic Science and Engineering," http://www.nap.edu/catalog.php?record
id=11741 (accessed January 15, 2012).
Committee on Science, Engineering, and Public Policy. 2006. *Rising Above the
Gathering Storm: Energizing and Employing America for a Brighter Economic Future.*
Washington, D.C.: National Academies Press.
"The Conceptual Framework for the 21st Century." 1994. *Journal of Family and
Consumer Sciences* 86(4): 38.
Coomer, Donna L. 1989. "Introduction to Critical Inquiry." In *Alternative Modes of
Inquiry in Home Economics Research*, edited by Francine H. Hultgren and Donna L.
Coomer, 167–184. Peoria, Ill.: Glencoe.
Coon, Beulah. 1961. *Home Economics in the Public Secondary Schools: A Report of a
National Study.* Washington, D.C.: Office of Education.
Council for Accreditation, American Association of Family and Consumer Sciences.
2010. *Accreditation Documents for Undergraduate Programs in Family and
Consumer Sciences.* Arlington, Va.: American Association of Family and Consumer
Sciences.
Creamer, Elizabeth G., Soyoung Lee, and Peggy S. Meszaros. 2007. "Predicting
Women's Interest in and Choice of a Career in Information Technology: A
Statistical Model." In *Reconfiguring the Firewall: Recruiting Women to Information*

Technology Across Culture and Continents, edited by Carol J. Burger, Elizabeth G. Creamer, and Peggy S. Meszaros, 15–38. Wellesley, Mass.: Peters.

Cremin, Lawrence A. 1980. *American Education: The National Experience, 1783–1876*. New York: Harper and Row.

Diner, Steven J. 1998. *A Very Different Age: Americans of the Progressive Era*. New York: Hill and Wang.

Engelhardt, Elizabeth, ed. 2005. *Beyond Hill and Hollow: Original Readings in Appalachian Women's Studies*. Athens: Ohio University Press.

Fiene, Judith I. 2002. "Gender, Class and Self-Image." In *Appalachia: Social Context Past and Present*, edited by Phillip Obermiller and Michael Maloney, 71–79. Dubuque, Iowa: Kendall/Hunt.

Gurer, Denise, and Tracy Camp. 1998. "Investigating the Incredible Shrinking Pipeline for Women in Computer Science." Final Report on NSF Project 9812016, http://women.acm.org/documents/finalreport.pdf (accessed June 9, 2006).

Hill, Catherine, Christianne Corbett, and Andresse St. Rose. 2010. *Why So Few? Women in Science, Technology, Engineering, and Mathematics*. Washington, D.C.: American Association of University Women.

Hultgren, Francine H., and Donna L. Coomer, eds. 1989. *Alternative Modes of Inquiry in Home Economics Research*. Peoria, Ill.: Glencoe.

Hunt, Caroline. 1980. *The Life of Ellen H. Richards*, 8th ed. Washington, D.C.: American Home Economics Association.

Hurst, Charles E. 1992. *Social Inequality: Forms, Causes and Consequences*, 6th ed. Boston: Allyn and Bacon.

ITAA (Information Technology Association of America). 2007. "IT Workforce Woes: Gartner Says 60 Percent of Organizations Ill Equipped to Build Workforce of the Future," http://www.itaa.org/sec/pubs/ecurrent.cfm (accessed September 22, 2007).

Lake Placid Conference on Home Economics. 1901. *Proceedings of the First, Second, and Third Conferences*. Lake Placid, N.Y.: n.p.

———. 1902. *Proceedings of the Fourth Conference*. Lake Placid, N.Y.: n.p.

McGrath, Earl J. 1968. "The Imperatives of Change for Home Economics." *Journal of Home Economics* 60: 505–514.

Meszaros, Peggy S., Soyoung Lee, and Anne Laughlin. 2007. "Information Processing and Information Technology: Career and Choice Among High School Students." In *Reconfiguring the Firewall: Recruiting Women to Information Technology Across Cultures and Continents*, edited by Carol J. Burger, Elizabeth G. Creamer, and Peggy S. Meszaros, 77–95. Wellesley, Mass.: Peters.

Meszaros, Peggy S., Ryan Brock Mutcheson, and Monica Kimbrell. 2013. *Appalachian Information Technology Extension Services Resource Compendium*, http://www.itpathways.org/userfiles/files/Resource_Compendium.pdf (accessed October 16, 2014).

Miles, Joyce B. 2009a. *Ellen Swallow Richards: In Her Own Words*. DVD available from American Association of Family and Consumer Sciences, Alexandria, Va.

———. 2009b. *The Life and Legacy of Ellen Swallow Richards*. DVD available from American Association of Family and Consumer Sciences, Alexandria, Va.

National Standards for Family and Consumer Sciences Education. 1998. Decatur, Ga.: Vocational Technical Education Consortium of States, http://ideanet.doe.state. in.us/octe/facs/natistandards.htm (accessed December 30, 2011).

NSB (National Science Board). 2008. *Science and Engineering Indicators 2008.* Arlington, Va.: National Science Foundation.

O'Brien, Karen M., and Ruth E. Fassinger. 1993. "A Causal Model of the Career Orientation and Career Choice of Adolescent Women." *Journal of Counseling Psychology* 40: 456–469.

Richards, Ellen H. Swallow, and Marion Talbot. 1882. *Home Sanitation: A Manual for Housekeepers.* Charleston, S.C.: Nabu Public Domain Reprints.

Rossiter, Margaret. 1982. *Women Scientists in America: Struggles and Strategies to 1940.* Baltimore, Md.: Johns Hopkins University Press.

———. 1995. *Women Scientists in America: Before Affirmative Action, 1940–1972.* Baltimore, Md.: Johns Hopkins University Press.

———. 1997. "The Men Move In: Home Economics, 1950–1970." In *Rethinking Home Economics: Women and the History of a Profession*, edited by Sarah Stage and Virginia B. Vincenti, 96–117. Ithaca, N.Y.: Cornell University Press.

Sax, Linda, and Cassandra E. Harper. 2005. "Origins of the Gender Gap: Pre-College and College Influences on Differences Between Men and Women." Paper presented at the annual meeting of the Association for Institutional Research, San Diego, Calif., May.

Sevo, Ruta. 2009. "The Talent Crisis in Science and Engineering." In *Apply Research to Practice (ARP) Resources*, edited by Barbara Bogue and Elizabeth Cady, http:// www.engr/AWE/ARPResources.aspx (accessed December 16, 2011).

Shaw, Thomas C., Alan J. DeYoung, and Eric W. Rademacher. 2004. "Educational Attainment in Appalachia: Growing with the Nation but Challenges Remain." *Journal of Appalachian Studies* 10(3): 307–329.

Simerly, Coby B., Penny A. Ralston, Lynda Harriman, and Barbara Taylor. 2000. "The Scottsdale Initiative: Positioning the Profession for the 21st Century." *Journal of Family and Consumer Sciences* 92(1): 75–80.

Solomon, Barbara. 1985. *In the Company of Educated Women.* New Haven, Conn.: Yale University Press.

Spafford, Ivor, ed. 1949. *Home Economics in Higher Education: Criteria for Evaluating Undergraduate Programs.* Washington, D.C.: American Home Economics Association.

Stage, Sarah. 1997a. "Ellen Richards and the Social Significance of the Home Economics Movement." In *Rethinking Home Economics: Women and the History of a Profession*, edited by Sarah Stage and Virginia B. Vincenti, 17–33. Ithaca, N.Y.: Cornell University Press.

———. 1997b. "Home Economics: What's in a Name?" In *Rethinking Home Economics: Women and the History of a Profession*, edited by Sarah Stage and Virginia B. Vincenti, 1–13. Ithaca, N.Y.: Cornell University Press.

Trilling, Mabel, et al. 1920. *Home Economics in American Schools.* Chicago: University of Chicago Press.

U.S. Department of Labor. 2012. "Labor Force Statistics from the Current Population Survey," http://www.bls.gov/cps/cpsaat11.htm (accessed July 5, 2013).

Vegso, Jay. 2005. "Interest in CS as a Major Drops Among Incoming Freshmen." *Computing Research News* 17(3), http://www.cra.org/CRN/articles/may05/vegso (accessed December 30, 2011).

Vincenti, Virginia B. 1990. "Home Economics in Higher Education: Communities of Convenience or Purpose?" *Home Economics Research Journal* 19(2): 184–193.

———. 1997. "Home Economics Moves into the Twenty-First Century." In *Rethinking Home Economics: Women and the History of a Profession*, edited by Sarah Stage and Virginia B. Vincenti, 301–320. Ithaca, N.Y.: Cornell University Press.

Walker, Melissa. 2000. *All We Knew Was to Farm: Rural Women in the Upcountry South, 1919–1941*. Baltimore, Md.: Johns Hopkins University Press.

IV. Home Economics
Identity and Continuity

The next two chapters examine some thorny issues faced by units of home economics in the context of institutional and cultural change, in order to better understand the decisions made in response to challenges to identity and continuity. Both group deliberation and quick-response activism—vastly different ways to deal with identity and perseverance—are solutions found in the history of the profession.

Gwen Kay, the author of chapter 12, "Changing Names, Keeping Identity," explores the issue of nomenclature for home economics, an ongoing question throughout the field's history. The outcome of discussions at the Lake Placid Conferences about a name for the nascent field was "home economics," and it remained uncontested for six decades. After several years of discussion, the American Home Economics Association (AHEA) formally examined the organization's mission, values, and indeed its name. Kay's chapter tells the story of how a new name was adopted in 1993, when the AHEA became the American Association of Family and Consumer Sciences (AAFCS). The core values of home economics continue in AAFCS and in institutions of higher education that have adopted other names.

Another issue related to identity and continuity is illustrated by the case of Kansas State University's College of Human Ecology, the subject of chapter 13, "Building a Legacy in Stone: Rocks in the Road" by Virginia Moxley. Kansas State was one of the first land-grant colleges and among the earliest coeducational colleges, and its faculty in domestic science provided early leadership in the western home economics movement beginning in 1873. The home economics program had an illustrious history, and thirteen campus buildings bear the names of significant leaders in home economics. The college was nationally recognized, yet it was targeted by campus administrators for elimination in 1990. Moxley's chapter recounts the mobilization of students, alumni, faculty, and staff to successfully advocate for the continuation of the college.

In the concluding chapter, "Looking Around, Thinking Ahead," Sharon Y. Nickols, Gwen Kay, and Billie J. Collier explore the interrelations of home economics and the changing contexts in which it functions. Responsiveness to the contemporary context has been prominent in several of the chapters, yet a dynamic field of study must invest some thought into anticipating the future. Nickols, Kay, and Collier emphasize the importance of attending to the vast demographic changes occurring in the United States as home economics works in the public interest in the future. Individual and family empowerment is a persistent theme in home economics, yet the profession itself has limited political power. Consequently, for the field to continue remaking itself, it needs the support of a constituency of advocates beyond the profession.

As an area of study and professional practice that is complex and multifaceted, home economics calls for joint endeavors among scholars from a variety of perspectives. Hopefully, this volume provokes new understandings and new questions that will continue the custom and necessity of innovating and remaking home economics. How will you be engaged?

12. Changing Names, Keeping Identity

GWEN KAY

"How would you like your name changed after all these years? What is a name? It's what people identify you by and what you go by. The most important title you hold" (Robinson 1990). In her letter to University of Georgia president Charles Knapp explaining why she did not want the name "home economics" to disappear from her alma mater, Jean Robinson, a proud College of Home Economics graduate, articulated her attachment to the name "home economics" and her reluctance to lose it. This discussion, and letters like this one, occurred over and over as colleges assessed themselves and positioned for the future. What happens when the discussion is on a much larger scale, such as a professional organization?

Home economics, like many other disciplines, continually evolves, redefining its mission, purpose, values, and educational goals. For a discipline firmly embedded in the educational system from junior high school through postgraduate work, which receives federal funding for "home economics," change can be challenging. For a discipline perceived by the American public as largely domestic, change can be powerful. One of the most visible ways a discipline can alert outsiders to its internal transformation and reconceptualization is by changing its name. In this chapter, I examine the complexity that surrounded the decision when a professional organization composed of a diverse group of practitioners—college and junior and senior high school educators, members of industry, extension personnel—sought change. Each constituency had its own agenda, its own population of "clients," its own reasons for being, and its own beliefs that informed its actions—and individual members had their own personal beliefs and opinions as well. In 1993, organizations interested in home economics convened in Scottsdale, Arizona, to participate in a conference with the title "Positioning the Profession for the

21st Century: Professional Unity and Identity." This meeting had been preceded by several other events that also scrutinized home economics. The Scottsdale conference was about more than the name of the profession, but this single issue—the name—became a symbol for how the conference has been remembered and interpreted.

Some participants at Scottsdale, particularly administrators, were from institutions that no longer carried "home economics" in the title of their college or school. The educational institutions from which these administrators came had changed their names in internally driven processes. For national organizations whose members were trained as home economists, including the Association of Administrators of Home Economics, the National Council of Administrators of Home Economics, the National Association of Extension Home Economists, the Home Economics Division of the American Vocational Association, and the American Home Economics Association (AHEA), change was more complex. The names of these organizations needed to reflect their members in terms of both self-identity and their sense of the profession.

As I examine the process, conversations, and decisions made before, at, and after Scottsdale and how the American Association of Family and Consumer Sciences emerged, transformed and poised to enter the twenty-first century, several questions are relevant. What were the experiences of colleges of home economics when they initiated their name change? What events in home economics professional associations, aimed at clarifying the philosophy and content of home economics, preceded the Scottsdale conference? What were the processes and outcomes of that meeting? What was the effect of the long delay in directly addressing the name of the professional organization on the processes and the outcomes?

For those organizations whose constituents were graduates of these programs, the name "home economics" had power and significance. Many home economics graduates belonged to the AHEA, the largest professional organization; in addition, many also belonged to more specialized and career-appropriate entities. For the AHEA's closely allied organizations to change their names, much communication was necessary. The term "home economics" had resonance, and some AHEA members were reluctant to let the name go. Had the AHEA acted even a decade earlier, the eventual chosen name might have been the obvious one for many programs seeking a new name. Instead, there were many names in use at the time (Horn 1981).

The issue of the name of this field has, almost from its beginning in the nineteenth century, been contested. "Domestic science" was an applied, practical science. At some institutions, the first two years of the domestic science curriculum were nearly identical to those of agriculture. To further complicate matters, domestic science was an umbrella term encompassing many different areas of study, including chemistry, food preparation and preservation, and textiles. Some college programs in the 1870s used "domestic science," while others used "sanitary science" for the parallel course of study offered for female students at land-grant institutions. The birthplace of domestic science is also contested, with Iowa State University, Kansas State University, and the University of Illinois each staking a claim (Eppright and Ferguson 1971; Hoeflin 1988; Miller 2004). From 1899 to 1908, a series of meetings were held at Lake Placid, New York. One outcome of the Lake Placid Conferences was consensus on a name for the discipline: home economics (Weigley 1974); other outcomes included curricula for primary, secondary, and collegiate levels and the formation of the American Home Economics Association (Lake Placid Conferences 1901–1908).

Federal legislation regarding the Cooperative Extension Service (Smith-Lever Act of 1914) and vocational education (Smith-Hughes Act of 1917) included home economics; subsequent legislation over the years continued this support. Federal funds often proved an important source of revenue for university and public school home economics programs. In addition, the creation of the federal Bureau of Home Economics within the U.S. Department of Agriculture in 1923, staffed by home economics scientists, provided the basis for Cooperative Extension's recommendations about nutrition and household management to the public (Betters 1930; Goldstein 2012).

In the mid-twentieth century, the profession reevaluated itself both nationally and locally. The former was visible at the 1961 Home Economics Seminar in French Lick, Indiana, which helped distinguish the educational goals of home economics at different levels (primary, secondary, and collegiate) ("Home Economics Seminar—French Lick, Indiana," n.d.). At universities, faculty members began to question if the name "home economics" was an accurate reflection of what they were teaching and training their students to do. Two of the earliest schools to engage in self-study were Pennsylvania State University (Henderson 1959) and the New York State College of Home Economics (New York State College of Human Ecology 1983; Benson 1999), housed at Cornell University. By 1969, each program had a new name. At both universities, the process was both thoughtful and time-consuming, taking ten and five years, respectively. But the names chosen by these two institutions were and continue to be an issue in terms of both clarity and public understanding.

At Penn State, the self-examination was spurred by the 150th anniversary of the university; every college projected its vision twenty-five and fifty years into the future. This included what they would be teaching and researching, and what their student population would be in terms of gender, major, and occupation upon graduation. The former home economics faculty chose the new name "human development," which emphasized the human relation-

ships and developmental aspects of their work. At Cornell, the president requested a self-study of the colleges of agriculture and home economics. That
led to an intense process of examination, with committees scrutinizing the
focus of academic areas and the name; admissions and recruitment; counseling and advising; public service; and field stations. The focus and name committee determined that "home economics" did not adequately represent the
program. Faculty voted to change the name, and given the choice of "human
development" or "human ecology," they selected human ecology. At both universities, the decision to change the name was part of a much larger (re)as-
sessment of home economics. The names selected were intended to capture
the complexity, depth, and connectivity that united seemingly disparate departments into one cohesive discipline.

In the 1970s, the perceptions of individuals and groups outside home economics jolted members of AHEA with the harshness of their interpretations of
the field. At the AHEA annual meeting in 1971, feminist Robin Morgan attacked
the organization and its practitioners for what she saw as fostering women's
traditional roles. She began her speech, "I gather from your literature and
from the way home economics has functioned in this country that the main
emphasis of your organization is to reinforce three primary areas: marriage,
the family, and the issue of consumerism. . . . Now these three areas—the institution of marriage, the institution of the nuclear family, and the incredible
manipulation of women as consumers—are three of the primary areas that
the radical women's movement is out to destroy. So one could say that as a
radical feminist, I am here addressing the enemy" ("What Robin Morgan Said"
1973). But Morgan had allowed popular stereotypes about home economics to
cloud her impression of the field. At that same meeting, resolutions passed by
AHEA called for the repeal of laws restricting or prohibiting abortion; supporting a commission on the status of women; helping the federal government
craft public housing policy; eliminating inequalities, real or perceived, of minority groups in the profession; and encouraging action following the White
House Conference on Aging.

Part of the challenge facing the AHEA was the unforeseen and external
threat of the women's movement. As a discipline long associated with domesticity, home economics had an identity problem even before the questioning
of gender roles became a national preoccupation (Elias 2008; Goldstein 2012).
Distancing themselves from this image had been part of the motivation for
the new names at Penn State and Cornell. The popular perception led to mis-
conceptions, as exemplified by Morgan's address. The AHEA, while uncertain
about how the women's movement would impact the organization and profession, did support many feminist issues, from day care to aiding displaced
homemakers to supporting women's employment outside the home. AHEA

members were conscious of and actively participating in the larger social issues. Although the AHEA may not have been able to position itself well as a
corporate body in terms of its name in this rapidly changing milieu, conversations—including those about the name of the field—were happening on the
floor of the annual meetings during the 1970s (P. Ralston, pers. comm.).

The new, and different, names chosen by Cornell and Penn State (and
other institutions) did not go unnoticed at the eleventh Lake Placid Conference sponsored by the AHEA. In 1973, the conference attendees were asked to
create "a new statement of philosophy and objectives for the profession." This
had evolved from an AHEA committee established in 1970, which was charged
with "deliver[ing] a statement to replace the 1959 statement on philosophy,
objectives and future direction in home economics, and to identify the areas for long-term program development" (O'Toole 1970). Participants at the
conference represented the bulk of AHEA members: elementary and secondary school educators; members of industry, government, and Cooperative
Extension; and college and university faculty and administrators. The three
hundred home economists at the meeting established recommendations and
priorities for consideration (Mann 1973). The conference "resulted in [a] massive collection of information. However, the outcome lacked focus and did
not provide direction or produce any new ideas. The intent was democratic
involvement of members" ("Development of Home Economics" n.d.).

In post-conference reflections, letters to AHEA leadership, and presentations at the conference itself, more than one person commented on the name
"home economics." Ruth Bonde (1973), a founder of the Council of Home Economics Programs, offered numerous proposals for action, such as to "discover,
if possible, what were the internal and external dynamics that caused several
institutions to discard the title Home Economics for other designations. An
alteration in title is a symptom of deeper problems. The matter of a common
designation should have high priority." Heather Kelly (1973), the president of
the Louisiana Home Economics Association, in a follow-up letter to Satenig
St. Marie, the president of the AHEA, observed, "As far as changing our name,
Home Economics, I think we should proceed with caution. If a change will
help us to help people in a more effective way then yes. . . . However, let us
not change our name just for the sake of change. Let us . . . think it through
carefully and logically, weighing every possibility of the pros and cons." AHEA's
"Summary Report" (1973) contained three statements on name change in the
section on philosophy and objectives. The final comments in the report were
perhaps the ones that resonated in the official organization for the next two
decades, including "Does name really matter if we are effectively meeting the
needs of people?"

Through the 1970s and 1980s, many college and university programs changed their names. In almost all instances, the change of name was one of many alterations to the program. Other, but less visible, changes included restructuring the majors, adding master's and doctorate programs, and updating the requirements in the core curriculum. The programs sought to attract more men (students and faculty), more grant-funded research, and more respect on campus (Trainor 1980; Royston 1993). The names chosen were varied but often consisted of some combination of the words human, family, consumer, science, development, and ecology. According to the AHEA (Weddle 1990), there were at least thirty-six variations in use by 1990.

Each time the administrators at a college or school contemplated changing its name, they gathered information on what other schools—regionally or of the same rank—were using, for comparative and informational purposes. Often, the names (new or contemplated) served to placate alumni, campus governance leaders, and boards of regents: the home institution was not alone in this endeavor to shed the moniker "home economics." When Ohio State's College of Home Economics proposed a new name in 1988, its supporting evidence documented change within the previous year at the peer institutions University of Tennessee, University of Alabama, University of North Carolina at Greensboro, Kansas State University, and Iowa State University, with change "under consideration" at University of Kentucky, University of Georgia, and University of Maine ("College Name Change" 1988).

For a discipline trying to remain relevant in the public's eye, a lack of unity over the name was often disconcerting. The public "knew," even if they were misperceiving it, what "home economics" meant; human ecology, family and consumer sciences, and the like were strange appellations, often explained as "formerly home economics." Had the AHEA been in front with a new name, a public education campaign could have clarified and consolidated public understanding of these various titles. For faculty doing research and applying for grants, changes of name carried a double-edged risk: some federal legislation explicitly allocated monies for "home economics," yet a name other than "home economics" might increase the chance of being funded.

In 1975, a committee charged with generating a statement of purpose and five new priorities for home economics reiterated the 1959 definition. In 1978, Marjorie Brown and Beatrice Paolucci were commissioned by the AHEA to "delineate the basic structure of the home economics profession for the present and the future" (Crabtree 1978). Upon completion, their position paper, *Home Economics: A Definition* (Brown and Paolucci 1979), was circulated and five forums were held across the country to give members a chance to respond to the paper prior to the AHEA annual meeting. *Home Economics: A Definition* has been profoundly influential, offering a philosophical rationale for the field (Brown 1985, 1993).

In the 1980s, home economics seemed to fragment. The economic recession and changes in American life led to fewer home economists in industry; secondary schools questioned the role of home economics in their curricula; and college and university programs changed their names to something other than home economics. For a discipline struggling to be seen as relevant, the fragmentation further threatened the loss of identity. In a 1985 letter to the editor of the *Journal of Home Economics*, the editor of the *Illinois Educator* submitted seventy-three reasons that the AHEA should not change its name to human ecology (Spitze 1985). A few years later, in a letter to the editor in which she examined different names for home economics, University of Nevada, Reno, professor Marilyn Horn (1989) asked, "why, then, should college issues be of concern to *all* AHEA members?" This was an essential question for the AHEA: did actions by a subset of its members need to impact everyone else? In her staunch support of the name "home economics," Horn may have missed, or ignored, the simmering tensions between collegiate members and everyone else. Fewer faculty members on university campuses were joining the AHEA, opting instead to join organizations that represented their specialized research interests.

Within academically minded groups, discussion and reassessment continued. In 1986, the title of the National Council of Administrators of Home Economics meeting was "Targeting the 21st Century: Transformation and Transition." One panel discussion examined name changes in home economics units. The two participants, Julia Miller of Virginia State University and Barbara Stowe of Kansas State University, and the moderator, Nancy Belck of the University of Tennessee, spoke from experience about the challenges of change. "Change is always difficult, the emotionalism accompanying a name change complicates the process, especially in certain regions of the country and on conservative campuses," they concluded ("Name Changes" 1986).

Simultaneously, two task forces examined the pressures and stresses on home economics programs in higher education from 1965 to 1985. Their goal was to "provide direction to the formulation of recommendations for strengthening home economics programs in higher education." Recognizing that technology, changing social patterns, and gendered role expectations impacted American families, the task force produced a document that examined the past, defined present goals, and suggested priorities for the future. Twenty-two recommendations for strengthening programs were developed, including the final recommendation, "solidarity of name," which neatly summarized: "By using one common name through the nation, solidification of this common purpose can be facilitated" (Bailey and Firebaugh 1986, 1, 16).

After five years of quiescence, two different but related meetings on home economics were held in 1991. The dean of the College of Human Ecology at

Cornell University hosted a think tank on the future of home economics in May. This small group met at a time when many home economics units were being disbanded or eliminated at institutions of higher education. All participants were senior administrators from institutions that had already changed their names. The questions with which they were grappling had already been worked through on their home campuses. These challenges in the field, and their willingness to engage, had been precisely how they had risen in the administrative ranks. Their goals were to "spark discussion; present a paradigm for the future of human ecology programs; and precipitate changes to help ensure the survival of human ecology as a field of study" (Bailey et al. 1993, 1). In their report, "Human Ecology in Higher Education: Surviving Beyond 2000," the authors worried about the disadvantages of human ecologists when applying for external funding. "The lack of a unified identity and name" (25) was a concern, as was the attention given to specializations in the field at the expense of a theoretical framework. They also brainstormed about the future and about how to become more visible in and more vital to higher education.

In October 1991, several organizations of home economics administrators sponsored a meeting in Pine Mountain, Georgia. The forty-six participants at the working conference "Creating a Vision: The Profession for the Next Century" tried to "assess the future trends and define the vision, mission and belief statements for the profession within that context" ("Creating a Vision" 1991). The attendees were nominated by the professional organizations sponsoring the meeting. In an attempt to get diverse opinions and a range of input, two-thirds of the participants were faculty and administrators, and the remaining one-third were "vital constituents" from entities—public and private—that hired graduates or used the research and resources generated by the programs.

But it had taken nearly two decades for AHEA to study itself anew. When the association took up the question in October 1993, the opening remarks at Scottsdale addressed this. "Many believe we are overdue in dealing with the issues before us," Lynda Harriman (1993), the immediate past president of the AHEA and co-organizer of the meeting, said. "During the past twenty years our profession has become fragmented in a number of ways." Harriman proceeded to outline the changes that had occurred, including name changes at academic programs of higher education.

The Scottsdale conference actually consisted of intensive pre-planning as well as the meeting itself. Once various organizations had committed to a conference to discuss the state of the field in the fall of 1993, a series of twenty-two "creative input sessions" were organized and led by a consulting firm, the McNellis Company, which had been hired to coordinate the conference. The purpose of the input sessions, held from May 1 to September 25, was to generate ideas and create visibility. These sessions posed big questions and gauged participants' responses to help determine what would be discussed at the Scottsdale meeting. Six such questions were asked, ranging from "how do we assure our profession remains indispensable to society in the twenty-first century?" to "what might we do to help unify our profession?" ("Positioning" 1993).

The answers were tightly bunched. For example, the top answer to the first question garnered sixty-four similar responses, and the second answer fifty-five; for the second question, the most popular answer had thirty-five similar responses and the second had thirty-two. The question on "potential names for the profession" was the exception to this pattern. The gap between the first potential name (home economics) and the second (human ecology resources) was vast: eighty-seven responses for the former and only twenty-three for the latter. That the potential "new" name was the same as the current name reflected the great discomfort at losing "home economics" as an identity and signifier, at least among those who attended these sessions; that the other names were so far back, and that there were so many of them, reflected the fracturing of the field, the diversity of the names used in different programs throughout the country, and the different identities of the field's members, from university faculty to Cooperative Extension personnel to secondary school teachers.

The meeting in Scottsdale, "Positioning the Profession for the 21st Century," like its antecedents, was co-sponsored by multiple organizations. The ninety-six participants included members from each of the constituent societies and other interested parties, including governmental agencies. A pre-meeting packet, sent out three weeks before the conference, included readings about the history, development, and philosophy of home economics, and a historical overview of home economics. The packet also included an overview of the decision-making model to be used; eleven commissioned papers, each with a proposed conceptual framework and recommended name; a list of participants, task force members, and facilitators; the names of financial contributors; and additional notes about the meeting. If people attending the meeting did not grasp the significance of what they were being asked to accomplish, they were reminded frequently, from the opening remarks, through the sessions, to the closing remarks. "We . . . know," Lynda Harriman (1993) gently reminded the audience at the beginning of the meeting, "that this conference affords us a window of opportunity that may not come our way again."

The goal of the Scottsdale meeting was to develop consensus among the many participants; that goal was met even though people wrestled with core sentiments about home economics. The potentially transformative power of the newly articulated vision was staggering. The conference was intense as participants spent long days engaged in discussion, working to reach a common viewpoint. In small groups, they grappled with and critiqued the eleven position papers, each of which presented a different model for the profession. In an attempt to keep the focus on the model rather than the author, each position paper appeared without attribution.

The authors of the commissioned papers were asked to delineate the breadth and scope of the profession; identify the mission; propose a model and identify its philosophical underpinnings; recommend a name and provide a rationale for it; and present a one- to two-sentence concise statement that would inform the public about the field. As an aid to the authors of the proposals, a list of some names in use was included in the instruction letter: family and consumer studies, education, or science; home economics; human ecology; human science; human environmental science. Some authors concluded that home economics was the best possible name, even though it was not on the list. As Kinsey Green (1993) noted, "The profession and critical science described herein *is Home Economics*. . . . It is neither reasonable nor ethical to compromise the essence of the critical science and profession of home economics in order to solve trends, expediency, resource limitations or other external demands." On the other hand, conference organizer Coby Simerly (1993) articulated a common belief in arguing for (any) new name: "The name 'home economics' has proved unsatisfactory and has caused so much inner turmoil that it has detracted from a more vigorous pursuit of the mission. We have not counteracted the negative home economics stereotype that has existed for many years. . . . I submit that we should not be committed to the name 'home economics' but to the mission which inspired the development of the field."

When no single paper received overwhelming support, the small groups were asked to identify specific elements that they liked, in order to create a new position paper. Each group shared their key ideas. A writing team then drafted a document incorporating the various elements; it was then revised after subsequent discussion and critique. Finally, a new document emerged. All of this occurred on the spot, with the writing, revising, and drafting often going late into the night so that, at the end of the conference, there would be significant accomplishments. The final position paper, either the twelfth or a summation of the best elements of the previous eleven, "described the unifying focus, basic beliefs, planning assumptions, statements regarding the professional practice and outcomes of the profession" (Gotting et al. 1993).

Simultaneously, but equally collaboratively and consensually, possible new names—to appropriately and adequately convey the meaning of the profession in the twenty-first century—were discussed. Again, the eleven discussion groups came up with alternatives, identifying strengths and weaknesses for each name. These names were then presented to all participants. Two names were eliminated in short order, and everyone was able to express their opinion about the nine remaining names. More discussion, and the placement of dots on boards next to each person's choice, led to "family and consumer sciences" as the consensus decision ("Final Boards" 1993). "Family and consumer sciences" was compared to "home economics." Seventy-two people favored "family and consumer sciences," while twenty-two supported "home economics." Each name also generated pluses and minuses, with twice as many positives as negatives for family and consumer sciences and an almost equal number of each for home economics. Two items appeared on both lists, as a plus for one name and a minus for the other: home economics as the term explicitly used in legislation; and family and consumer sciences as appealing to men. As noted in the McNellis Company report issued after the conference, "an extensive period of discussion allowed all participants to share their thoughts and feelings regarding the pros and cons of a name change. While this clearly was not an easy task, there was a clear commitment from the group to consider what was best for the future of the profession as it prepares to move into the 21st century" ("Decision Making" 1993).

The goal of the conference was to emerge with a clear and unified vision of home economics, a name, and a mission around which all of the sponsoring organizations could rally. This urgency and sense of purpose—the opportunity to seize this unique moment—helps explain why, when none of the pre-circulated position papers were quite right, the conference attendees were willing to work through their differences to create a new position paper and emerge with something tangible.

Each sponsoring organization developed a plan of action at the meeting to build support among their own members for the new name and mission that emerged from the Scottsdale meeting. AHEA's plan was similar to other organizations' plans. The post-Scottsdale packet detailed forty-eight ways the AHEA leadership could sell "family and consumer sciences" to its members; offered a timetable for change, from notifying state association presidents to the annual meeting the following June; and concluded with strategies. For AHEA, as for the other organizations present, adopting the new mission statement was less of a challenge than the name change. For that, members needed to be informed and educated, boards of directors' and trustees' approval was necessary, articles needed to be written for newsletters and journals explaining the whys and wherefores of the process, and bylaws needed to be changed. For AHEA, the culmination was a report and an open session at the next annual meeting to ensure that the earlier steps to disseminate information and educate members had been successful enough to merit passage of the changes by the Assembly of Delegates ("AHEA: Ways to Build Support" 1993).

By sitting on the sidelines for twenty-five years while academic units changed their names, the AHEA was behind the curve. The delay reflected other tensions in the organization, such as between university faculty and secondary school educators. The former were educating students for future employment in professional careers; the latter were teaching important but undervalued life skills. For the former, their identity was created through research interests; for the latter, their professional identity was as home economists. In reality, both struggled against popular misperceptions. Changing the curriculum emphasis to technical career paths and teaching human development, budgeting, and other life skills were all doable for teachers, but explaining what they did—without the comfortable tag "home economics"—was a challenge. Other entities within AHEA, such as the Home Economists in Business group, formerly a sizable portion of its membership, had disengaged by the 1980s. Had the AHEA changed its name sooner rather than later, it could have been in a stronger position to lead its membership into the last third of the twentieth century and the beginning of the twenty-first century.

Choosing to make significant decisions about the breadth and scope of the organization and profession, and finding just the right name to convey that message to the public at large, legislators, practitioners, and academicians in the last decade of the twentieth century did, ultimately, have at least two impacts. First, just as the first Lake Placid Conference happened at the end of one century and set the stage for the next, so too did the Scottsdale conference occur at the end of one century and set the stage for the next. Second, the AHEA was able to use the best practices for rethinking its mission, vision, and name by examining and learning from what had happened on myriad college and university campuses. The process before, during, and after Scottsdale was based on building consensus, engaging all constituents in discussion, examining the list of names currently in play, and trusting the process. Ultimately, Scottsdale worked—the name "family and consumer sciences" does articulate the mission of the discipline—but rather than the AHEA leading to Scottsdale, Scottsdale led to the AAFCS.

REFERENCES

"AHEA: Ways to Build Support for 'Family and Consumer Sciences.'" 1993. American Association of Family and Consumer Sciences Records, Cornell University Library (hereafter AAFCS), box 222.

Bailey, Lena, and Francille Firebaugh. 1986. *Strengthening Home Economics Programs in Higher Education.* Columbus: Ohio State College of Home Economics.

Bailey, Lena, Francille Firebaugh, Elizabeth Haley, and Sharon Y. Nickols. 1993. "Human Ecology in Higher Education: Surviving Beyond 2000." *Journal of Home Economics* 85(4): 3–10.

Benson, Lynne Byall. 1999. "Gender and the Marginalization of Women at Cornell University: A History of Home Economics/Human Ecology." Master's thesis, Cornell University.

Betters, Paul V. 1930. *The Bureau of Home Economics: Its History, Activities, and Organization*. Washington, D.C.: Brookings Institution.

Bonde, Ruth. 1973. "The Memory of Lake Placid, 1973." AAFCS, box 95.

Brown, Marjorie. 1985. *Philosophical Studies of Home Economics in the United States: Our Practical-Intellectual Heritage*. East Lansing, Mich.: College of Human Ecology, Michigan State University.

———. 1993. *Philosophical Studies of Home Economics in the United States: Basic Ideas by Which Home Economists Understand Themselves*. East Lansing, Mich.: College of Human Ecology, Michigan State University.

Brown, Marjorie, and Beatrice Paolucci. 1979. *Home Economics: A Definition*. Alexandria, Va.: American Home Economics Association.

"College Name Change Proposed." 1988. *Focus* (Spring). Ohio State University, College of Home Economics Records (hereafter OSU CHE), Oregon State University, box 2.

Crabtree, Beverly. 1978. "From the President: Report of 1977–78 Activities," *Journal of Home Economics* 70(4): 39.

"Creating a Vision: The Profession for the Next Century Final Report." 1991. AAFCS, box 222.

"Decision Making Process." 1993. AAFCS, box 222.

"Development of Home Economics: An Historical Overview." N.d. AAFCS, box 222.

Elias, Megan. 2008. *Stir It Up: Home Economics in American Culture*. Philadelphia: University of Pennsylvania Press.

Eppright, Ercel Sherman, and Elizabeth Storm Ferguson. 1971. *A Century of Home Economics at Iowa State University: A Proud Past, a Lively Present, and a Future Promise*. Ames: Iowa State University, Home Economics Alumni Association.

"Final Boards." 1993. AAFCS, box 222.

Goldstein, Carolyn. 2012. *Creating Consumers: Home Economists in Twentieth-Century America*. Chapel Hill: University of North Carolina Press.

Gotting, Karen, Barbara MacDonald, and Jerry McNellis. 1993. "The Decision Making Process—The McNellis Facilitators." AAFCS, box 222.

Green, Kinsey. 1993. "Professional Unity and Identity: The Case for Home Economics." AAFCS, box 222.

Harriman, Lynda. 1993. "Opening Remarks." Presented at the Scottsdale Meeting on Professional Unity and Identity, October 21–24. AAFCS, box 222.

Henderson, Grace. 1959. "Long-Range Plan, College of Home Economics, 1959." Penn State University Archives, College of Home Economics (hereafter PSU CHE), Special Collections, box 24.

Hoeflin, Ruth. 1988. *History of a College: From Woman's Course to Home Economics to Human Ecology*. Manhattan, Kans.: Ag Press.

"Home Economics Seminar—French Lick, Indiana." N.d. PSU CHE, box 45, folder 45: "Home Economics Seminar"; and "Home Economics Seminar, French Lick, Indiana." N.d. AAFCS, box 286.

Horn, Marilyn. 1981. "Home Economics: A Recitation of Definition," *Journal of Home Economics* 73(1): 19–23.

———. 1989. "Letter to the Editor: College Programs Affect All AHEA Members." *Journal of Home Economics* 81(3): 2.

Kelly, Heather. 1973. Letter to Satenig St. Marie, November 19. AAFCS, box 95.

Lake Placid Conference on Home Economics. 1901–1908. *Proceedings of the Conferences 1899–1908*. Lake Placid, N.Y.: n.p.

Mann, Opal. 1973. "Home Economics Issues of Concern as Perceived by a 1973 Lake Placid Conference Participant." AAFCS, box 95.

Miller, Elisa. 2004. "In the Name of Home Economics: Women, Domestic Science, and American Higher Education, 1865–1930." PhD diss., University of Illinois, Urbana-Champaign.

"Name Changes in Home Economics Units." 1986. Paper presented by unknown author at the Association of Administrators of Home Economics, National Council of Administrators of Home Economics meeting. OSU CHE, box 2.

New York State College of Human Ecology. 1983. "A 1983 Look at a 1966 Document: A Review of the Final Report of the President's Committee to Study the College of Home Economics." New York State College of Human Ecology Records, Cornell University, box 13.

O'Toole, Leila. 1970. "From the President: 1969–70 Report of AHEA Activities." *Journal of Home Economics* 62(7): 471.

"Positioning the Profession for the 21st Century: Creative Input Sessions Response and Summary." 1993. AAFCS, box 222.

Robinson, Jean D. 1990. Letter to Dr. Charles Knapp, May 1. Family and Consumer Science Papers, Hargrett Rare Book and Manuscript Library, University of Georgia, box 17.

Royston, Lawrence. 1993. "Men and Home Economics in the United States, 1900–1975." *Journal of Home Economics* 85(1): 22–25.

Simerly, Coby. 1993. "Family Science: Concepts for Consideration." AAFCS, box 222.

Spitze, Hazel Taylor. 1985. Letter to Constance Burr, March 23. AAFCS, box 6.

"Summary Report: Lake Placid Conference, October 14–17, 1973." 1973. AAFCS, box 95.

Trainor, Rhonda. 1980. "Home Economics: Where (Some of) the Boys Are." *Florida Vocational Journal* 5(7): 22–25.

Weddle, Karl. 1990. Letter to Kinsey Green, June 6. OSU CHE, box 2.

Weigley, Emma Seifrit. 1974. "It Might Have Been Euthenics: The Lake Placid Conferences and the Home Economics Movement." *American Quarterly* 26(1): 79–96.

"What Robin Morgan Said at Denver." 1973. *Journal of Home Economics* 65(1): 13.

13. Building a Legacy in Stone

Rocks in the Road

VIRGINIA MOXLEY

> The State of Kansas has the honor of being the first to open its Agricultural College to young ladies as students, and to appoint a lady to one of the Professorships. Other states, we believe, have followed or are preparing to follow the example, but to Kansas belongs the credit of being the first to do an act, which is not the less honorable because it is merely a deed of justice. We know that it often requires more courage to be just than to be liberal. (Hale 1870, 190)

This announcement by the editor of the most popular ladies' magazine of the 1800s—*Godey's Lady's Book and Magazine*—recognized the pioneering role of a pioneering state by announcing the admission of women to the new land-grant college. That action would be just the beginning of years of innovation and leadership in higher education, especially in human ecology.

The College of Human Ecology, identified over the years by various names, has been an integral part of Kansas State University since the 1870s. The institution, originally known as Kansas State Agricultural College (KSAC), was founded in 1863 as one of the first land-grant universities and one of the earliest coeducational state universities. In 1931, reflecting the expanded mission of the college, the name was changed to Kansas State College of Agricultural and Applied Science, and in 1959 the name became Kansas State University of Agriculture and Applied Sciences (Hoeflin 1988).

Kansas State University's College of Human Ecology has a distinguished history, including early leadership in the western home economics movement, graduates who pioneered in establishing home economics at other colleges, and prolific textbook authorship. On the university's campus, human ecology has architectural as well as intellectual significance. Thirteen buildings, more than any other land-grant university, bear the names of home economics faculty and administrators, attesting to the leadership of the women they honor. This chapter chronicles the early development of domestic science at Kansas State University and the response to an unexpected threat to its continuity as human ecology in its second century.

To fully understand the centrality of the College of Human Ecology to Kansas State University, and how it came to be that so many campus buildings are named for women in the field, it is instructive to understand the formative years of KSAC and domestic science. The university came into being at a time of great turbulence in the new state of Kansas. The difficulties of founding a college in Manhattan, Kansas, in 1863 were nearly insurmountable.

Prior to the 1850s, the territory was occupied sparsely by Native Americans, and few other people lived there. Massive herds of buffalo traversed the area until they were hunted to extinction in the 1870s. The Kansas-Nebraska Act of 1854 allowed residents of the Kansas and Nebraska territories to use popular sovereignty to determine whether each prospective state would be free or slaveholding. New England abolitionists led the movement to promote the emigration of anti-slavery settlers, including Isaac T. Goodnow, who led an emigrant aid company that selected Manhattan, Kansas, as its town site in 1855. One month later, at a meeting of the trustees, the idea of a college was proposed. In 1858, Bluemont Central College was opened in Manhattan; however, the few students who attended were at an elementary level (Willard 1940).

Kansas was admitted to the Union as a free state in 1861, and the 1862 Homestead Act encouraged westward expansion by providing 160 acres of land to any head of family. President Abraham Lincoln signed the Morrill Act in 1862, and Kansas accepted the land grant for a college on February 3, 1863. The next month, on March 3, Kansas State Agricultural College was approved by the Kansas legislature to occupy the site of Bluemont Central College. According to the formula of 30,000 acres for each of its U.S. congressional representatives, the state of Kansas received 82,313 acres of land (*Second Annual Catalogue Kansas State Agricultural College* 1865). The state's new inhabitants mostly resided in tents, dugouts, lean-tos, and other hastily constructed houses, often on land they were homesteading. Manhattan's population was remarkable in its level of education and its commitment to furthering the education of all in the state. In 1866, three years after KSAC was founded on the "very frontier of human settlements" (Willard 1940, 2), rail service reached Manhattan from the East. The population in the state grew rapidly from 100,000 in 1860, to 364,000 in 1870, to 996,000 in 1880, to 1.4 million in 1890 (*Population Growth, Kansas and the U.S.* 1860–2012).

In the early years of KSAC, funding was extremely problematic. The legislature provided little money from 1863 to 1871 other than small loans against future income from the sale of the land grant (Willard 1940). Students paid no tuition. The land grant was not fully sold until the mid-1880s (*Catalogue of the State Agricultural College of Kansas: 1885–86* 1886). KSAC's first president, Joseph Denison, mortgaged his house twice to keep the college afloat (Gunn 1992). Following a grasshopper plague in 1874, state revenues were particularly bleak. The college's trustees reduced faculty salaries in 1875 and again in 1878 (Gunn 1992).

In the first decade, although more than a thousand students had received some education, only nine women and six men had completed the full course of instruction (Gunn 1992; Willard 1940). A new board of regents sought to transition the college curriculum from a classical to an industrial focus in keeping with its mission as a land-grant institution. In June 1873, the regents asked all ten members of the faculty to resign. All but President Denison were rehired (Willard 1940). In July 1873, the board appointed the Reverend John A. Anderson as president, and during his six-year tenure he transformed the college, making it a model for emerging land-grant institutions. Anderson left the presidency to serve the state as a congressman (Willard 1940).

"Narrowly interpreting the Morrill Act, Anderson dropped most of the classical curriculum and submitted a plan for a six-year program with practical courses geared to farm, mechanical, commercial, and domestic needs" (Gunn 1992, 62). Students at this time qualified for admission by completing a rigorous admission test and reaching the minimum age of fourteen (*Catalogue of the State Agricultural College of Kansas: 1877–80* 1880). Anderson stated that the college would give a woman "an education as an industrialist, one by the practice of which she can earn money" (Gunn 1992, 65). The initial courses of study offered to women were accounting, printing, telegraphy, and sewing.

As the curriculum developed, KSAC helped set the land-grant standard for a balanced combination of liberal, scientific, and practical courses. "Women at Kansas State completed the regular co-educational courses in organic chemistry and inorganic chemistry, and in botany, entomology, geology, mineralogy, physics, physiology, and zoology required of all students" (Gunn 1995, 16). Anderson worked quickly to establish opportunities for women to become "industrialists." By November 1873, three months after being named president, he received approval from the board of regents to offer industrial work in sewing. Hattie Cheseldine, a forty-year-old widow with four children who ran her own dressmaking and millinery business in Manhattan, was hired at a salary of $35 per month (Gunn 1992). The work could not have been easy due to the absence of sewing machines in the laboratories during the first year.

In March 1875, Cheseldine broke her leg and was replaced by Mary Cripps, a fifty-five-year-old widow with children who had a successful wholesale and retail millinery business in New York City in the 1850s and 1860s (Gunn 1992). Cripps's salary, the lowest at the university, was $500 per year (Hoeflin 1988).

Laboratories for thirty students now had four sewing machines. Although Elias Howe had patented an interlocking sewing machine in 1846, and in the 1850s the machines became commercially available, they were not common items in most Kansas homes in the 1870s. Knowing how to construct garments and how to maintain the early sewing machines proved to be highly marketable skills for students in the sewing classes.

The domestic science program that began in 1873 with clothing construction courses was quickly expanded as courses in household economy and household chemistry were added in 1875. Beginning in 1876, Cripps taught lectures on health and cooking. Faculty wives and Manhattan friends brought recipes and samples of food to class for students to try. They became Cripps's "Assisting Society of Ladies," indicative of the community's interest in and support of this formal educational opportunity for young women (Hoeflin 1988). This forerunner of an external advisory board later renamed itself the Domestic Science Club, a Manhattan women's organization that continues into the twenty-first century. Cripps made the cooking classes self-supporting by selling the prepared food. She and her classes began serving popular ten-cent noon dinners to students and professors in 1880. Under Cripps's leadership, the domestic science program became an important and integral component of KSAC.

K-State's third president, George Thompson Fairchild, took office in 1879. Fairchild, like his predecessors, was committed to both women's education and industrial education. He served until 1897, when the regents again fired the entire faculty; he declined to be a candidate for reappointment (Willard 1940). At Cripps's retirement in 1882, President Fairchild hired one of the college's own brightest and best domestic science graduates of the class of 1876, Nellie Sawyer Kedzie, then a young widow, to lead the program. Under Kedzie's seventeen-year leadership, KSAC developed the largest and strongest academic program of domestic science in the country (Gunn 1995).

The domestic science laboratory had only a few kitchen tools, and Kedzie taught cooking with no icebox, no piped hot water, and no power in the building. Bread dough sometimes froze in the bowls overnight, because the building lacked central heat. Like her male counterparts, Kedzie wrote articles for the *Industrialist*, the campus newspaper; she discussed household management themes. Elida Winchip, a thirty-five-year-old widow with three children, was hired in 1884 to teach the sewing classes in laboratories that now had six sewing machines (Gunn 1992).

Kedzie expanded the role of a university professor. She responded to student needs and began to function as a dean of students. A forceful and articulate speaker, she also filled the role of (future) extension agents, transmitting homemaking information to the people in the state through publications and presentations. The board of regents raised her salary to $1,000 annually, "an attractive salary for a woman, although still less than most of her male counterparts" (Gunn 1992, 116).

In 1885, the faculty formalized the requirements for earning a master's of science degree (Gunn 1992). Thirty percent of the 423 undergraduates at KSAC were female, and three of the four registered postgraduate students were women (*Catalogue of the State Agricultural College of Kansas: 1885–86* 1886). Kedzie helped initiate postgraduate research in domestic economy. "As the only academic institution offering a terminal M.S. degree in domestic economy in the late 1880s and early 1890s, Kansas State would have major influence in shaping [the home economics] programs which began to emerge at several other institutions" (Gunn 1992, 129). In keeping with the KSAC philosophy of practical education, Kedzie was committed to preparing graduates for gainful employment. When the Kansas legislature mandated county high schools in 1886, teaching opportunities rapidly expanded. By 1888, Kedzie was preparing her graduates to provide instruction in domestic science in those schools, and enrollment in the program at KSAC expanded dramatically.

In recognition of her teaching, writing, speaking, and student advising, the board of regents designated Kedzie as the professor of household economy and hygiene in 1887 (Hoeflin 1988). Kedzie was a force for change. She developed the program in domestic science at KSAC at a time when there were no others to emulate. Graduates from the program went on to found other university programs, expanding the influence of Kedzie's work. Yet, in 1897 when, due to a change in state politics, the entire faculty was fired, Kedzie and Winchip both refused the offer to be rehired and left KSAC (Willard 1940). Of the nineteen professors employed in 1896, only eight returned in 1897 (*Kansas State Agricultural College Catalogue 1896–97* 1897). However, Kedzie's legacy was not finished. She had secured a commitment from the legislature for a domestic science building. In *History of the Kansas State College of Agriculture and Applied Science*, Willard (1940, 87–88) described the genesis of the building:

> Largely through the personal efforts of Prof. Nellie S. Kedzie the legislature of 1897 was persuaded to make an appropriation of $16,000 for the erection of a building for the work in domestic economy. This was built that year by the succeeding administration, and dedicated in January 1899. It was given the name Kedzie Hall in honor of Professor Kedzie in 1902. This is believed to be the first building in the country provided wholly for work in home economics.

Naming a public university building for a woman in 1902 was a singular event, made more significant by the fact that the three buildings in the 1902 resolution were the first buildings on the campus to be named, and the other

PHOTO 13.1. Kedzie Hall, Kansas State Agricultural College, 1908. Photograph courtesy Morse Department of Special Collections, Kansas State University Libraries.

PHOTO 13.2. Nellie Kedzie, professor of domestic science, Kansas State Agricultural College, 1882–1897. Photograph courtesy Morse Department of Special Collections, Kansas State University Libraries.

two honored the second and third presidents of KSAC. Even more remarkable is the eloquent tribute by Regent Foster Dwight Coburn recorded in the minutes of the board of regents meeting:

> Whereas, it has long been customary among educational institutions to perpetuate the memory of men who have been great in their history, and
>
> Whereas, the Kansas State Agricultural College has won a fair fame that is not

bounded by state lines, and has reached an age when the commemoration of the work of its builders and founders should be made secure in some concrete form,

Therefore, be it

Resolved, that in order to perpetuate the memory of the one man . . . who was in reality the founder of the Kansas State Agricultural College, it is hereby ordered that in remembrance of the splendid services of John A. Anderson, the principal college building commonly known as the "Main Building" shall be named and hereafter known as "Anderson Hall."

And further: As a library building is always typical of wisdom and learning and as this one marks the most important accession to the group of buildings made during the administration of President George T. Fairchild . . . the building now known as "The Library" shall be named and hereafter known as "Fairchild Memorial Hall."

And further: In view of the fact that women's no less than men's deeds live after them, and in recognition of her skillful and efficient labors and of the fact that Nellie S. Kedzie was in reality the founder of the Domestic Science department of this institution, as well as a pioneer whose well-timed efforts have been recognized throughout the country by the establishment of many like departments whose model this has been, it is ordered that the building now known as "Domestic Science Hall" shall be named and hereafter known as "Kedzie Hall." (Kansas State Agricultural College Board of Regents 1902, 436–437)

The resolution was approved.

While Kedzie Hall was the first building at Kansas State University named for a home economist, three others would follow in 1925 and more in subsequent years (Hoeflin 1988). In its early years, KSAC rarely named buildings, but for the next fifty years it had a practice of naming buildings for prominent campus leaders. After the 1902 resolution, the next three named buildings (Nichols in 1909, Denison in 1913, and Waters in 1919) were dedicated to former college presidents. The following three named buildings honored home economics administrators (*K.S.U. Buildings* 2002). Calvin Hall, constructed in 1908 to accommodate the growing domestic science program, was named in 1925 for Henrietta Willard Calvin, a librarian, 1901–1903, and a professor of domestic science, 1903–1908. Thompson Hall, constructed in 1922 to serve as the KSAC cafeteria, was named in 1925 for Dr. Helen Bishop Thompson, the dean of home economics, 1918–1923. Van Zile Hall, named in 1925 and constructed in 1926 as the first women's residence hall, was named for Mary Pierce Van Zile, the dean of home economics, 1908–1918, and the dean of women, 1908–1939 (Lindemuth 2001).

The impetus for naming Calvin Hall, Thompson Hall, and Van Zile Hall appears to be related to the impending Diamond Jubilee celebration of the home economics program, scheduled for 1925. Dr. Margaret Justin, who would serve as the dean of home economics for thirty-one years, 1923–1954, had recently been appointed to her position. Although the new designations for Calvin Hall (State Board of Administration 1925a, 127) and for Van Zile Hall (State Board of Administration 1925c) were officially approved by the board of administration, the naming of Thompson Hall, although discussed at a meeting of the college faculty (Kansas State Agricultural College Faculty Records 1925, 174), occurred without formal board action. Apparently, Dean Justin persuaded Acting President F. D. Farrell to approve the naming of the building immediately before the Diamond Jubilee celebration in April 1925. Additionally, honorary doctoral degrees for three distinguished alumnae of home economics were approved by the board of administration and were awarded during the Diamond Jubilee (State Board of Administration 1925b, 132). Prior to the board of administration action, the council of deans and the faculty had also approved of these degrees. The honorees were Nellie Sawyer Kedzie Jones and Henrietta Willard Calvin, who received the degree of doctor of laws, and Abby Lillina Marlatt, who received the degree of doctor of science.

By 1940, the campus consisted of twenty-six buildings, ten of which had been named—four extant buildings were named for college presidents, one for a vice president, and one for an administrator in horticulture; four honored home economics faculty or administrators (*K.S.U. Buildings* 2002). These buildings remained in use and retained their 1940 designations as of 2014. Over the years, the campus has continued its architectural growth. All buildings were constructed of limestone native to the region, creating a campus of distinction that reflects its setting. Although buildings today are customarily named for major donors because the state no longer funds construction, throughout most of Kansas State University's history, buildings were named for the institution's leaders. Nine additional campus buildings were named for home economists, the most prominent being Justin Hall, the current home of the College of Human Ecology. Groundbreaking occurred in 1957, and Justin Hall was dedicated and opened in 1960. It was built at a cost of more than $2 million and named for Dr. Margaret M. Justin, who took the program first envisioned by Nellie Kedzie and grew it to national prominence during her thirty-one years as dean (Hoeflin 1988).

The home economics administrative structure and program offerings have changed markedly over the 140 years since the first course was taught in 1873. From 1873 to 1912, the programs were organized within frequently changing departmental configurations that reflected the growth in the breadth of course offerings. In 1912 KSAC organized into divisions, and the home economics programs were organized within the Division of Home Economics. In 1942 the former division became the School of Home Economics, and in 1963 the school became the College of Home Economics. Following a review of its mission, vision, and comprehensive interdisciplinary scope, it became the College of Human Ecology in 1985 (Hoeflin 1988).

Not only was the legacy of home economics leaders etched in stone on the Kansas State University campus, but the College of Human Ecology expanded its course offerings and majors at the undergraduate and graduate levels in keeping with the changing opportunities available to home economics graduates; placed strong emphasis on student-faculty relationships, leading to a strong sense of loyalty among alumni; established relationships with international colleagues; attracted men to the majors in the college; supported a strong Cooperative Extension program for youth and adults; and provided distinguished leadership in professional associations connected with home economics (Hoeflin 1988). At the end of the twentieth century, the College of Human Ecology was nationally recognized among its peers. However, despite its 117-year history and its national prominence, the college was targeted for elimination in 1990.

Influences both internal and external to the university played a role in the proposal to eliminate the College of Human Ecology. Externally, the 1980s was fraught with rapid change in higher education. Among the strategies for dealing with the issues that were perplexing administrators, George Keller, the author of *Academic Strategy: The Management Revolution in American Higher Education* (1983), suggested eliminating outdated programs. Keller targeted home economics as an illustration of a field where cuts could be made in order to realign funding so that salaries could be raised in some (other) science and business fields. His rationale was that universities "are able to shave salaries in declining fields such as home economics, which many regard as an increasingly anachronistic nineteenth-century academic invention now that 52 percent of all women are in the workforce" (ibid., 23). Keller failed to acknowledge that employed adults, particularly women, engaged in significant household work regardless of their employment status—which was confirmed by research conducted by home economists in programs he suggested could be eliminated. He mistakenly equated the profession of home economics and the practice of homemaking, and he undervalued the professions for which home economics students were prepared. He and others did not comprehend the vast array of goods and services that home economists were developing and providing to make it possible for adults and children to have comfortable home lives whether or not women were in the paid labor force.

Keller's book seems to have been widely read by higher education administrators, one of whom proposed closing the Home Economics Department at Emporia State University, where I served as department head in 1983. His justification, echoing Keller's words, was "home economics is an anachronism."

Ultimately, rather than eliminate all subject matter in the department, Emporia State University merged home economics with sociology and anthropology and moved the department to a less desirable location on campus. In 1985, I took a position at Kansas State University, serving as associate dean of the newly named College of Human Ecology. The next year, 1986, Jon Wefald was appointed the twelfth president of K-State.

A press release issued by Stanley Koplik, the executive secretary of the Kansas Board of Regents, reflected the internal challenges facing Kansas State University in the mid-1980s: "John [*sic*] Wefald was selected by the Kansas Board of Regents to be the new president of Kansas State University in July, 1986, with the following charge: to recruit outstanding students; to reverse declining enrollment; to lead in the efforts for higher faculty salaries in the Regents system; to restore competitiveness to KSU's intercollegiate athletic programs; and to initiate a process of strategic planning" (Creighton 1990, A3).

Wefald took bold steps to reverse the trend of downward enrollment. In 1986 there were 17,630 students. By 1990, enrollment had grown to over 20,000 students—a first in the history of the university. This growth gave new vibrancy to the university, but it also created resource pressures because the Kansas legislature did not provide funding to support the increased numbers. President Wefald understood the vital role athletics had come to play in universities, and he invested heavily in its support.

University administrators are planners. As financial pressures mount, plans are increasingly about what to eliminate and less about what to enhance. Fiscal constraints were central to the development of a 1987 strategic plan for Kansas State University in which the colleges participated. The College of Human Ecology developed and implemented its plan and, by 1990, had achieved the university directives of reducing programs and state expenditures, while increasing undergraduate enrollment and extramural funding for research (Kansas State University College of Human Ecology 1987).

In early 1990, a university-wide committee of faculty leaders was appointed by central administrators to develop a proposal for a university-wide reorganization. Fiscal constraints were again a central concern in the process. A set of seven criteria for reorganization decisions was publicly announced, including the existing quality of the program, current and projected demand for the program, cost, and the historical commitment of the university to the program. Using these benchmarks, the College of Human Ecology expected to fare rather well in the priority-setting. However, while the publicly announced criteria guided faculty planning, it did not drive the final round of campus-level planning, where substantive changes in the priorities and their definitions were made.

After the planning process was under way, the university experienced even more fiscal jolts, somewhat reminiscent of its early history. In January 1990, the university took a mid-year budget rescission of $1.2 million of its state appropriations. In April, when the next fiscal year's budget was being finalized in the state legislature, the third year of the state's Margin of Excellence program, designed to create more competitive faculty salaries, was not funded. Further, a $2.1 million enrollment growth adjustment was not funded, and $500,000 was removed from salary support. As a final blow, $1.9 million was removed in an end-of-year, across-the-board budget reduction. It was stating the obvious when the provost said there was no question that resources were insufficient (Coffman 1990).

These fiscal pressures gave rise to yet another institutional reorganization process in which faculty expected to have full campus engagement. In late August 1990, the campus newspaper reported President Wefald saying that "he hopes that by working with faculty leadership, a plan acceptable to both the administration and faculty can be designed in 30 [to] 60 days. The plan could be implemented within a year" (Henry and Sack 1990, 1). On September 11, 1990, Provost James Coffman proposed to the faculty senate "to develop a draft plan for reorganizing the academic programs, administrative structures and support services at Kansas State University" (Wright 1990, A1). That day, the faculty senate approved the following resolution: "The Faculty Senate of Kansas State University endorses the Provost's proposal to develop a draft plan for reorganizing the academic programs, administrative structures, and support services at Kansas State University. The President, President-elect, and Past President of Faculty Senate should be included in the development of the draft plan. Faculty Senate will ensure that appropriate faculty input and discussion are solicited" (Kansas State University Faculty Senate 1990, sec. V.A.2, par. 3). The draft plan, which was never shared outside the committee in written form, was created in private by a team of institutional administrators and three faculty senate leaders. Deans whose colleges would be impacted were given only hints of what the plan contained, and no dean saw a written copy of the draft plan (Wright 1990).

Once the reorganization planning process was introduced to the faculty senate, it was fast-tracked. Dean Barbara Stowe reported to the College of Human Ecology's administrative council on September 18 that the criteria for the reorganization plan had been revised and redefined. The criteria to be used to evaluate the reorganization initiatives would be centrality to Kansas State University, centrality to a university, avoiding redundancy with programs at another university in Kansas, necessity to the state of Kansas, quality, and demand (College of Human Ecology Dean's Administrative Council 1990).

Noting the changed criteria, and the redefinitions given to these criteria, administrators and faculty in the College of Human Ecology were on high alert. Differences from the previous planning criteria were subtle, but skewed in ways that disadvantaged the college. The revised priorities discounted the strengths of the College of Human Ecology. Centrality to the land-grant mission was undercut by the criterion to be central to *any* university. Uniqueness in the state was undercut by the potential of the planners to determine that the state did not need any of the programs in human ecology. Quality simply did not matter, because it was stated that quality alone would not be sufficient to decide whether to maintain a program or not. Program enrollment did not seem to be a factor in the criterion of demand; rather, projections for the future needs of the state were to guide decisions. Furthermore, professions dedicated to creating solutions for persistent and emerging human needs appeared not to be a workforce concern of the planners.

The College of Human Ecology Faculty Council (1990) met on September 19 and discussed the revised criteria for the university reorganization. Members of the council agreed to review and update the departmental and program plans of their respective units, working with department heads and directors to delineate program strengths and weaknesses according to the provost's announced revised criteria. Additionally, they would focus on the university's five strategic planning themes, which had been in place since September 1989 (Kansas State University Dean's Council et al. 1989).

Each unit agreed to provide input to Dean Stowe before her September 26 scheduled meeting with the provost (College of Human Ecology Faculty Council 1990). Following that meeting, Stowe sent a letter to department heads noting that, at the provost's request, discussions with deans were confidential at this point. She stated, "It was clear that *there is no plan yet developed*" (Stowe 1990a). However, it is apparent from an eloquent confidential letter Stowe (1990b) wrote to the provost that the possibility of the dissolution of the college was discussed at this meeting, but was not a foregone conclusion.

On October 26, in a follow-up conference, Provost Coffman told Dean Stowe what the dean of architecture, planning, and design had already announced to his college the day before. Both colleges were proposed for elimination. In that plan, some departments in human ecology would be moved to other colleges; some majors would be completely eliminated. No mention was made of the fate of the PhD program in human ecology or the general undergraduate programs. At this point, a written plan had not been released, even to the deans. Dean Stowe immediately called a meeting of all College of Human Ecology faculty, staff, and students to discuss the university reorganization. Defending the college's integrity was the chosen plan of action. Following the meeting, a writing team met to develop talking points for students, faculty, and alumni. That same evening, the Human Ecology Faculty Council met to plan responses to the proposed elimination of the college. The defense strategy was guided by advice provided by Dr. Bea Smith, the dean of the College of Human Environmental Sciences at the University of Missouri, another nationally prominent college that had been proposed for elimination in a 1982 university planning process. Among the points of advice from Dean Smith (1990) were these:

1. Focus on these points: affirmative action, land-grant mission, accreditation, support for [Cooperative] Extension programs, peer esteem, and national stature.
2. Assign writing committees to articulate the contemporary need for the College, accomplishments of the College, and mission.
3. Act quickly.
4. Work with the press.
5. Do not assume campus colleagues will be advocates for your position—they have a conflict of interest.

On October 27, at the request of the college's faculty council, the presidents of the human ecology alumni board and the student council wrote a joint letter to the twelve thousand human ecology alumni, informing them of the university's plan to dismantle the college, soliciting input, and giving the university president's contact information. Attached to the letter was a fact sheet about the college and its programs. The College of Human Ecology's alumni board paid for printing and distribution costs.

On October 29, students gathered to prepare the letter for mailing to all college alumni. Administrators and faculty prepared for a "seminar" scheduled for October 31, to be held in front of the university's administration building, Anderson Hall. Students established a calling tree to assure that all human ecology students understood the extent of the changes proposed for their programs of study. Students also organized a petition drive to retain the integrity of the college and asked for contributions of $1 or $2 from each student to defray the costs of mailings, posters, and the upcoming seminar. By October 30, responses from alumni began to flood the university president's office.

On October 31 at 10:30 a.m., students, faculty, alumni, and friends of the College of Human Ecology participated in the seminar in front of Anderson Hall. The purpose of the seminar was to substantiate the need for the college. It began with a walk from Justin Hall, the college's main building, to Anderson Hall. Participants donned T-shirts with this message on the front: "H*/‡@! NO WE WON'T GO." Speakers (faculty, students, and prominent alumni) described the value that the college and its programs provided to the university, the state, and the world. The seminar was staged concurrently with President Wefald's press conference to release the university's reorganization plan.

PHOTO 13.3. Speakers at the October 31, 1990, rally for the College of Human Ecology, Kansas State University, including Virginia Moxley (*left of speaker*) and Dean Barbara Stowe (*right with sign*). The sign held by Stowe reads "Immoral Act Against the Morrill Act" and the large banner reads "Keep KSU Comprehensive." Photograph courtesy Virginia Moxley, personal collection.

Over two thousand people, including representatives from every major newspaper and television station in the state, were present on the lawn next to Anderson Hall. Dean Stowe set the tone with her remarks:

> Your presence here today together with the tremendous numbers of phone calls, voluntary offers to help, and student, faculty, alumni, and community concern tells us we must be doing something right. KSU and the state of Kansas need a College of Human Ecology. . . . You want the information base for [Cooperative] Extension, and social services [that] we provide. Our students value the kind of instruction and advisement they get in the CHE. . . . This College may appear from the *outside* to be an odd collection of specializations. . . . It may *appear* that those practical specializations belong with their base disciplines. . . . [However] those of us who work inside CHE, and you who like hiring our graduates and using our information base know that the concerns and interests of *people* do not occur along *academic lines*—they are complex issues requiring interdisciplinary study and understanding. (Stowe 1990c, pars. 1–3)

She continued, "A quality college education requires a good basic general education, but a quality professional education requires a context where those basic disciplines are synthesized into people-based, as well as profit-based careers" (ibid., pars. 5–6).

Remarks at the event by Carolyn Roby, the president of the Human Ecology Alumni Association, described the historical and contemporary significance of the college as a part of the university:

> I represent 12,000 [alumni] voices who say—WE WILL NOT BE DISSOLVED! 117 years of tradition are not wiped out with a First Draft Reorganization Plan. . . . Regardless of the years we alumni have walked this campus or stood in this spot, we have something in common with you students—the recognition of names such as Kedzie, Calvin, Thompson, . . . Van Zile, Justin . . . , buildings on this campus named for Home Economists, all graduates or members of the faculty of the College of Human Ecology. We have a heritage of pioneers in our field second to none! (Roby 1990)

At his press conference, occurring at the same time as the seminar, President Jon Wefald announced that the plan to eliminate the College of Human Ecology was no longer being considered.

While Kansas State University's planners had initially determined that human ecology was not needed to meet the state's future needs, at Cornell University's College of Human Ecology's Sixty-Fifth Anniversary Institute in October 1990, Cornell President Frank H. T. Rhodes stated:

> I believe that the chief challenge our nation faces in the '90s and into the next century, is to deal with the very issues that are the focus of this College: an aging population, the structure (or lack of structure) of the American family, human development, youth at risk, nutrition, and the general range of human services on which we have become increasingly reliant as a society. If one were to pick one particular set of issues which threaten to undermine our strength as a nation, I think it would be this set of issues which are the responsibility of the College of Human Ecology. (Firebaugh 1990)

Scores of letters from friends and alumni of the Kansas State University College of Human Ecology were sent to the president and provost. One of the most compelling philosophical arguments, rooted in the origins of home economics, for retaining the college as a cohesive whole was made by Dr. Elizabeth W. Crandall, professor emerita at the University of Rhode Island and a Kansas State University College of Human Ecology alumna. Crandall wrote: "Implicit in the term 'Human Ecology' is the concept of a system in which individuals, families, and households interact with and are affected by their environments—physical (including man-made and natural), social, economic, and political—to list only one possible categorization. One of the advantages of a systems approach is that its total impact is much greater than the sum of its parts" (1990, par. 2). Crandall continued the letter with her objection to dispersing departments of the college throughout the university. She expressed outrage that "a University that gives great emphasis to animal nutrition and food science is willing to ignore human nutrition!" (ibid., par. 3).

The editorials in the press and the appeals of alumni, students, and colleagues from other universities led President Wefald, who seemed to find himself in charge of a plan he had little part in creating, to take action to control the damage to the university's reputation. He met with the Human Ecology Faculty Council; he met with students; he sent a letter rescinding the plan to all human ecology alumni; and he wrote to all current and prospective students in the college. On November 28, one month after the draft plan to eliminate the College of Human Ecology, Wefald and his administrative team met with representatives of all College of Human Ecology departments. He described the events of the previous month as an "incredible affirmation" of the college. He concluded, "Nobody will suggest that the College of Human Ecology be merged or eliminated from Kansas State University ever again. It is here to stay. As long as K-State is here, the College of Human Ecology will be here" (Wefald 1990).

Throughout the College of Human Ecology's history, from its founding in 1873, to the turbulence in 1990, to the present, both Kansas State University and the college have evolved in ways that assure the continuing relevance of each. The College of Human Ecology is larger, more diverse, and more central to the university's mission now than it was in 1990. Yet, as of this writing, another university-wide strategic plan is under development, and the outcome is inherently uncertain.

What has not changed, as noted by alumni board president Carolyn Roby in her 1990 seminar speech, is the silent presence of the prominent buildings at Kansas State University that are named for home economists who were leaders in the work of the university and in the profession. These thirteen buildings of solid native limestone are an enduring symbol of the prominence of domestic science/home economics/human ecology at Kansas State University and beyond. The enduring centrality of human ecology to Kansas State University is evidenced in the buildings, but it comes to life in the classrooms, laboratories, and studios where knowledge is discovered and disseminated. When threatened by an ill-conceived university reorganization plan, the College of Human Ecology was sustained by engaged students, faculty, and alumni who knew the value of their education, and by citizens' recognition of its heritage and contemporary importance. The buildings bearing the names of home economists stand in testimony to the enduring relevance of the mission they pioneered.

REFERENCES

Catalogue of the State Agricultural College of Kansas: 1877–80. 1880. Manhattan,
    Kans.: Printing Department, Agricultural College, http://archive.org/details/
    CatalogueOfTheStateAgriculturalCollegeOfKansas (accessed March 25, 2013).

Catalogue of the State Agricultural College of Kansas: 1885–86. 1886. Manhattan,
Kans.: Printing Department, Agricultural College, https://archive.org/details/
CatalogueOfTheStateAgriculturalCollegeOfKansas_844 (accessed March 25, 2013).

Coffman, James. 1990. Letter to Kansas State University Faculty, November 13. In
author's possession.

College of Human Ecology Dean's Administrative Council. 1990. Meeting minutes,
September 18. In author's possession.

College of Human Ecology Faculty Council. 1990. Draft meeting minutes, September
19. In author's possession.

Crandall, Elizabeth W. 1990. Letter to President Jon Wefald, November 12. In Notebook
of Correspondence, 1990, Human Ecology. In author's possession.

Creighton, Robert. 1990. "Regents Office: Give K-State Proposals a Chance to Be
Heard." *Manhattan Mercury*, November 22, A3.

Firebaugh, Francille M. 1990. Letter to Cornell University Alumni, October 29. In
author's possession.

Gunn, Virginia R. 1992. "Educating Strong Womanly Women: Kansas Shapes the
Western Home Economics Movement, 1860–1914." PhD diss., University of Akron.

———. 1995. "Industrialists Not Butterflies: Women's Higher Education at Kansas
State Agricultural College, 1973–1882." *Kansas History* 18(1): 2–17.

Hale, Sarah. 1870. "Editors' Table: Ladies in Agricultural Colleges." *Godey's Lady's Book
and Magazine* (February): 190.

Henry, Eric, and Rebecca Sack. 1990. "Reorganization Set for 1990–91." *Collegian*
(Kansas State University) (August 27): 1.

Hoeflin, Ruth. 1988. *History of a College: From Woman's Course to Home Economics to
Human Ecology.* Manhattan, Kans.: Ag Press.

Kansas State Agricultural College Board of Regents. 1902. Meeting minutes, June 18.
File: Board of Regents, Minutes, 1902–1904, Richard L. D. and Marjorie J. Morse
Department of Special Collections, Kansas State University Libraries, Manhattan,
Kansas (hereafter Morse Department of Special Collections).

Kansas State Agricultural College Catalogue 1896–97. 1897. Topeka, Kans.:
J. S. Parks, State Printer, http://ia601508.us.archive.org/25/items/
CatalogueOfTheStateAgriculturalCollegeOfKansas_960/1896-97.pdf (accessed
March 25, 2013).

Kansas State Agricultural College Faculty Records. 1925. Vol. E, March 10. Morse
Department of Special Collections.

Kansas State University College of Human Ecology. 1987. "5-Year Plan," April 3. In
author's possession.

Kansas State University Dean's Council, the Strategic Planning Committee, and the
Faculty Senate Committee of Planning. 1989. *Report of Strategic Planning Themes
for Kansas State University, 1992–1997.* In author's possession.

Kansas State University Faculty Senate. 1990. Meeting minutes, September 11. File
U95.36, Faculty Senate, Minutes, 1990, September, Morse Department of Special
Collections.

Keller, George. 1983. *Academic Strategy: The Management Revolution in American
Higher Education.* Baltimore, Md.: Johns Hopkins University Press.

K.S.U. Buildings. 2002. Information circular. Morse Department of Special Collections, http://www.lib.ksu.edu/depts/spec/flyers/ksu-bldgs.html (accessed March 27, 2013).

Lindemuth, Tim. 2001. "Building a Legacy, Buildings Named for Women." *K-Stater* (August): 20–23.

Population Growth, Kansas and the U.S. 1860–2012. http://www.ipsr.ku.edu/ksdata/ksah/population/2pop1.pdf (accessed March 27, 2013).

Roby, Carolyn. 1990. "Remarks." Speech presented at Anderson Hall lawn at Kansas State University, Manhattan, Kans., October 31. In author's possession.

The Second Annual Catalogue of the Officers and Students of the Kansas State Agricultural College, for 1864–5. 1865. Manhattan, Kans.: J. H. Pillsbury, Printer, http://ia601508.us.archive.org/32/items/SecondAnnualCatalogueOfTheOfficersAndStudentsOfTheKansasState/1864-65Ocr.pdf (accessed March 25, 2013).

Smith, Bea. 1990. FAX to Virginia Moxley, October 26. In author's possession.

State Board of Administration. 1925a. Minutes. Box 1, folder 12. Morse Department of Special Collections.

——. 1925b. Minutes. Box 1, folder 12. Morse Department of Special Collections.

——. 1925c. Minutes. Box 1, folder 12. Morse Department of Special Collections.

Stowe, Barbara. 1990a. Letter to College of Human Ecology Department Heads, September 27. In author's possession.

——. 1990b. Letter to Provost James Coffman, October 10. In author's possession.

——. 1990c. "Human Ecology Seminar." Speech presented at Kansas State University, Manhattan, Kans., October 31. In author's possession.

Wefald, Jon. 1990. Presentation to College of Human Ecology Faculty at Kansas State University, Manhattan, Kans., November 28. In author's possession.

Willard, Julius Terrass. 1940. *History of the Kansas State College of Agriculture and Applied Science.* Manhattan, Kans.: Kansas State College Press.

Wright, Sherry. 1990. "Plan: Two KSU Colleges Cut." *Manhattan Mercury*, October 28, A1.

14. Looking Around, Thinking Ahead

SHARON Y. NICKOLS, GWEN KAY, *and* BILLIE J. COLLIER

Since its beginning home economics has been remaking itself. Members of the public have a fairly clear idea of what the field was in the past, but they may not recognize its present diverse forms. Home economics was both an area of study and a cluster of professional occupations concerned with the home, household management, and the near environment. It focused largely on the role of women. Now it includes many areas of specialization that build on the understanding of individuals and families and their interdependence with their physical and cultural environments. A vast amount of research exploring all aspects of daily life has accumulated over more than a century. Today the career possibilities are remarkably diverse, as are the audiences for family- and consumer-related information, products, and services. As the chapters in this book have demonstrated, home economics and its contemporary counterparts offer rich possibilities for exploration by scholars from history, women's studies, science and technology, journalism, the field itself, and others.

The names for the field have changed. Now most college and university comprehensive units are known as human ecology, human sciences, or family and consumer sciences. Family and consumer sciences is the nomenclature used in Cooperative Extension and in most school programs.[1] Elements of home economics are woven into the fabric of U.S. culture, sometimes highly visible and yet often in the background. Given the contemporary challenges of everyday life in an interdependent, fast-paced, technologically oriented, global world, human sciences is needed—both for the lenses of its specializations and for the prism of its interrelated, holistic perspective.

The chapters in *Remaking Home Economics: Resourcefulness and Innovation in Changing Times* have offered a variety of perspectives on core features of home economics and the experiences of significant individuals who helped lay its foundation, as well as others who had careers in the profession. Their work continues to have relevance to our personal and collective quality of life. This concluding chapter prompts the reader to reflect on the contents of the book, to look around and consider the continuing currency of the profession, and to think ahead toward how human sciences will contribute in the future.

Home Economics: Ever Timely

Calls in the popular press to "bring back home economics" and awareness among other professions of the role home economics has played and can continue to play in addressing issues of food quality and availability, nutrition, fitness, child development, financial literacy, family relations, balancing paid work and family responsibilities, aging, textiles and clothing, household technology, aesthetics in living spaces, consumer product safety, and environmental sustainability, among others, reinforce the appropriateness of Gentzler's (2012) description of the field as "ever timely and forever complex." Home economics is a renewable resource for addressing the well-being of individuals, families, and communities.

Each generation must learn what it means to be human: to understand the meaning of family and to learn basic skills for caring for oneself and others, what to eat and when, how to form relationships, how to care for possessions and other resources, and what values are prized in one's culture. These lessons are the responsibility primarily of parents. Yet every culture has other institutions to supplement that teaching role. For many years, home economics courses in the schools supplemented what children and youth were taught at home, and as each new generation passed through home economics classrooms, good teachers updated their curricula and teaching methods to address the changes in society and technology. As family composition and roles changed, beginning in the 1960s and 1970s and continuing in the twenty-first century, it became apparent that many children were learning little in the way of these life skills at home. Contemporary commentators have pointed out that this gap could once again be filled through family and consumer sciences courses (Graham 2013; Lichtenstein and Ludwig 2010; Plenda 2014; Veit 2011). Traister (2014) proposed that even the radical feminists of the 1970s who denigrated home economics would be gratified to see the reintroduction of these classes—for boys as well as girls—to teach fundamental information and skills about household work and relationships, and indirectly to "remind us of the tremendous value of housework, which has been regarded as unserious for too long—precisely because one population has been assigned to it by dint of biology."

The general public may agree that family and consumer sciences courses teaching practical life lessons should provide youth with the tools needed to build a healthy, fulfilling life; yet, contemporary standards for academic performance are based on mathematics and reading comprehension. Consequently, these "academic" courses take priority in the curriculum. Still, the current situation offers opportunities for family and consumer sciences to contribute to science, technology, and math education. Home economics is a science-based field of study and learning. In the hands-on world of today, the applied nature of family and consumer sciences lends itself to teaching science and math concepts. Indeed, measurements in recipes and sewing instructions have taught about fractions forever. The applications of science and mathematics in home-related activities are things with which young people are familiar and about which they may be inquisitive. What makes bread rise? How do detergents clean clothes? What will it cost to have my own apartment? Family and consumer sciences educators in middle and high schools have the knowledge, experience, and often the laboratory setting to help students pose and answer such questions. Increasingly STEM education does not occur just in science, math, and engineering courses, but extends to many applied fields. Food and textiles continue to attract students, especially girls, as subjects for school science projects, offering the potential for the collaboration of family and consumer sciences teachers with their biology, chemistry, and physics colleagues, and a strategy for attracting more women to STEM careers.

Human ecology, human sciences, and family and consumer sciences departments and colleges in institutions of higher education provide academic preparation, leadership and research experiences, and global understanding to prepare graduates for a wide range of careers. Many of these programs are structured, such as dietetics, personal financial planning, and family life education, leading to credentialing in specific occupations. Other majors, often with internships to explore the workings of businesses and governmental and private agencies, provide students with opportunities to match their particular interests. Family and consumer sciences in higher education has taken on many of the characteristics of colleges of arts and sciences, yet the underlying principles of interdependent relationships in physical and social environments, and an ethic of service to humanity endure. Do people with degrees in human ecology get jobs? The answer is a resounding yes, as it has been since the beginning. Degrees from these colleges are a pathway to employment and the foundation for meaningful lives.

Human sciences' responsiveness to the contemporary context is ongoing and it is vitally important, not only to collective survival and well-being, but to personal self-fulfillment and social cohesion. The backstory, which the many chapters of this book have provided, gives greater shape and context to both past experiences and some current features of the remaking of home economics. The chapters reflect the various complexities of home economics as the field has addressed issues of personal and public concern, often centered on the experiences of women, as well as professional identity and continuity over its more than one-hundred-year history.

Home economics has flourished, sometimes floundered, and regained its footing throughout its history. In this, it has been no different than many other disciplines in their evolution. Almost every decade during the first half of the twentieth century, an event propelled the field forward, highlighting its necessity even as some people may have dismissed its relevance. Home economics was instrumental in opening doors for women into higher education and careers. From the challenges wrought by two world wars and the intervening Depression of the 1930s, all of which required food preservation, careful budgeting, conservation techniques, and human perseverance, the United States recovered and moved forward, often on the shoulders of this discipline.

The second half of the twentieth century also benefited as home economics proved critical in the formation of many Great Society programs, aided displaced homemakers, supported women's paid employment, championed day care, promoted change in banking policies and women's access to credit, and advocated for consumer product safety. Home economics provided avenues for achievement for both men and women through expanded graduate programs and research in higher education, especially during the 1970s and 1980s and again in the twenty-first century. Concurrently, the expanding opportunities for women in other college majors and careers contributed to diminishing the profile of home economics professions. Toward the end of the twentieth century, fewer jobs in business explicitly for home economists, the canceling of home economics courses in some public schools, and cuts to county Cooperative Extension programs closed or restricted the traditional pathways for home economics graduates.

Although home economics was in the vortex of these elements of a perfect storm, which could have led to the demise of the profession, yet again the great resonance of the field for addressing the fundamental issues of daily life provided ways to deal with the turmoil of the economic crisis of 2007–2010 in the United States. Family and consumer sciences personnel in Cooperative Extension ramped up educational programs on debt management, financial literacy, and resource conservation. Innovative faculty at universities with expertise in marriage and family therapy and family financial planning joined forces to develop courses, practicum programs, and a professional organization, the Financial Therapy Association, to more effectively address the interpersonal and other issues when families face financial problems. The nexus of health and family finances became more prominent as concerns mounted regarding the costs of chronic disease and the financial crisis, and this provided yet another opportunity for consumer educators to develop responses to help increase health and financial literacy.

People turn to professionals in times of crisis. Social historian Megan J. Elias (pers. comm.) observed: "Home economics has been most visible in times of crisis (e.g., the Great Depression, the obesity epidemic), but such flashpoint attention overlooks the holistic connections in home economics and the core principles and practices of the field, which focus on ordinary, daily experiences and are essential to a well-functioning society." The main focus of family and consumer sciences has been to prevent human crises, but the knowledge in the profession also enables families and communities to address the effects of crises. Family and consumer sciences educators and counselors assist individuals and families to identify ways to mitigate problems, secure resources, and promote the resiliency needed for coping with and recovering from unemployment, loss of family members, natural disasters, and other traumatic events. Child life specialists, members of pediatric medical teams serving hospitalized children and their families, receive their training in colleges of human sciences. The recognition of a national crisis of childhood obesity brought together university researchers in human ecology, dietitians, and school lunch personnel with school board members, principals, and teachers to develop healthier food choices, redesign the placement of food items in school cafeterias, and provide age-appropriate nutrition education. Agricultural and family and consumer sciences educators work together to engage children and adults in local food systems. Other human sciences professionals collaborate with city planners and exercise scientists to design environments that promote active lifestyles and to develop better nutrition to address obesity among adults.

From the beginning, home economics has targeted its work at improving conditions for everyone, including at-risk populations. The increased variety of living patterns is changing the composition of and attitudes about families in the United States. Many children are members of fragile families; they and their parents need support systems to create pathways to well-being. The CYFAR (Children, Youth, and Families at Risk) program of the USDA's National Institute of Food and Agriculture supports collaboration to build resiliency and protective factors in youth and adults in at-risk environments (NIFA 2013). Family and consumer sciences professionals have a proven track record of using the human ecological principles of working across the lifespan in the context of the family and community to implement CYFAR projects since 1991. Other community programs for youth, shelters for homeless families, and agencies serving elderly adults are staffed and led by human ecology professionals.

Whereas the research activities of the profession were concentrated in the Bureau of Home Economics in the past, today college faculty members in human sciences produce a vast array of research applicable to the well-being of individuals, families, and communities, much of which is on the cutting edge of technology. Individual researchers and teams of human ecology scientists collaborate with scholars in a wide variety of disciplines. Researchers across the spectrum of human ecology study material science, the development of new products and processes, the interface of families and technology, strategies for family resiliency, and the effectiveness of intervention methods, among many other topics. The route to multidisciplinary approaches in research is facilitated by the holistic approach in human ecology, but the research process and the outcome can only be successful if the collaborators are equally strong. The future strength of the research enterprise in human sciences will be achieved by staying on the path of strong graduate programs and success in garnering the resources to conduct relevant, impactful studies. The fundamental soundness of the family and consumer sciences body of knowledge likewise offers a platform for addressing current issues of sustainability related to the environment and for thinking globally while acting locally.

The Twenty-First-Century Social Fabric

Speaking at the fourth Lake Placid Conference, the home economics and women's education pioneer Marion Talbot (1902, 22) sketched the broad scope of home economics: "that the activities of the home are far wider than physical well-being, that the obligations of home life are not by any means limited to its own four walls, that home economics must always be regarded in the light of its relation to the general social system, that men and women are alike concerned in understanding the processes, activities, obligations and opportunities which make the home and the family effective parts of the social fabric." The social fabric of the United States was being dramatically rewoven as the country moved into the twentieth century and the profession of home economics became formalized. Likewise the social fabric of the twenty-first century is being rewoven by significant demographic and economic changes.

Demographers, historians, and family sociologists have analyzed a number of trends whose cumulative effects have significantly changed the form, function, and purpose of the "family" in the United States. Taylor (2014, 1) observed: "Demographic transformations are dramas in slow motion. They unfold incrementally, almost imperceptibly.... But every so often, as the weight of change builds, a society takes a hard look at itself and notices that things are different." The changes in U.S. household composition are rippling through all the other aspects of society and culture, and they have vast implications for family and consumer sciences.

Marriage is in decline (Pew Research Center 2010). In 2011, only half (51 percent) of U.S. adults were married, and less than half (48 percent) of U.S. households were composed of a husband-wife family (Taylor 2014; U.S. Census Bureau 2012). The median age at first marriage rose to 27.4 for men and 25.6 for women in 2008 (Cherlin 2010). Cohabitation may be replacing marriage as a living arrangement, particularly in Generation X (those born from 1965 to 1980) and the millennial generation (those born after 1980) (Taylor 2014). Family historian Elizabeth Pleck (2012) reported that there were 8 million cohabiting households in the United States in 2010 (compared to about 230,000 in 1960) and that this living arrangement occurs at all economic and educational levels, but is more common among less well-educated and lower-income men and women. However, Cherlin (2010) pointed out that cohabitation has become common among people across educational levels.

The co-residence of grandparents and grandchildren has been increasing since 1970 with about 10 percent of all children (7.5 million) living with grandparents in 2011 (Ellis 2013). Concurrent with the bursting of the housing bubble and the economic recession beginning in 2007, the incidence of children and their parent(s) co-residing with grandparents increased substantially.

Births outside of marriage have increased markedly. In 2011, 41 percent of all births in the United States were to unmarried mothers, compared to 28 percent in 1990 (Taylor 2014). The increase in births to unmarried mothers is occurring among women in their late twenties and thirties, not among teenagers (Brown 2013; Cherlin 2010). The family structures experienced by many children in the United States are increasingly complicated. Whereas in 1980, 77 percent of children lived with their biological mothers and fathers (Amato et al. 2007), in 2012, 35 percent of children lived in single-parent families (Kids Count Data Center 2013). Today's children are much more likely to have a parent who lives elsewhere, and children are more likely to have ties to multiple households due to their parents' transitions in spouses and/or cohabiting partners (Cherlin 2010; Crosnoe and Cavanagh 2010). "Multifamily children," who go through numerous relationship and living transitions, are at risk for developmental delays and behavioral problems (Amato 2010; Cherlin 2010; Crosnoe and Cavanagh 2010; Pleck 2012; Sweeney 2010).

As practitioners in the field of human sciences engage in critical self-awareness with the goal of becoming more resourceful and innovative in the teaching, outreach, and research dimensions of the profession, it is essential that attention be given to the increasing complexity in contemporary families. Previous conventions about how children and adults designate the members of their family (or families), and how they experience "family," are being replaced by multiple living arrangements, relationship networks, and terminology. For example, while the traditional theory of life course development was helpful in anticipating what a family would need in the way of housing, furniture, and transportation as children grew and developed, a contemporary family with divorced and remarried parents who share child custody and who weekly alternate the children in residence (and perhaps also have an older child who has returned to live at home) have more complex management and interpersonal relationships, as well as housing needs. Family sociologist Paul Amato (2014, 3–4) suggested that using "subjective definitions" in which people specify whom they consider "family" will move researchers, educators, and program leaders to a clearer understanding of "the lived reality of people's lives . . . [and] to identifying the extent to which family networks are sources of social capital."

Attention has also turned to the role of fathers and fathering in the midst of dramatic social, economic, and historical changes. Roy (2014, 91) observed that at the turn of the twenty-first century, "the place of men in families is anything but stable or well understood," and he urged professionals who work with and study families to take note of "the diversity of men's experiences, specifically in an era of rising inequality." As the expectations of fatherhood are shifting from paternal rights and responsibilities vested in one individual toward multiple "fathering" individuals, who may include a child's biological father, nurturing father, and/or financially supporting father, the intersection of families and family members with systems of education, health, insurance, medical institutions, and the legal system will grow increasingly complex. Attention has been given to women's roles as mothers (married, single, and cohabiting), employed workers, and managers of family life, but these roles are also in flux. These new realities challenge professionals in human ecology to look around and think ahead as academic programs and service careers continue to develop.

The U.S. population is getting older. At the upper end of the age spectrum, the Baby Boom generation (those born between 1946 and 1964) is becoming a "silver tsunami" with ten thousand people turning sixty-five years of age every day (Alliance for Aging Research 2006). The older generations represented 8 percent of the total population in 1950 and 12 percent in 2000, and are projected to reach 18 percent in 2025 (Shrestha and Heisler 2011).

Poverty rates among older adults have declined since the 1960s due to the success of government policies favoring the old (Taylor 2014). Yet many face a precarious economic future because their resources are insufficient for their increasing longevity. Women have particular concerns about meeting their financial needs during their later years for a variety of reasons: on average women earn less than men and consequently have contributed less to retirement savings; they have more gaps in their careers; and they have longer life expectancy compared to men. Caregiving for older people will become more complicated as roles, relationships, resources, and longevity are increasingly in flux. With the decline in marriage and the instability of cohabitation, at some point in the future, tenuous family bonds may create a cohort of "elderly orphans" (Taylor 2014).

The U.S. poverty rate increased during the economic downturn that began in 2007. Families at the margin experienced economic hardships, and families with heavy credit card and mortgage debt were in economic crisis. Nationally, the percentage of people in poverty increased from 12.2 percent in 2000 to 15.9 percent (48.8 million people) in 2012 (Bishaw 2013). The largest number of people living in poverty are White, but poverty is experienced disproportionately by race and ethnicity; it is highest among Black and Hispanic individuals (approximately one in four) but affects less than one in ten among non-Hispanic White individuals (Edelman 2012; Edin and Kissane 2010). One in five children in the United States lives in a household that is economically poor. In 2013, the poverty rate among female-headed families with children was 39.6 percent compared to 16.9 percent among all families with children (Mishel et al. 2012–2013). Edelman (2012) credited SNAP (the Supplemental Nutrition Assistance Program, formerly known as food stamps) and the Earned Income Tax Credit for alleviating some of the burdens of poverty. Meanwhile, neighborhoods in the United States have become "more integrated by race but more segregated by income" (Taylor 2014, 4).

Increased racial and ethnic diversity is among the major demographic and social changes characterizing the United States in the twenty-first century. The United States is on a demographic track to become a "majority minority" (i.e., majority nonwhite) nation by the mid-twenty-first century (Taylor 2014). There are many correlates of race and ethnicity that influence the well-being of groups in the United States. For example, Hispanic and Black households fall at the lower end of household median income and educational attainment, whereas Asian Americans are the highest-income, best-educated, and fastest-growing racial group in the United States (Taylor 2014).

Although few people would agree that demographics are destiny, it is clear that demographic changes can be transformative. Since human ecology is a field of study and a profession focused on people and their daily lives, anyone who is looking around will recognize that the opportunities (and perhaps the challenges) for human ecology are unlimited.

Innovation in Changing Times:
Thinking Ahead

The growing diversity in the United States mandates increased diversity in the human sciences profession, including personnel in all settings, students, paraprofessionals, teachers, college administrators, and practitioners in business and service agencies. Identification with role models is a powerful influence on young people's choice of academic majors and careers. One of the functions of history is to probe, and bring to the present, information from the past, including awareness about pivotal figures in the history of home economics, not only those who attended the Lake Placid Conferences, but others rarely in the spotlight.

The "discovery" of two pioneering home economists is a case in point. Willie Lee Glass was an African American home economics teacher, college administrator, and philanthropist. As a consultant with the Texas Education Agency, she monitored the implementation of racial integration plans across the state. Her career spanned the 1930s to the 1970s (Greer and Kenner 2008). Fabiola Cabeza de Baca Gilbert taught in a multilingual one-room school in New Mexico, and then in 1927 earned a degree in home economics (Makela 2012). She was the first Cooperative Extension agent in New Mexico who spoke Spanish, and she learned Tewa and Tiwa to work with Pueblo women, teaching gardening, canning, and sewing. Later, she was a consultant for the Peace Corps. Knowing more about the diversity of home economics specialists contributes to remaking the profession because the arrays of role models and experiences are expanded. Previously unknown individuals were not peripheral. Many made substantive contributions to the field, and their stories deserve to be told.

The increase in Hispanic and Asian segments of the U.S. population offers opportunities for family and consumer sciences to expand its programs and services, as well as to enroll a more diverse student population and enlist new professionals, whose perspectives and experiences will enrich the field. Asians are now well represented among human sciences faculty and graduate students. They are having a significant impact on cross-cultural research on family dynamics, nutrition, financial practices, and the purchase of consumer products, as evidenced in frequent articles in the *Family and Consumer Sciences Research Journal* and publications of the specialized disciplines within family and consumer sciences.

Those who advocate reinstating the family and consumer sciences curriculum in the schools would do well to move their support to the level of a coordinated public voice. Action beyond attention-getting headlines is necessary to reinstate and remake home economics into a universally available program for youth in the schools. Thinking ahead: what if expanding the length of the school day to incorporate life skills courses had the same level of support as high school sports currently enjoy?

Another route to developing life skills in the nation could be to expand programs at community colleges beyond technical training by offering courses in financial literacy, personal and family relationships, parenting, and food and nutrition. As a developmental stage of life, young adulthood (and the transitions of older returning students) provides a teachable moment and could be a pathway toward a better quality of life for individuals and a stronger social fabric.

The venues for information related to family and consumer sciences to reach the public have increased exponentially. Social media, particularly the internet, offer the democratization of knowledge, providing ready access to a wide range of topics. Anyone from the amateur enthusiast to the professional can create and post information, goods for sale, tweets, or videos on a range of topics. Still, there is a paucity of accurate information on a wide variety of household activities and family relationships that could be addressed by brief lessons and instructions for time-constrained consumers and novices. Family and consumer sciences innovators will increasingly use social media to expand the reach of the profession.

Issues related to environmental sustainability will continue to challenge personal and community decisions about air, water, land, and nonrenewable resources. Family and consumer sciences researchers, educators, and practitioners have for many years championed environmental awareness and the wise use of resources. Apparel and interior designers can have an increased impact because they are often decision makers in selecting materials for the clothing and interior furnishings people use daily. The content of high school and college courses and extension programming will increasingly include an emphasis on repurposing, reusing, and recycling, as well as selecting products made from renewable materials. Not only will these contributions be related to technical competencies, but the ethics of social justice and the municipal housekeeping characteristic of the early home economists are central to these concerns.

There is ample talent and leadership in family and consumer sciences, but the focus on educating and empowering others has precedence over advocating for the profession itself. Thirty-five years ago, Marjorie East (1980, 107) observed about home economics: "we aren't much interested in power, influence, and renown." Rather, home economists were and continue to be altruistic, concerned about social well-being, practical, and focused on enabling others. Many in the profession today are attuned to and engaged in shaping public policy, but for a variety of reasons, family and consumer sciences has limited political clout to further its own interests.

Thinking ahead: a higher profile for the profession and greater understanding of the many areas of expertise in human sciences might well be achieved if its practitioners ratchet up their efforts to gain visibility. For example, we could better prepare graduates of the human sciences to articulate how their education is important to their abilities and their success, seize opportunities to appear in public forums as experts, increase the use of social media, and engage marketing expertise to tell the family and consumer sciences story.

Historically, home economics provided an avenue for leadership development for women, primarily in institutions of higher education. Those opportunities have continued to expand as department heads and deans of home economics units have been appointed to administrative posts at the central campus level. Beyond college and university campuses, the expertise of human sciences graduates is adding value to agencies and foundations that are addressing broad societal and environmental issues. Election to public office is another avenue that human ecology professionals could pursue to influence public policy for the benefit of children, families, and communities.

Home economics started with women in mind as its students and its practitioners. A future historian will note the substantial growth in the number of men in college preparing for careers in dietetics, financial planning, housing, family counseling, interior design, and fashion merchandising and entrepreneurship; some use the field as pre-professional preparation for medical or law school. At each successive level in higher education, the proportion of men increases, from undergraduate to graduate programs to faculty. Ellen Richards, Caroline Hunt, Nellie Kedzie Jones, and others in their cohort probably never imagined that the field would become so diverse in terms of gender, race, ethnicity, or vocation.

Much of this book has chronicled the history and changes in home economics. Its purpose also has been to encourage consideration of the future. Thus, we challenge you. Thinking ahead, what will be the keys to remaking home economics in the future? What aspects need to be rethought? What should be reclaimed? Remembering that much change is nonlinear, what is in store for the future?

The history of home economics, its current manifestations, and prospects for the future provide an abundance of opportunities to explore topics beyond those in this book. Scholars from an array of disciplines have much to contribute to the ongoing exploration and dialogue about home economics, and practitioners have many stories to tell. A discipline such as home economics at the intersection of so many issues is destined to be remaking itself for decades to come.

ACKNOWLEDGMENTS

We express our appreciation to Virginia Moxley for her review of an earlier draft of this chapter.

NOTE

1. In this chapter, the various names adopted by units originating as home economics are used interchangeably: human ecology, family and consumer sciences, and human sciences. "Home economics" is mostly used with reference to the field of study and the profession up to 1994.

REFERENCES

Alliance for Aging Research. 2006. "Preparing for the Silver Tsunami," www.agingresearch.org/content/article/detail/826 (accessed October 19, 2013).

Amato, Paul R. 2010. "Research on Divorce: Continuing Trends and New Developments." *Journal of Marriage and Family* 72(3): 650–666.

———. 2014. "What Is a Family?" *National Council on Family Relations Report* 59(2): 3–4.

Amato, Paul R., Alan Booth, David R. Johnson, and Stacy J. Rogers. 2007. *Alone Together: How Marriage in America Is Changing*. Cambridge, Mass.: Harvard University Press.

Bishaw, Alemayehu. 2013. *Poverty: 2000 to 2010*. U.S. Census Bureau, U.S. Department of Commerce, www.census.gov/prod/acsbr12-01.pdf (accessed May 12, 2014).

Brown, Sarah. 2013. "Start Spreading the News: The Remarkable Declines in Teen Pregnancy and Childbearing." *Population Connection Reporter* 45(1): 12–19.

Cherlin, Andrew J. 2010. "Demographic Trends in the United States: A Review of Research in the 2000s." *Journal of Marriage and Family* 72(3): 403–419.

Crosnoe, Robert, and Shannon E. Cavanagh. 2010. "Families with Children and Adolescents: A Review, Critique, and Future Agenda." *Journal of Marriage and Family* 72(3): 594–611.

East, Marjorie. 1980. *Home Economics: Past, Present, and Future*. Boston: Allyn and Bacon.

Edelman, Peter. 2012. *So Rich, So Poor: Why It's So Hard to End Poverty in America*. New York: New Press.

Edin, Kathryn, and Rebecca Joyce Kissane. 2010. "Poverty and the American Family: A Decade Review." *Journal of Marriage and Family* 72(3): 460–479.

Ellis, Renee. 2013. "Changes in Coresidence of Grandparents and Grandchildren." In *Family Focus*, F13–F15, F17. Minneapolis, Minn.: National Council on Family Relations.

Gentzler, Yvonne S. 2012. "Home Economics: Ever Timely and Forever Complex." *Phi Kappa Phi Forum* 92(2): 4–7.

Graham, Ruth. 2013. "Bring Back Home Ec! The Case for a Revival of the Most Retro Class in School." *Boston Globe*, October 12, http://www.bostonglobe.com/ideas/2013/10/12/bring-back-home/EJJi9yzjgJfNmgxWUIedgO/story.html (accessed October 15, 2013).

Greer, Rebecca W., and Janie O. Kenner. 2008. "Willie Lee Glass: A Lady of Remarkable Influence." *Family and Consumer Sciences Research Journal* 37(2): 140–148.

Kids Count Data Center. 2013. "Children in Single-Parent Families." Annie E. Casey Foundation, http://datacenter.kidscount.org/publications (accessed May 9, 2014).

Lichtenstein, Alice H., and David Ludwig. 2010. "Bring Back Home Economics Education." *Journal of the American Medical Association* 303(18): 1857–1858.

Makela, Carole J. 2012. "Interrelationships of a Home Economist: Legacy of an Extension Agent in New Mexico." *Journal of Family and Consumer Sciences* 104(1): 10–13.

Mishel, Lawrence, Josh Bivens, Elise Gould, and Heidi Shierholz. 2012–2013. *The State of Working America*, 12th ed. www.stateofworkingamerica.org/economic-indicators/income-poverty (accessed October 6, 2014).

NIFA (National Institute of Food and Agriculture). 2013. "Communities at Risk," www.csrees.usda.gov/nea/family/cyfar/overview.html (accessed June 6, 2014).

Pew Research Center. 2010. "The Decline of Marriage and Rise of New Families." *Social and Demographic Trends*, www.pewsocialtrends.org/2010/11/18/the-decline-of-marriage-and-rise-of-new-families (accessed August 5, 2013).

Pleck, Elizabeth H. 2012. *Not Just Roommates: Cohabitation After the Sexual Revolution.* Chicago: University of Chicago Press.

Plenda, Melanie. 2014. "Home Economics Classes Are Not What They Used to Be: Today's Family and Consumer Science Classes Are Teaching Kids Real-Life Skills," www.parentingnh.com (accessed May 16, 2014).

Roy, Kevin. 2014. "Invited Commentary: Fathers on the Frontiers of Family Change." *Journal of Family Theory and Review* 6 (March): 91–96.

Shrestha, Laura B., and Elayne J. Heisler. 2011. *The Changing Demographic Profile of the United States.* Congressional Research Service, www.crs.gov (accessed March 18, 2013).

Sweeney, Megan M. 2010. "Remarriage and Stepfamilies: Strategies for Family Scholarship in the 21st Century." *Journal of Marriage and Family* 72(3): 667–684.

Talbot, Marion. 1902. "Discussion." In *Lake Placid Conference on Home Economics, Proceedings of the Fourth Annual Conference.* Lake Placid, N.Y.: n.p.

Taylor, Paul. 2014. *The Next America: Boomers, Millennials, and the Looming Generational Showdown.* New York: Public Affairs.

Traister, Rebecca. 2014. "Feminists Killed Home Ec. Now They Should Bring It Back— for Boys and Girls." *New Republic*, May 28, www.newrepublic.com/article/117876/feminists-should-embrace-home-economics (accessed May 29, 2014).

U.S. Census Bureau. 2012. *Households and Families: 2010.* Washington, D.C.: U.S. Department of Commerce, www.census.gov/prod/cen2010/briefs/c2010br-14.pdf (accessed October 15, 2013).

Veit, Helen Zoe. 2011. "Time to Revive Home Ec." *New York Times*, September 5, http://www.nytimes.com/2011/09/96/opinion/revive-home-economics-classes-to-fight-obesity.html (accessed October 15, 2013).

Suggested Readings and Resources

PUBLISHED SOURCES

Andress, Elizabeth L., Sharon Y. Nickols, Gina G. Peek, and Sharon M. Nickols-Richardson. 2010. "Seeking Food Security: Environmental Factors Influencing Home Food Preservation and Wellness, Part II: 1960–2010." *Family and Consumer Sciences Research Journal* 39(3): 233–245.

Apple, Rima D. 1996. *Vitamania: Vitamins in American Culture.* New Brunswick, N.J.: Rutgers University Press.

———. 2006. *Perfect Motherhood: Science and Childrearing in America.* New Brunswick, N.J.: Rutgers University Press.

Bailey, Lena, and Francille Firebaugh. 1986. *Strengthening Home Economics Programs in Higher Education.* Columbus: Ohio State College of Home Economics.

Betters, Paul Vernon. 1930. *The Bureau of Home Economics: Its History, Activities, and Organization.* Washington, D.C.: Brookings Institution.

Biltekoff, Charlotte. 2013. *Eating Right in America: The Cultural Politics of Food and Health.* Durham, N.C.: Duke University Press.

Brown, Marjorie M. 1985. *Philosophical Studies of Home Economics in the United States: Our Practical-Intellectual Heritage.* Vols. 1 and 2. East Lansing, Mich.: Michigan State University.

———. 1993. *Philosophical Studies of Home Economics in the United States: Basic Ideas by Which Home Economists Understand Themselves.* East Lansing, Mich.: Michigan State University.

Brown, Marjorie M., and Beatrice Paolucci. 1979. *Home Economics: A Definition.* Alexandria, Va.: American Home Economics Association.

Brumberg, Joan Jacobs. 1988. *Fasting Girls: The History of Anorexia Nervosa.* New York: Vintage.

Cherlin, Andrew. 2012. *Public and Private Families: An Introduction,* 7th ed. New York: McGraw-Hill Humanities.

Clifford, Marie. 2003. "Working with Fashion: The Role of Art, Taste, and Consumerism in Women's Professional Culture, 1920–1940." *American Studies* 44(1–2): 59–84.

Coontz, Stephanie. 1997. *The Way We Never Were: American Families and the Nostalgia Trap*. New York: Basic.

Cravens, Hamilton. 1990. "Establishing the Science of Nutrition at the USDA: Ellen Swallow Richards and Her Allies." *Agricultural History* 64(2): 122–133.

deMarrais, Kathleen, and Stephen D. Lapan, eds. 2004. *Foundations for Research: Methods of Inquiry in Education and the Social Sciences*. Mahwah, N.J.: Erlbaum.

Dewhurst, Yvonne, and Donna Pendergast. 2011. "Teacher Perceptions of the Contribution of Home Economics to Sustainable Development Education: A Cross-Cultural View." *International Journal of Consumer Studies* 35(5): 569–577.

Duran, Nancy. 2004. "Farmers' Bulletins: Advice to Women on Diet, Food, and Cooking." *Journal of Agriculture and Food Information* 6(1): 49–75.

Elias, Megan J. 2008. *Stir It Up: Home Economics in American Culture*. Philadelphia: University of Pennsylvania Press.

Gentzler, Yvonne S. 2012. "Home Economics: Ever Timely and Forever Complex." *Phi Kappa Phi Forum* 92(2): 4–7.

Goldstein, Carolyn. 2012. *Creating Consumers: Home Economists in Twentieth-Century America*. Chapel Hill: University of North Carolina Press.

Gordon, Lynn D. 1990. *Gender and Higher Education in the Progressive Era*. New Haven, Conn.: Yale University Press.

Harper, Alfred E. 2003. "Contributions of Women Scientists in the U.S. to the Development of Recommended Dietary Allowances." *Journal of Nutrition* 133(11): 3698–3702.

Hayes, Shannon. 2010. *Radical Homemakers: Reclaiming Domesticity from a Consumer Culture*. Richmondville, N.Y.: Left to Write Press.

Helveston, Sally I., and Margaret M. Bubolz. 1999. "Home Economics and Home Sewing in the United States, 1870–1940." In *The Culture of Sewing: Gender, Consumption and Home Dressmaking*, edited by Barbara Burman, 303–325. Oxford: Berg.

Hesse-Biber, Sharlene Nagy, and Patricia Leavy. 2011. *The Practice of Qualitative Research*, 2nd ed. Thousand Oaks, Calif.: Sage.

Holt, Marilyn Irvin. 1995. *Linoleum, Better Babies, and the Modern Farm Woman, 1890–1930*. Albuquerque: University of New Mexico Press.

Lake Placid Conference on Home Economics. 1901–1908. *Proceedings of the Conferences*. Lake Placid, N.Y.: n.p. http://hearth.library.cornell.edu.

Lane, Ruth, and Andrew Gorman Murray, eds. 2011. *Material Geographies of Household Sustainability*. Burlington, Vt.: Ashgate.

Leach, William. 1984. "Transformations in a Culture of Consumption: Women and Department Stores, 1890–1925." *Journal of American History* 71(2): 319–342.

Leavitt, Sarah. 2002. *From Catharine Beecher to Martha Stewart: A Cultural History of Domestic Advice*. Chapel Hill: University of North Carolina Press.

Levenstein, Harvey. 2003a. *Paradox of Plenty: A Social History of Eating in Modern America*. Berkeley: University of California Press.

———. 2003b. *Revolution at the Table: The Transformation of the American Diet*. Berkeley: University of California Press.

————. 2012. *Fear of Food: A History of Why We Worry About What We Eat.* Chicago: University of Chicago Press.

Lichtenstein, Alice H., and David Ludwig. 2010. "Bring Back Home Economics Education." *Journal of the American Medical Association* 303(18): 1857–1858.

Miller, Julia R., Dorothy I. Mitstifer, and Gladys Gary Vaughn, eds. 2009. *African American Women: Contributions to the Human Sciences.* East Lansing, Mich.: Kappa Omicron Nu.

Mudry, Jessica. 2009. *Measured Meals: Nutrition in America.* Albany: State University of New York Press.

Nerad, Maresi. 1999. *The Academic Kitchen: A Social History of Gender Stratification at the University of California, Berkeley.* Albany: State University of New York Press.

Nickols, Sharon Y., Elizabeth L. Andress, Gina G. Peek, and Sharon M. Nickols-Richardson. 2010. "Seeking Food Security: Environmental Factors Influencing Home Food Preservation and Wellness, Part I: 1910–1959." *Family and Consumer Sciences Research Journal* 39(2): 122–136.

Nickols, Sharon Y., Penny A. Ralston, Carol Anderson, Lorna Browne, Genevieve Schroeder, Sabrina Thomas, and Peggy Wild. 2009. "The Family and Consumer Sciences Body of Knowledge and the Cultural Kaleidoscope: Research Opportunities and Challenges." *Family and Consumer Sciences Research Journal* 37(3): 266–283.

Pendergast, Donna, Sue L. T. McGregor, and Kaija Turkki, eds. 2012. *Creating Home Economics Futures: The Next 100 Years.* Bowen Hills: Australia Academic Press.

Przybyszewski, Linda. 2014. *The Lost Art of Dress: The Women Who Once Made America Stylish.* New York: Basic.

Richards, Ellen. 1911. "The Social Significance of the Home Economics Movement." *Journal of Home Economics* 3(2): 117–130.

Rossiter, Margaret W. 1982. *Women Scientists in America: Struggles and Strategies to 1940.* Baltimore, Md.: Johns Hopkins University Press.

————. 1995. *Women Scientists in America: Before Affirmative Action, 1940–1972.* Baltimore, Md.: Johns Hopkins University Press.

————. 2012. *Women Scientists in America: Forging a New World Since 1972.* Baltimore, Md.: Johns Hopkins University Press.

Schneider, Dorothy, and Carl J. Schneider. 1993. *American Women in the Progressive Era.* New York: Facts on File.

Stage, Sarah, and Virginia B. Vincenti, eds. 1997. *Rethinking Home Economics: Women and the History of a Profession.* Ithaca, N.Y.: Cornell University Press.

Sullivan, Joan L. 1999. "In Pursuit of Legitimacy: Home Economists and the Hoover Apron in World War I." *Dress* 26: 31–46.

Veit, Helen Zoe. 2011. "Time to Revive Home Ec." *New York Times*, September 5, http://www.nytimes.com/2011/09/06/opinion/revive-home-economics-classes-to-fight-obesity.html.

Weigley, Emma Seifrit. 1974. "It Might Have Been Euthenics: The Lake Placid Conferences and the Home Economics Movement." *American Quarterly* 26(1): 79–96.

SPECIAL COLLECTIONS ON HOME ECONOMICS

American Association of Family and Consumer Sciences Archives, Special
   Collections, Carl Kroch Library, Cornell University, Ithaca, N.Y.
Elsie Carper Collection on Extension Service, Home Economics, and 4-H,
   USDA National Agricultural Library, http://specialcollections.nal.usda.gov/
   guide-collections/elsie-carper-collection-extension-service
Home Economics Research Archive: Research, Tradition, History (HEARTH), http://
   hearth.library.cornell.edu/h/hearth

Contributors

Elizabeth L. Andress is a food safety and preservation specialist with Georgia Cooperative Extension and a Professor in the Department of Foods and Nutrition. She has been the Director of the National Center for Home Food Preservation, partially funded by NIFA–USDA, since 1999 and is a co-author of the USDA's *Complete Guide to Home Canning* and *So Easy to Preserve*.

Rima D. Apple is Professor Emerita, University of Wisconsin, Madison. Her books include *Perfect Motherhood: Science and Childrearing in America* and *The Challenge of Constantly Changing Times: From Home Economics to Human Ecology at the University of Wisconsin-Madison, 1903–2003*. Most recently she was a visiting professor at Glasgow Caledonian University.

Jorge H. Atiles is a Professor and the Associate Dean for extension and engagement in the College of Human Sciences at Oklahoma State University. He holds degrees in architecture, urban and regional planning, and housing. He leads the family and consumer sciences unit of Cooperative Extension in Oklahoma.

Susan F. Clark is an Associate Professor in the Department of Horticulture, College of Agriculture and Life Sciences, at Virginia Tech, with an adjunct appointment in the Department of Human Nutrition, Foods and Exercise. She is the director of the interdisciplinary Civic Agriculture and Food Systems Program and a member of the Southwest Virginia Community Food Security Assessment Team.

Billie J. Collier is Dean Emerita of the College of Human Sciences at Florida State University and has taught textiles and research methods at five universities for more than thirty years. She is the co-author of two textbooks on textiles and holds six patents for the development of textile products.

Caroline E. Crocoll is the Director of the Division of Family and Consumer Sciences at the USDA–NIFA. She provides national leadership for family and consumer sciences program development and collaboration; identifies mission-relevant opportunities, priorities, and issues; and evaluates the impacts of these programs.

Stephanie M. Foss completed the master of science degree in the Department of Foods and Nutrition at the University of Georgia in 2013. Her research on vitamin D and biomarkers of muscle metabolism was part of a multisite clinical trial. She is a registered dietitian working as a diabetes educator in Dallas, Texas.

Gwen Kay is a Professor in the History Department and the Director of the Honors Program at the State University of New York, Oswego. She is the author of *Dying to Be Beautiful: The Fight for Safe Cosmetics* and is currently working on a book manuscript called *Not Just Stitchin' and Stirrin': Changing Identities in Home Economics*.

Emma M. Laing is a registered dietitian nutritionist and an assistant research scientist at the University of Georgia's Bone and Body Composition Laboratory. Her osteoporosis and obesity prevention research focuses on improving health during childhood in order to reduce the risk of chronic diseases in adulthood.

Richard D. Lewis is a University of Georgia Foundation Professor in the Department of Foods and Nutrition, College of Family and Consumer Sciences, and is the Director of the UGA Bone and Body Composition Laboratory. His research focuses on understanding how micronutrients and physical activity impact obesity and bone development during the growing years.

Peggy S. Meszaros is the William E. Lavery Professor of Human Development at Virginia Tech, where she is also the Director of the Center for Information Technology Impacts on Children, Youth and Families. She is the author of over eighty publications, a former Senior Vice President and Provost of Virginia Tech, and a past president of the American Association of Family and Consumer Sciences.

Rachel Louise Moran teaches in the History Department at the University of North Texas. She earned her PhD in history and women's studies from Penn State University in 2013 and is currently working on a book manuscript called *The Muscular State: Modern Politics and American Physique*.

Virginia Moxley is Dean Emerita of the College of Human Ecology, Kansas State University. She is a founder of the Great Plains Interactive Distance Education Alliance and served as a Co-Director of the Institute for Academic Alliances. Moxley is a past president of Omicron Nu Honor Society (now Kappa Omicron Nu Honor Society).

Sharon Y. Nickols is Dean Emerita of the College of Family and Consumer Sciences, University of Georgia, where she held the Janette M. Barber Distinguished Professorship. She is a past president of the American Association of Family and Consumer Sciences and the recipient of the Nellie Kedzie Jones Lifetime Achievement Award from the Board on Human Sciences.

Margarete Ordon is Curator of history at the Montana Historical Society. Previously, she was a postdoctoral research associate at the Helen Louise Allen Textile Collection in the School of Human Ecology, University of Wisconsin, Madison. She received the PhD in design studies and a certificate in material culture from the University of Wisconsin, Madison. She is the 2011 recipient of the Schurch Scholar Award for Outstanding Graduate Research.

Linda Przybyszewski is an Associate Professor in the History Department and a Concurrent Associate Professor in the Law School at the University of Notre Dame. Her interest in the use of gender, power, and authority in the context of racial, moral, and religious reasoning led to the publication of two books on John Marshall Harlan and his wife, Malvina Shanklin Harlan. She is also the author of *The Lost Art of Dress: The Women Who Once Made America Stylish*.

Penny A. Ralston is Dean Emerita at the College of Human Sciences, Florida State University. She is a Professor and the Director of the Center on Better Health and Life for Underserved Populations. She is a past president of the American Association of Family and Consumer Sciences.

Jane Schuchardt is the Executive Director of Cooperative Extension, Association of Public and Land-Grant Universities, Washington, D.C. With the Extension Committee on Organization and Policy, she works to provide visibility for exemplary programming and create partnerships to support local and online extension programming. Formerly, she was a national program leader at the USDA–NIFA.

Index